I.B.TAURIS SHORT HISTORIES

I.B.Tauris Short Histories is an authoritative and elegantly written new series which puts a fresh perspective on the way history is taught and understood in the twenty-first century. Designed to have strong appeal to university students and their teachers, as well as to general readers and history enthusiasts, *I.B.Tauris Short Histories* comprises a novel attempt to bring informed interpretation, as well as factual reportage, to historical debate. Addressing key subjects and topics in the fields of history, the history of ideas, religion, classical studies, politics, philosophy and Middle East studies, the series seeks intentionally to move beyond the bland, neutral 'introduction' that so often serves as the primary undergraduate teaching tool. While always providing students and generalists with the core facts that they need to get to grips with the essentials of any particular subject, *I.B.Tauris Short Histories* goes further. It offers new insights into how a topic has been understood in the past, and what different social and cultural factors might have been at work. It brings original perspectives to bear on the manner of its current interpretation. It raises questions and – in its extensive bibliographies – points to further study, even as it suggests answers. Addressing a variety of subjects in a greater degree of depth than is often found in comparable series, yet at the same time in concise and compact handbook form, *I.B.Tauris Short Histories* aims to be 'introductions with an edge'. In combining questioning and searching analysis with informed history writing, it brings history up-to-date for an increasingly complex and globalized digital age.

www.short-histories.com

'Rich in erudition, this book wears its learning lightly and engages the reader throughout by posing as many questions as it answers. Texts, artefacts and historical events are deftly interwoven. Dr Leyser shrewdly negotiates the complex interactions between faith and politics in the period, grounding her assumptions in a wholly convincing context. A truly excellent short history.'

– Susan Irvine, Quain Professor of English Language and Literature,
University College London

'In eight invigorating chapters, Henrietta Leyser covers a period of six hundred years from the settlement of Germanic peoples across eastern and southern Britain, in the fifth and sixth centuries, to the Norman Conquest of England in 1066. She provides a lively and well-balanced assessment of the ways in which social, cultural, economic and political forces interacted with each other, leading to the emergence of a unified kingdom of the English – and its conquest. It is over thirty years since a book of this scope and nature has appeared; and Dr Leyser is a very skilful guide to all that has changed in our perception of the Anglo-Saxon world-order.'

– Simon Keynes, Elrington and Bosworth Professor of Anglo-Saxon,
University of Cambridge

'*A Short History of the Anglo-Saxons* opens new windows on a distant yet very present world at a corner of early medieval Europe. The book provides a valuable guide for the newcomer and yet still throws up surprises for those already familiar with the period. Henrietta Leyser revels in the new work undertaken on the Anglo-Saxon period in recent years. She reveals how much we now do know, while at the same time reminding us how much we still don't, and raises provocative questions that those of us who wish to understand the period should think about. This little book packs in a great deal.'

– Ryan Lavelle, Reader in Early Medieval History,
University of Winchester

'Henrietta Leyser not only sets out the tumultuous events of Anglo-Saxon history with elegant clarity and eloquent cogency, but also explores many of its byways with a pithy wit. General readers will be drawn into a compelling narrative ranging over many centuries, and illustrated throughout with a wealth of translated quotations from contemporary sources. Students and specialists, meanwhile, will appreciate the breezy ease with which this sometimes baffling and always complex material is summarized and analysed by its distinguished author. This is a beautifully crafted and well-researched book.'

– Andy Orchard, Rawlinson and Bosworth Professor of Anglo-Saxon,
University of Oxford

A Short History of . . .

the Ottoman Empire	Baki Tezcan (University of California, Davis)
the Phoenicians	Mark Woolmer (Durham University)
the Reformation	Helen Parish (University of Reading)
the Renaissance in Northern Europe	Malcolm Vale (University of Oxford)
Revolutionary Cuba	Antoni Kapcia (University of Nottingham)
the Risorgimento	Nick Carter (Australian Catholic University, Sydney)
the Russian Revolution	Geoffrey Swain (University of Glasgow)
the Spanish Civil War	Julián Casanova (University of Zaragoza)
the Spanish Empire	Felipe Fernández-Armesto (University of Notre Dame) and José Juan López-Portillo (University of Oxford)
Transatlantic Slavery	Kenneth Morgan (Brunel University London)
Venice and the Venetian Empire	Maria Fusaro (University of Exeter)
the Vikings	Clare Downham (University of Liverpool)
the Wars of the Roses	David Grummitt (University of Kent)
the Weimar Republic	Colin Storer (University of Nottingham)

A SHORT HISTORY OF THE ANGLO-SAXONS

Henrietta Leyser

I.B. TAURIS

LONDON · NEW YORK

Published in 2017 by
I.B.Tauris & Co. Ltd
London • New York
www.ibtauris.com

ISBN: 978 1 78076 599 0 (HB)
ISBN: 978 1 78076 600 3 (PB)
eISBN: 978 1 78672 140 2
ePDF: 978 1 78673 140 1

A full CIP record for this book is available from the British Library
A full CIP record is available from the Library of Congress

Library of Congress Catalog Card Number: available

Typeset by Fakenham Prepress Solutions, Fakenham, Norfolk NR21 8NN
Printed and bound in Great Britain by T.J. International, Padstow, Cornwall

MIX
Paper from
responsible sources
FSC® C013056

To my children
Conrad, Ottoline, Crispin and Matilda
and my grandchildren
Francesca, Joshua, Hester, Hildie, Riddley, Felix and Tenar

Contents

List of Maps and Illustrations

MAPS

FIGURES

For contextual further details regarding the figures, see the appendix. All figures, unless stated otherwise, are public domain.

Preface

It was an act of great faith on the part of Alex Wright to ask me to write this book and of considerable temerity on my part to have agreed. In my research as a historian I have generally worked on periods after the Norman Conquest of 1066, but in my teaching the Anglo-Saxons have long held my attention. The need to consider so many different kinds of evidence and the problems to be faced in scrutinizing written such sources as have survived was a challenge that before long became something of a preoccupation. In the chapters that follow I chart a rapid journey from what used to be called 'the adventus', when various migrants arrived in England in the fifth century, until the Norman victory at Hastings in 1066. Since the days when I was myself an undergraduate both these events have come to be seen as considerably more complex than once was thought; it is some of this complexity that I hope to have shown in the following pages.

The great historian of the Anglo-Saxons, James Campbell, died as this little book was nearing completion. During visits I paid to him in his final months, I told him, with some trepidation, what I was doing: 'I hope' (he said) 'you have plenty to say about the Germanic homelands of all those who came.' I had to confess I had not and it fills me with considerable apprehension to consider in what other ways this book would have disappointed him. But he will also have known how behind it lay the inspiration of his scholarship and its power to transform our understanding of this period of English history.

I have many debts: to St Peter's College, Oxford for entrusting me with undergraduates to teach and for the pleasure and privilege

Henrietta Leyser

of still being able to use its library; to my friends for their continued encouragement, support and incomparable fellowship. I would like also to thank Kate Sykes for her careful reading of the whole manuscript and to Lisa Goodrum, David Campbell and the I.B.Tauris team together with Kim Storry at Fakenham Prepress Solutions for all their work in the book's final stages; Susannah Jayes for invaluable help with the illustrations and Gustav Zamore for his patience and exemplary copy editing of a very messy manuscript. Errors that remain are of course my own.

Timeline

410	Roman legions leave Britain.
429	Visit of St Germanus.
	[further fifth-century dates in general too uncertain for inclusion]
592	Aethelfrith: king of Bernicia (604 also of Deira).
597	St Augustine, sent by Pope Gregory, arrives in Kent to convert the English.
616	Penda, king of Mercia defeats and kills Aethelfrith. Accession in Northumbria of Edwin of Deira.
627	Baptism of Edwin.
633	Death of Edwin at the Battle of Hatfield Chase.
634	Oswald (son of Aethelfrith) becomes king of Northumbria.
635	Aidan (from Iona) arrives at Lindisfarne as Northumbria's missionary.
642	Battle of Maserfelth: Mercian victory. King Oswald is killed.
651	Death of Aidan.
655	Battle of the Winwaed: death of Penda of Mercia. Christianization of Mercia.
c.657	St Hilda: abbess of Whitby.
c.660	Wilfrid: abbot of Ripon.
664	Synod of Whitby: disputed date of Easter settled.
668	Theodore of Tarsus: archbishop of Canterbury.
671/3	Foundation of Hexham by Bishop Wilfrid.
673	Foundation of Ely community by Aethelthryth (formerly Queen of Northumbria).

673/4	Foundation of Wearmouth by Benedict Biscop.
c.681	Foundation of Jarrow by King Ecgfrith of Northumbria.
687	Death of Cuthbert, bishop of Lindisfarne.
688	Death of Cadwalla of Wessex, last pagan king (but dies baptized). Succeeded by Ine.
705	Aldhelm appointed Bishop of Sherborne.
c.731	Bede completes his *Ecclesiastical History of the English People*.
754	Martyrdom of St Boniface.
757	Death of Aethelbald, king of the Mercians. Accession of Offa.
787	Lichfield given archiepiscopal status.
793	Vikings sack Lindisfarne.
797	Death of Offa.
871	Accession of Alfred as King of Wessex.
878	Alfred's victory over the Viking army at Edington
899	Death of King Alfred; accession of Edward the Elder.
924	Accession of Athelstan. Reconquest of territory from Vikings.
937	Athelstan's victory at Brunanburh.
939	Death of King Athelstan.
959	Accession of Edgar as 'king of the English'.
973	Council of Winchester endorses *Regularis Concordia*. Coronation of Edgar at Bath.
978	Accession of Aethelred the Unready.
991	Battle of Maldon signals Viking return.
1016	Death of Aethelred the Unready. Cnut completes his conquest of England and becomes its king.
1037	Harold Harefoot succeeds Cnut.
1040	Harthacnut succeeds Harold.
1042	Edward the Confessor succeeds Harthacnut.
1051/2	Rebellion of Godwine family against Edward.
1066	January: death of Edward. Accession of Harold. September: Battle of Fulford Bridge. October: the Battle of Hastings. December: Crowning of William the Conqueror.

Map 1: Bishoprics and selected minsters

Map 2: English kingdoms *c.*850

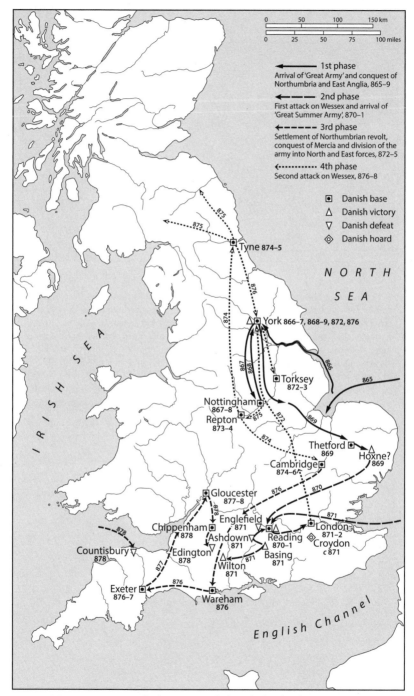

Map 3: Movement of Viking Armies before the battle of Edington, 878

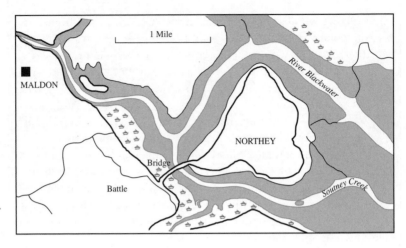

Map 4: The Battle of Maldon, 991
The Battle of Maldon was fought between Ealdorman Byrhtnoth of East Anglia
and a newly arrived Viking army. The Vikings had offered to sail away in return for
tribute but this Byrhtnoth refused, challenging the Vikings instead to fight. In the
course of the battle Byrhtnoth allowed the Vikings to cross the causeway (illustrated
here). The result was disastrous for the Anglo-Saxons. Byrhtnoth himself was killed
as were many of his men but the battle was commemorated in a poem notable for
its insistence on the heroic nature of both Byrhtnoth and his loyal followers, as well
as its indictment of those who fled once Byrhtnoth had been killed. Here, from the
poem, is Byrhtnoth's speech to the Viking messenger who has asked for tribute:

> Go, viking herald, answer back again,
> Tell your men a much more hostile tale:
> Here stands an earl undaunted with his troop,
> One who intends to save this fatherland,
> Ethelred's kingdom, and my liege lord's land
> And people. It shall be the heathen host
> That falls in fight. It seems to me too shameful
> That you should take our tribute to your ships
> Without a fight, now that you have advanced
> So far onto our soil. You shall not win
> Treasure so easily; but spear and swords
> Must first decide between us, the grim sport
> Of war, before we pay our tribute to you.'

trans. Richard Hamer, *A choice of Anglo-Saxon Verse* (London, 1970), p. 53.

Introduction

You see, my boy, before the Normans, the English had no real civilization:
they had been living in the Dark Ages, after all.
(Field Marshal Montgomery in conversation with Michael Wood,
in 1966, quoted in Michael Wood, *In Search of England*)[1]

Anglo-Saxon history, consigned once to the 'Dark Ages' that were
thought to have followed on from the collapse of the Roman
Empire in the fifth century, has for some time now been enjoying
a renaissance. The unearthing of the great ship burial at Sutton
Hoo in 1939 scotched forever any idea that the Germanic peoples
who had migrated to England after the departure of the Roman
legions in 410 were no more than poverty-stricken barbarians,
reduced to subsistence farming. The development now of new
techniques – DNA samples, for example, and the use of isotopes –
is providing innovative ways of deciphering the incomers' origins
and population patterns. Moreover, quite unexpected and random
discoveries are, with seeming regularity, being unearthed through
the use of metal detectors, the Staffordshire Hoard of 2009 being the
most spectacular to date. Anglo-Saxon history is then a fast moving
field, exciting in its interdisciplinarity. Even at the time of writing
news is coming in of important archeological work in progress at St
Cuthbert's original monastery of Lindisfarne.

The chapters that follow aim to provide an introduction to
some of the current debates in Anglo-Saxon history thrown up by
such discoveries as these and to show why the period is an essential
part of English history. England was not born fully fledged but it
was in this period that it emerged, assuming a shape that is still

recognizable today. Up until 1974, when the shires of England were reorganized, the boundaries were essentially those which Anglo-Saxon rulers had determined; the great monasteries of Anglo-Saxon England now serve as Anglican cathedrals but their earlier traditions have not been forgotten. Edward the Confessor's abbey of Westminster has remained the principal site of coronations ever since its re-foundation by Edward, the form of service derived from the 973 ceremony mandated by King Edgar.

But history is never, of course, only or even principally about the search for roots or continuities. Above all, it is about understanding the complexity of the past and how it is always possible to ask new questions from what we know and indeed from what we do not. My hope therefore is that the chapters that follow will provide not so much answers but rather frameworks for enquiry which readers can pursue for themselves in their search for the making of Anglo-Saxon England.

The book was completed in the summer of 2016 at the time of the referendum which asked all British citizens whether they wished to remain in the European Union or whether to leave it. Many 'leavers', having won the vote, expressed their delight at having 'won back England from Europe'. It was impossible, as I wrote my final pages during those days, not to be struck by how differently both Europe and England (not even named then as 'England' for most of the book) were seen during my time period. Around AD 400 Europe, originally a mythical land, now shared the universe with Asia and Africa, and was fast becoming equated with Christendom. Britain was still (just) a Roman province and all freeborn Britons were, automatically, Roman citizens.

What may have happened to these 'Romano-British' after the departure of the Roman legions in 410 is discussed in Chapter 1. Chapter 2 begins with the mission sent by a pope to bring Christianity to the 'English people' but it is not until after the Viking invasions and the reconquest of territory the Vikings had won that the country known as 'England' came into being (Chapters 5 and 6), to be conquered some 125 years later in 1066 (Chapter 8) by second-generation Vikings from Normandy whose descendants would in time come to see themselves as 'English'.

The story this book tells is then complex – the telling of it made all the more so by the fragmentary and partisan nature of the written evidence and by the challenge of absorbing the new archaeological finds that over recent years have come thick and fast. To quote the late James Campbell, writing about the fifth and sixth centuries:

> The natural vice of the historian is to claim to know about the past. Nowhere is this more dangerous than when it is staked in Britain between 400 and 600. We can identify some events and movements: make a fair guess at others: try to imagine the whole as a picture in the fire. That is all. Knowledge will creep forward by the accumulation of facts, especially archaeological facts and by the dialectic of hypotheses. But what really happened will never be known.[2]

Welcome, then, to what Campbell himself calls 'a quagmire' ...

1

AFTER THE ROMANS

As the Romans went back home, there eagerly emerged from the coracles that had carried them across the sea-valleys the foul hordes of the Scots and Picts, like dark throngs of worms who wriggle out of the narrow fissures in the rock when the sun is high and the weather grows warm ... [then was] devised [a plan] for our land ... that the ferocious Saxons ... hated by man and God should be let into the island like wolves into the fold, to beat back the peoples of the north. Nothing more destructive, nothing more bitter has ever befallen the land.

(Gildas, *The Ruin of Britain*)[1]

'410: In this year the Goths stormed Rome and the Romans never afterwards reigned in Britain.' Thus did the *Anglo-Saxon Chronicle*, first compiled in the ninth century, recount with unwavering certainty the abrupt end of Roman Britain. The urgent need for troops to withstand barbarian attacks on the continent had indeed led to the sudden withdrawal of the Roman armies stationed on the island and, in many parts of the country, the economic consequences were swift, devastating and remembered as such. In 418, continued the *Chronicle*, 'the Romans collected all the treasures which were in Britain, and hid some in the ground, so that no one could find them afterwards, and took some with them into Gaul'.[2] The reference is enigmatic but telling: with the withdrawal of the army, and the need to pay its soldiers, the monetary economy and the urban life of Roman Britain had swiftly collapsed. For the better part of 200 years, no new coins were minted. Meanwhile, the nearest contemporary record, from the sixth century, entitled *The Ruin of Britain*, was unsparing in its description of the chaos and internecine fighting that was to follow the aftermath of the Roman departure: 'fragments of corpses, covered (as it were) with a purple crust of congealed blood, looked as though they had been mixed up in some dreadful wine-press'.[3]

The *Ruin of Britain* was the work of Gildas, a scholar, possibly a monk, who was most probably based in the south-west of Britain. In *The Ruin*, Gildas describes how after the departure of the Roman legions, Scots and Picts from the north of the island relentlessly pushed southwards, whereupon the Britons beseeched the Romans to return and come to their aid, but the Romans refused; in their despair the Britons turned for help to pagan mercenaries, the Saxons, from across the sea. Through this act of 'crass stupidity', as Gildas saw it, Christian Britain became ravished and plundered by these Saxon barbarians: 'All the major towns were laid low by the repeated battering of enemy rams; laid low, too, all the inhabitants – church leaders, priests and people alike, as the swords glinted all around and the flames crackled.'[4]

Historians have long been wary of prose as colourful as Gildas'. But Gildas was no tabloid writer. He was a learned and a brilliant writer, well-schooled in Latin oratory.[5] Uncertainties as to exactly when and where he was writing continue, however, to puzzle historians and make it difficult to use his work to establish any kind of chronology of events. He himself tells us that he took up his pen 44 years after a spectacular British victory over the Saxons at the Battle of Mount Badon (*Mons Badonicus*). Gildas' target was the five British kings whom he castigates for indolence, complacency and the squandering of the opportunity which this great battle had offered them. The dates of at least one of Gildas' kings can be calculated with a reasonable degree of confidence and on this basis it would seem as if the famous battle took place sometime near the end of the fifth century, with 530–50 as a likely time then for the composition of *The Ruin*.[6] Such a date, well over a hundred years after the departure of the Roman legions in 410, together with the very western setting of Gildas' work – the kings he addresses ruled in what is today Wales and in the West Country – means that there is every reason to read his narrative of the fifth century with caution. The scenario he painted may have seemed plausible to his own contemporaries, and no doubt it satisfied his own rhetorical needs, but it is now clear that, however closely it depicted events in his own locality, there was never any one story which could have been applied to the whole of the country. With that proviso in mind, let us, nonetheless, take a closer look at Gildas' Britain.

Excavations make it clear that in some areas of the west of Britain the departure of the Romans was followed by a notable revival of earlier ways of living. Precisely in those areas where there is no evidence of early Saxon settlement there is, by contrast, considerable evidence of British hill-forts being restored and re-occupied – and in style. South Cadbury (in what is now Somerset) provides just one example of how, in the fifth century, such places gained a new lease of life. Here, major new building works were undertaken, trade with the Mediterranean was maintained and, to judge by the quantity of pottery, wine and glass that was imported, life continued to be enjoyed and celebrated in (to follow Gildas) a spirit of hedonism, dangerously oblivious of the advance westwards of Saxon conquerors. When, at last, the Britons awoke to the perils confronting them and their way of life, the one victory they then won (at Mount Badon) only lulled them into a false sense of security.

Fans of the 'real King Arthur' have long been tantalized by the failure of Gildas to mention their hero by name, all the more since Gildas attributes the victory at Mount Badon not to Arthur, but to a certain 'Ambrosius Aurelianus', whom he described as 'the last of the Romans'. Valiant attempts to prove that Ambrosius and Arthur are one and the same notwithstanding, it is more fruitful to widen the Arthurian search and to accept that, rather than one heroic figure, it is more likely that there were indeed many such, of whom Arthur, 'real' or not, became in time the totemic leader. Thus, the long-cherished suggestion that South Cadbury was the original Camelot should be abandoned; but the possibility that every restored hill-fort (and the sites stretch from the south-western peninsula of Britain up to modern-day Scotland) had its own collection of 'Arthurian' figures seems highly likely.[7] These are the figures long remembered in heroic poetry, not least in the battle poem, *The Goddodin*.[8] This poem, in the form we have it, is usually dated to *c*.600. It is thought to have been composed somewhere near Edinburgh, in a northern dialect of Brittonic, a language cognate with Welsh. The poem records an epic battle, seemingly fought at Catterick in Northumberland, between a carefully picked troop of native Christians against a much larger force of Saxon 'heathens'. The heathens annihilate the Christians – there are only three survivors (of whom one is the poet), but nothing is allowed to dull the excitement of the preparation for the battle, nor the heroism of the fight:

> The men went to Catraeth, they were famous; wine and mead from gold vessels was their drink for a year, according to the honourable custom; three men and three score and three hundred wearing torques. Of those that hastened forth after the choice drink none escaped but three ... the two battle-hounds of Aeron and Cynon ... and I, with my blood streaming down ...[9]

In one verse, the hero is explicitly described as brave, generous and fearsome, 'though he was no Arthur' – a reference which has caused much spilt ink.[10] It is very probably an interpolation. *The Goddodin* was at first an oral poem and, since the earliest manuscript is thought to date only from the ninth century, the reference here to 'Arthur' may do no more than add to the evidence, by then plentiful, of the legendary Arthur, victor of Mount Badon, a figure of whom any Saxon should beware.

But Mount Badon, with or without an 'Arthur', was undoubtedly a telling British victory. That it was (as Gildas feared) only a pause in the advance westward of the Anglo-Saxons seems confirmed by the entry in the *Anglo-Saxon Chronicle* for 577, which reports:

> In this year Cuthwine and Ceawlin fought against the Britons and killed three kings, Conmial, Condidan and Farinmail, at the place which is called Dyrham; and they captured three of their cities, Gloucester, Cirencester and Bath.[11]

'Dyrham' is six miles north of Bath along the A46 and the annal can reasonably be suspected of reflecting West Saxon claims to the three named cities, and not a report of an actual battle, but nonetheless it clearly mattered in the annals of Anglo-Saxon history that these particular cities should be recorded as having been captured. Even if these cities were derelict, they still represented the grandeur of Rome and a very different way of life from that of the nearby (and newly restored) British hill-fort Cadbury Congresbury.

The years after 577, and after the supposed battle at Catterick, witnessed new, shifting alliances. Linguistic evidence, the survival notably of both Welsh and of Cornish, makes it plain that despite any victories they may have had, nonetheless there were limits as to how far west the new immigrants were prepared to venture, so much so that it has even been suggested that it is only with Edward I's defeat of the Welsh in 1282 that the final collapse of Roman Britain should be dated.[12] That the fate of post-Roman Britain has so often been simplified must of course be attributed in large part to the master narrative presented by the Northumbrian monk Bede in his *Ecclesiastical History of the English People,* completed *c.*731.

It was once said that:

> if one were given the chance to interview any character in English history in the hope of increasing the sum total of our knowledge, one would be likely to obtain more really significant information from an hour's talk with the Venerable Bede than with any other figure at any period.[13]

Bede certainly had further material at his disposal than had Gildas and, in any case, his magisterial style and didactic purpose gave his account a credibility which Gildas' rhetoric had forfeited. Thus it was Bede's *History* which soon came to be seen as authoritative. As Bede told the story, after the failure of the British appeal to the Romans to return to come to their aid, it was a certain king named Vortigern who suggested that the Britons should seek help from nearer home.[14] And so it was that in 449 three warships, bearing 'Angles or Saxons', arrived on British shores. So successful seemed this scheme (and so astute were the Saxons who spotted both 'the fertility of the island and the slackness of the Britons') that before long more and more Saxons and their allies arrived, coming, according to Bede, from 'three very powerful Germanic tribes, the Saxons, Angles and Jutes'. Their leaders Hengist and Horsa (now thought to be no more than mythical founding figures, whose names mean 'horse' and 'stallion') were, Bede assures us, of royal stock, descended from the pagan god Woden. But before long, 'hordes of these peoples' began to crowd into the island and to settle it.[15] The Jutes took Kent and the Isle of Wight; the Saxons occupied what is now Essex, Sussex and the South-West, while the Midlands and the North went to the Angles.

But far from defending the Britons, the Angles now allied with the Picts so that the British position was even worse than it had been before, and then, when the Britons failed to provide the provisions the newcomers demanded, a mutiny followed. The Britons were shown no mercy. Some were massacred; some fled overseas; others died of starvation or at best were condemned to a life of slavery.

In his description of the years of terror in post-Roman Britain, Bede's debt to Gildas has long been recognized and for some years now Bede's knowledge, as well as his purposes, has been subjected to ever closer scrutiny and many new approaches have been adopted towards his work. Questions which had once seemed relatively simple to answer now appear to be considerably more complex. Could it really be possible, for example, to accept that the newcomers belonged to groups as distinct as the three which Bede had named? Material culture (such as the brooches men and women wore; their pots; their dress fastenings and the remains of their burial rites; and notably whether they practised inhumation or cremation) had once seemed to hold all the clues necessary to decode tribal identities and had made it possible for the historian to colour in his or her map of England accordingly and to adorn it with arrows to show the relationship of the newcomers to their continental homelands. Closer analyses have shown how highly problematic such uses of the evidence can be. In the light of World War II, moreover, historians, increasingly wary of concepts that smacked of 'racial purity', began to question the beguiling simplicity of such arrows and labels and to wonder whether Bede's tribes had any objective reality: might these not simply be useful names acquired by heterogeneous peoples after they had settled their new lands? Could it not be that the people of Kent became notably 'Jutish' only after their arrival on the Isle of Wight and in Kent, and not before? Was it not possible that particular fashions signalled aspirations rather than inalienable birthrights? In much the same way, the Britons, it was suggested, could easily have become assimilated into the families of the incomers. Dressed, housed and buried according to the fashions of those who had conquered them, the Britons thus became in no time every bit as 'German' as their new masters. ('Masters' who in turn would soon be doing their very best to appear 'Roman'.) No need, then, to believe in the labels provided by Bede, nor in the massacres of

Britons both he and Gildas had described. All that is needed instead is some understanding of ethnogenesis.[16]

Ethnogenesis notwithstanding, questions relating to the fates of the Britons and to the original homes of those who came to be known as 'Anglo-Saxon' have failed to go away. Not so long ago, a flurry was caused by the possibility that DNA testing would reveal all. Doubts have now been cast on the viability of this evidence and yet another method (the analysis of isotopes) has been suggested instead. Such work is still in its infancy, and cannot help, for example, with the analyses of cremated bodies, but it seems likely to support the conclusion that the particular interest of the fifth century may well lie in the range and number of stories that can be told, rather than in any breakthrough discovery delivering a master narrative. The evidence provided in this way from a cemetery in West Heslerton, in North Yorkshire, for example, has produced intriguing results: out of 24 buried there only four are likely to have come from Scandinavia; 13 from west of the Pennines; seven were local.[17] Consequently, in what follows the emphasis has been placed on the variety of communities across fifth-century Britain, and on the many different ways in which they shaped the legacy Rome had left behind. In time such communities would indeed become absorbed into the new kingdoms of Bede's England but in the fifth century no such grand enterprise could possibly have been conceived. The places to be looked at have therefore been chosen to give a sense of variety and should not be taken as necessarily 'typical' of any particular category of site; the variables and the gaps in our knowledge make it impossible to suggest patterns of settlement with the kind of conviction later periods can command. Generalizations must, on the whole, be limited to expressions not of what we know but of what we do not. The evidence is seldom transparent. Even the location of many early Anglo-Saxon settlements is uncertain. Thus pottery, so often used to identify Roman or later medieval sites, may in the case of early Anglo-Saxon settlements be entirely absent from the record, either because the settlers were not as yet making pots or because those they had were of such poor quality that they have broken into tiny fragments, leaving only an extremely meagre harvest of shards for the archaeologist to find.[18] The meaning of objects may be imponderable. Cremation combs, for example, frequently (but not always) found at many of the cremation sites of East Anglia and the East Midlands, turn out to be impossible to sort by gender, age or status; nor can any explanation be found as to why some of the combs had been burnt along with the body while others had not been put through the flames. In inhumations, combs by contrast are seemingly rare, but is this simply because they keep less well in the ground than when placed in a funeral urn?[19] With such reservations in mind, let us move to Mucking in Essex, one of the earliest Anglo-Saxon sites to be extensively excavated.[20]

Mucking is situated on the northern bank of the Thames. In origin it was a Roman foundation, perhaps even an adjunct to those Saxon shore forts which the Romans kept manned by cohorts of Germanic mercenaries to help protect both the coastline and in particular London; the discovery during early excavations of an elaborate copper and silver buckle, kept now in the British Museum, of the type known to have been issued to Roman military personnel in the fourth century and often found in graves both in England and in Scandinavia, first suggested this possibility. But whatever the origin of the settlement, by the fifth century a cluster of Germanic settlers was establishing itself on the deserted farmlands of Mucking, though they shunned the established Romano-British cemeteries, choosing instead to bury their dead in new plots. Yet despite this, and even though Mucking was a comparatively large settlement (with eventually perhaps as many as 90 inhabitants), there is nothing about its development to suggest confrontation or competition, either among themselves or with any previous inhabitants. As the land under cultivation became exhausted the settlement shifted, but there is no evidence that the newcomers ever tried to establish clear property boundaries and very little to suggest anything beyond the loosest of social systems. Both cremation and inhumation were practised. One or two of the men were buried with swords, one or two of the women with brooches, but such differentiation was not reflected in the Mucking housing.

Excavated at Mucking were over 200 wooden huts, known by archaeologists as *grubenhauser* or SFBs (sunken-featured buildings) since typically each such hut (measuring on average around 3 × 4 metres) was erected over a pit – sometimes the pit formed a cellar, but this was by no means always the case. Such buildings have a long history on the continent but were unknown in England until the fifth century and much about their use remains controversial.[21]

Fig. 1: Spong Hill man: pottery lid

Fig. 2: Mucking belt fitting

Archaeologists interpreted them at first as evidence of the primitive living standards to be expected of barbarian invaders but it soon became clear that *grubenhauser* were never intended to provide housing; categorized now as workshops and storage huts, they have been found at early Anglo-Saxon settlements across England. The precise uses to which such huts were put remain hard to recover since they were regularly dismantled; much of the archaeological deposit is therefore likely to have accumulated only after the abandonment of each hut and as the settlement itself shifted. It has, however, been suggested that the Mucking huts may have clustered around two main areas, thus forming 'industrial' centres of the settlement for the making both of cloth and for the working of iron and lead. But absent at Mucking, as elsewhere in Anglo-Saxon England, is any evidence for wheel-thrown pottery. For almost 300 years no such pottery was made anywhere in England. The technology and the expertise had simply disappeared.[22]

From Mucking to the centre of London is some 30 miles, but whereas by the year 500, Mucking seems to have established itself as a viable community, London had become a ghost town. With no army to defend it (not even a putative mercenary from Mucking), and with little or no coinage to support trade, city-life had very quickly collapsed. This was not, as we shall see, true of cities everywhere in Britain, but there can be no doubt that in the South and South-East of the country the evidence of any urban Anglo-Saxon life is negligible. In London, a few squatters may have settled within its deserted streets, but the layers of 'black earth' within the city, made up of the debris of collapsed buildings, provide ample testimony to the desolate nature of the city. London's walls, however, still stood and if we are to believe the *Anglo-Saxon Chronicle*, then these walls provided a place of refuge for the Britons of Kent during an attack in 456 (led by the legendary figure of Hengist), but we have no evidence of any permanent settlement within the city. In time, Roman walls and Roman buildings would come to inspire both emulation and imitation among Anglo-Saxons, but in the fifth and sixth centuries none among them had any experience of building in stone. All living accommodation, and all *grubenhauser*, was therefore built of timber. And while occasionally (as at Canterbury) some evidence has been found of early wooden buildings within the walls, more often (as at London), the earliest Anglo-Saxon settlements are to be found outside the city walls.[23]

The best that could be done to prop up a 'failing' Roman town was achieved at Wroxeter in the South-West of England.[24] Wroxeter, a Roman fort inhabited also by the *Cornovii* tribe (inhabitants originally of the Iron Age fort at Wrekin), was the fourth largest city in Roman Britain. Even after the army had moved from it to Chester (in AD 88), the city still flourished: tanning, weaving and the mining of lead and copper were among the industries that ensured its prosperity. What is surprising is the extent to which the city managed to adapt to the circumstances of post-Roman Britain, when there was no longer a money economy in operation. Goods were seemingly bartered and, at first, buildings repaired if not to former standards at least so they could be functional. By the mid sixth century, however, more radical steps seemed necessary: substantial demolition work now began, new buildings were put up and a new gravel street laid. Roman measurements were used for these, but the buildings themselves were different from anything the city had seen before. Thus, on the site of the Roman baths complex, the plentiful supply of rubble now available was converted into a huge platform suitable to bear the weight of a substantial timber-framed building. On the same site, as many as 33 other buildings were erected, some timber-framed, others with walls built of clay. How, logistically, was all this work possible? How was it financed? Questions rather than answers abound.

Whoever it was who was master-minding the reconstruction of Wroxeter, of this we can be certain: he was not an Anglo-Saxon. In the mid-sixth century, there is as yet no trace of any Anglo-Saxon settlement as far west as Wroxeter. What there may be, however, is enough evidence to suggest that sixth-century Wroxeter was under the command of its bishop. To questions relating to the survival of British Christianity we will need to return in Chapter 2, to the time when Wroxeter became caught up in a world of shifting and messy alliances and power struggles between pagan and Christian, British and Anglo-Saxon, Northumbrian and Mercian. But, for fifth- and sixth-century Wroxeter, it was seemingly not fear of conquest that was at issue; what mattered was how to improvise, how to adapt, how to survive.

It is perhaps the instinct for survival which helps explain the 'disappearance' of Britons of the South and South-East. These were the areas of England which from the archaeological record seem to have been extensively settled by incoming groups of Germanic settlers, but which yield no clues as to the fate of the native population. But nothing indicates that they were massacred; they simply 'disappear'. Outside the Roman garrison town of Dorchester, for example, two cemeteries have been excavated. The earlier of the two at Queensford contain burials from the fourth to fifth century, unaccompanied by grave goods. It is thus reasonable to assume that here lie the bodies of British Christians. But at some point in the fifth century, burials at Queensford stop and a new cemetery is opened up at close-by Berinsfield. These burials have grave goods. The conclusion seems inescapable: the customs and fashions of Germanic newcomers are now dominant. The Britons have 'vanished'; seemingly they have chosen to assimilate.[25] In some areas it is indeed possible that Britons were enslaved, but this would seem most likely to have been the case in the west of England, at the time when the new Anglo-Saxon kingdom of Wessex was emerging, and therefore in the sixth century, rather than in the fluid world of the fifth.

The plausibility of a scenario in which communities of Britons and immigrants from various parts of Europe found ways of living together is, of course, likely to have depended on the numbers involved. For a long time, it was assumed that the Anglo-Saxons arrived *en masse*, ready to impose their will and their customs with due belligerence. The archaeological record, however, now suggests otherwise. The farmland the newcomers took over, as at Mucking, was often not of top quality, while the methods of its cultivation were frequently unchanged. For quite some time spelt continued to be grown, to be only gradually replaced by wheat; new methods of weaving were introduced, but the flocks of the white-fleeced sheep introduced by the Romans were still maintained, providing in time textiles for high-status use.[26] The co-existence this agricultural continuity suggests becomes perhaps intelligible when it is remembered that, under the Romans, the Britons had long become accustomed to the presence of Germanic peoples (the mercenaries of the Roman army). The 'new Germans' at least did not expect tax. They may well have been accepted as less onerous masters than those whom the Britons had long endured. It is of course also clear that in some places at least the expectation that the Romans would re-appear may well have been entertained. Even after the legions had left, it must still have been considered a possibility that, once the crisis for which they had been recalled had been settled, they would return, since it is evident that Britain was still considered a part of the new Roman world which Christianity was now shaping.

So much is evident from the visit of Bishop Germanus from Gaul in 429 (and possibly a return visit a decade or so later) in order to combat the heresy of Pelagianism (a heresy which denied the existence of original sin). Germanus made the journey to the shrine of the British martyr St Alban, a shrine thought to be situated outside the great Roman city of Verulamium, a city rivalled in size only by London and Cirencester. Here Germanus found British Christians and a decaying city, but as yet, little evidence of Saxon occupation or hostility – or rather nothing, according to the hagiographical account, that could serve to intimidate the Christians in any way. Priests chanting 'Alleluia' provided more than enough protection.[27]

The paradox, however, is clear: whatever further archaeological discoveries may yet reveal and, however small the number of immigrants might prove to be, nothing can obscure the fact that English is a Germanic language and England the land of the Angles.[28] The extent of this cultural conquest is such that it remains hard

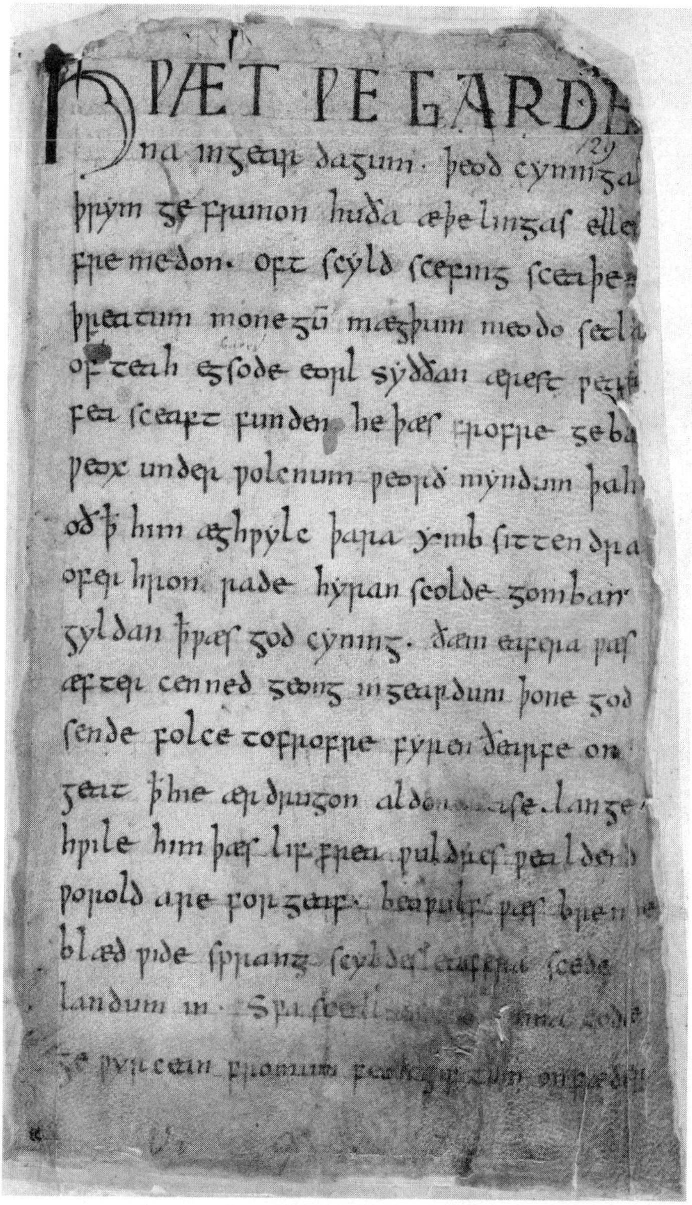

ᚻPÆT PE GARDE
na mᵹeaᵱ daᵹum · þeod cynniᵹa
þrym ᵹefrunon huða æþelinᵹaſ elle
fremedon. oft ſcyld ſceþinᵹ ſceaþe
þreatum moneᵹū mæᵹþum meodo ſetl
of teah eᵹſode eopl syððan æreſt peſ
fea ſceaft funden he þær froffre ᵹeba
peox under polcnum peorð myndū þah
oð þ him æᵹhpylc þara ymb ſittendra
ofer hron rade hyran ſcolde ᵹomban
ᵹyldan þ pæſ ᵹod cyninᵹ. ðæm eafera paſ
æfter cenned ᵹeonᵹ in ᵹeardum þone ᵹod
ſende folce to frofre fyren ðearfe on
ᵹeat þ hie ær druᵹon aldor aſe lanᵹe
hpile him þæſ lif frea puldreſ pealdend
porold are for ᵹeaf · beopulf pæſ bren
blæd pide ſpranᵹ ſcyldeſ eafera ſcede
landum in · Spa ſceal
ᵹe pyrcean fromum feoh ᵹiftū on fæder

Fig. 3: The first folio of the poem *Beowulf*

Fig. 4: Replica of the helmet from the Sutton Hoo burial ship, mound 1

Fig. 5: Belt buckle from the Sutton Hoo burial ship, mound 1

to believe that so complete a take-over could have been achieved without, at the least, a trickle from those rivers of blood bemoaned by Gildas. And there can be no doubt that, eventually, much blood was indeed spilt, but it seems increasingly likely that the bitterest battles belonged to the sixth and seventh centuries, rather than to the fifth. The fifth century indeed witnessed the withering away of Roman Britain and the gradual ascendancy of Germanic peoples over the native population of much of what would become known as England, but it is only for the sixth century that we have significant evidence of warfare and then it is, on the whole, between rival groups of 'invaders' rather than between 'invaders' and 'natives'.

What mattered in the fifth century was settlement; the sixth-century scenario was very different. Communities across the country were becoming increasingly hierarchical and as every leader seized power, so too did he attempt to extend his territory and to proclaim his authority. In this process unexpected help would come, ultimately, in the shape of Christian missionaries sent from Rome, though the old gods would still have their part to play. For reasons that are unlikely ever to be fully understood the apparently peaceable and self-sufficient communities of the fifth century became caught up in wars fought under first pagan and then Christian banners in the sixth and seventh centuries. Relative prosperity seemingly fuelled ambition, so that the proverbial ploughshares were now turned into spears and pruning forks into swords. Settlements became subject to kinglets; cemeteries of modest and equally ranked graves were replaced by the fabulously rich graves of the dead, whose resting place depended on carefully calibrated hierarchies.

In the fifth to mid sixth centuries, both cremation and inhumation of the dead had been practised. In various ways, the rank of the deceased had been displayed but without any particular flamboyance. In both rituals the body was dressed and provided with a range of artefacts – jewellery, combs, weapons (the weapons seemingly signs of status, rather than of military prowess, since they are found with the very young as well as the very old). Regional variations, however, were marked, with cremation considerably more usual in the 'Anglian' midlands, whereas inhumation predominated in the 'Saxon' south. Jewellery fashions, too, differed: 'Anglian' women, for example, secured the wrists of their garments with sleeve-clasps, and showed a preference for a particular style of great square-headed brooches, while 'Saxon' women favoured smaller brooches, often worn in pairs. But the late sixth to seventh century witnessed dramatic changes. On the one hand, the distinctive variations of the earlier sixth century now disappeared; on the other, certain graves (both of those inhumed as well as of those cremated) were now singled out for particular attention. Such graves were furnished with spectacular richness and were positioned in the landscape in mounds or barrows so that they would be highly visible.

The best known of these ostentatious graves remains that at Sutton Hoo, in Suffolk, first excavated in 1938 and studied much more intensively in subsequent decades.[29] Initial interest focused on the evidence of the great ship burial of mound 1. Here was displayed for the first time incontrovertible evidence of the wealth and richness of seventh-century Anglo-Saxon England – the discovery in the nineteenth century of the rich barrow burial at Taplow in Buckinghamshire had been so hampered by inadequate techniques, compounded by the damage caused by the collapse of the yew tree growing by the barrow, that its importance has often been overlooked. Not so with Sutton Hoo. Further excavations, finally completed in 1997, have thrown up a host of new questions about the identities of the dead, about the comparative wealth of the site and the meanings behind the furnishing of the barrows and of the ceremonies that must have accompanied each interment. Even now, the whole site has not been excavated leaving as many as five mounds for future exploration by scholars who may have new skills and new techniques as well as new questions to ask.

Of the twenty mounds excavated so far, the grave in mound 1 remains unsurpassed in terms of its treasures, but these have now been analysed much more firmly than before within the context of the site as a whole. Here clearly was a cemetery designed not for the needs of a community, but only for use by an elite group. The inhabitant of mound 1 had companions – a young man, in mound 17, buried with weapons, cauldron and bucket and a very splendid harness for a horse; the horse was in a pit nearby. In mound 14 lay a woman whose grave had been robbed, but some modest grave goods still remained to her; in mound 2 there were again spectacular treasures to be found, this time placed around a man in a chamber on top of whom a ship had been placed; close to mound 5 were the remains of three young people – possibly children. Six mounds were built over cremations. The gruesome surprise came with the discovery of 37 bodies who had been executed; it now seems that these victims belong to a later date and that they are probably the graves of those considered so wicked as to be unfit for a Christian burial.

At the time of its discovery, Sutton Hoo seemed quite unsurpassable in its wealth but recent evidence suggests that there is no knowing what the building of new roads or new housing estates or metal detectors may yet reveal; in 2003, roadworks at Prittlewell in south-east Essex revealed the barrow burial of an aristocrat. Nearby, at Rayleigh, there is a meagrely furnished cremation site, but at Prittlewell itself excavators found an elaborate burial chamber furnished with a spectacular copper-alloy hanging bowl, a Byzantine flagon – a rarity in England – and an equally rare folding stool. The gold buckle had probably been made in Kent; it is only the third such buckle to have been recovered from an Anglo-Saxon burial.[30] In the last few years at Coddenham, in Suffolk, the building of new Wimpey homes has led to the unearthing of a seventh- to eighth-century burial ground containing mainly unfurnished burials, but three of these had barrows erected over them, in one of which was found the body of a woman buried in a bed.[31] Excavations at Street House, near Loftus, between 2005 and 2007 also unearthed the bed burial of a woman, upsetting preconceptions that this form of burial was unknown so far North.[32] The body was adorned with a rich gold pendant, inset with garnets. In 2012, a further bed burial (the fifteenth to date) was found at Trumpington near Cambridge. The young woman here was buried with a gold and garnet cross, similar to the pectoral cross found in the grave of St Cuthbert.[33]

Despite items such as the Trumpington cross, and, at Prittlewell, the little crosses of gold foil placed (or so it is thought) over the eyes of the dead man, we cannot be entirely certain of the faith of those buried. Christian symbols could have been adopted for a variety of reasons, only loosely connected with religious belief or practice. Archaeologists place such rich burials of the seventh century to a 'final phase' since grave goods would soon fall out of fashion. This 'final phase' denotes then a very specific period of religious and political ferment and transition rather than a world of settled beliefs. This, arguably, is the world too, to which the poem *Beowulf* belongs.

Fig. 6: Detail from the south face of the Ruthwell Cross, Dumfries and Galloway

Debates as to when *Beowulf* was composed are unlikely ever to be resolved. The manuscript in which it has been preserved dates only from around 1000, but the Scandinavian setting of the poem and its focus on the exploits of the Geats and Danes, in contrast to the English who get no attention and Christian beliefs very little, make it seem probable that it is in origin a much older tale. In it, the eponymous hero goes off in search of fame, fortune and adventure. He offers his services to a Danish king whose country, for 12 years, has been terrorized by a man-eating monster named Grendel. Beowulf kills Grendel but he has then to contend with his wrathful mother. He tracks her down to a watery lair (the description of its horrors will later be borrowed by a Christian writer attempting to depict Hell) and after a mighty struggle succeeds in killing her. Stories within stories are included in the poem and the finale comes only many years after Beowulf's feats as a young man. After a successful reign as king of the Geats, Beowulf, now nearing the end of his life, has to face the calamity that has struck his kingdom in the shape of a perilous dragon. The dragon has been provoked to anger because one of its treasures has been stolen; its enraged attacks of revenge are such that Beowulf, despite his great age, determines that he will take it upon himself to track it down and kill it. His heroism stands in sharp contrast to that of his retainers all of whom, bar one, flee during the ensuing fight. Both dragon and Beowulf die of their wounds. With much lamentation, Beowulf's body is carried to a magnificent funeral pyre, hung about with helmets, battle-shields and coats of mail:

> Heaven swallowed up the smoke. Then the people of the Weders constructed on the promontory a mound which was high and broad, to be seen far and near by those voyaging across the waves, and in ten days they had built up a monument to the man renowned in battle; they surrounded the remains of the fire with a rampart, the finest that the most skilful men could devise. In the barrow they placed rings and brooches, all such trappings as men disposed to strife had earlier taken from the hoard; they let the earth keep the warriors treasure, gold in the dust, where it remains now, as useless to men as it was before.[34]

Over these ceremonies hangs not only a sense of futility of war but also a deep sense of foreboding, a fear that without their leader, the kingdom will be prey to attack: feuds and cycles of revenge will surely follow.

How to use *Beowulf* as a historical source has long exercised scholars, but just as the discovery of the Sutton Hoo ship burial transformed understanding of the opening scene of the poem (in which the body of Beowulf's father Scyld is sent out to sea in a ship laden with treasure), so too must the discovery of the Staffordshire Hoard alter all perceptions of the treasure found throughout the poem, not least that of treasure plundered in battle. The full story of the Staffordshire Hoard has yet to be told (since it was discovered only in 2009) and it may, of course, never be known, just as no one is ever likely to be certain who was buried in the mounds at Sutton Hoo. But *Beowulf*, Sutton Hoo and the Staffordshire Hoard do, together, tell a story of ambition, wealth, political insecurity and precarious Christianity.[35]

The re-introduction of Christianity will be considered in the next chapter, but the new political order that welcomed it needs some introduction here.

Bede, writing his *Ecclesiastical History*, had a clear conception of the political and ethnic make-up of England. As we have seen, Bede believed the invaders had come from three distinct Germanic tribes: Saxons, Angles and Jutes. The Jutes had settled themselves in the Isle of Wight and in Kent; the Saxons had created the kingdoms of the East Angles, the Middle Angles and Mercia. North of the Humber, the kingdoms of Deira and Bernicia, both made up of Angles, united to form the kingdom of Northumbria, a kingdom which at times stretched far into the north of what is today Scotland. For Bede, the history of these kingdoms is intimately tied up with the conversion story and how each kingdom came to play its part in the creation of a Church which would transcend political boundaries. Thus Bede's kingdoms, populated from the start by distinct peoples, would in time come to accept a new God and a new political identity. But once this grand narrative is discarded, it becomes much more difficult to know how it was that kingdoms emerged. On what were they built?

One of the most revealing, as well as the most enigmatic, documents to have survived from this period is the so-called Tribal Hideage. This document (possibly, but not certainly, a tribute list) names 34 territories south of the Humber. The territories vary enormously in size – ranging from as many as 30,000 hides (a hide being the amount of land thought necessary to support a peasant household) down to 300. Included are the major kingdoms of the South – Mercia, East Anglia, Essex, Kent, Surrey and Wessex – but what is most striking is the appearance of small communities, of clusters of peoples, who otherwise have no place in the historical record and whose territories seem to have been recorded at a very particular moment in the settlement of Anglo-Saxon England. These territories include the 'ingas' group, once thought to represent the very earliest settlements and their leaders (so Reading would be where Read or Reada's people lived) but which it is now estimated to belong to a later period, to the sixth rather than to the fifth century. 'Reada' then, should be seen not as founding father, making his way up the River Thames; rather, he belongs to the generation of those buried at Sutton Hoo, to those with an eye for prestige and the consolidation of power.[36]

Christianity, as the next chapter will show, indeed did what it could to support the emergence of the new political order, but it would be a mistake to think it held a monopoly. *The Anglo-Saxon Chronicle*, first compiled in the ninth century, provides genealogies of these early kingdoms which take care to link every dynasty to the pagan god of war, Woden. Indeed, even Bede gave due place to Woden 'from whose stock the royal families of many kingdoms claimed their descent'.[37] The conclusions are unavoidable: power, to be acceptable, had to be canonized and particularly in a period of transition it was as well to co-opt both old gods and new.

2

THE ARRIVAL OF CHRISTIANITY

About 150 years after the coming of the Angles to Britain, [Pope]
Gregory, prompted by divine inspiration, sent a servant of God named
Augustine and several more God-fearing monks with him to preach the
word of God to the English race.

(Bede, *Ecclesiastical History*, i, 23)

The installation of any new archbishop of Canterbury includes the
placing upon the altar of his cathedral of a sixth-century gospel
book. This is the book traditionally claimed to have been brought
to Canterbury by St Augustine on his arrival in 597 to fulfil the
commands of Pope Gregory I to convert the English. Gregory, so
the story went (a story preserved in our main source for the history
of the conversion, Bede's *Ecclesiastical History of the English
People*), had come across some strikingly beautiful slave boys up
for sale in the market in Rome. On enquiring who these boys
were, Gregory was told they were *Angli*. 'Good', replied Gregory,
'they have the face of angels, and such men should be fellow-heirs
of the angels in heaven.'[1] Gregory had not yet been elected pope
and thought that he might himself go to England to convert its
people. His subsequent elevation made such a plan impossible but,
as Bede went on to tell us, Gregory did not forget the *Angli* and in
due course he dispatched missionaries under the leadership of the
Roman monk Augustine, in order to 'preach the word of God to
the English race'.[2]

26

Gregory's mission would establish him as 'the apostle of the English', but Christianity had, of course, been introduced to England long before the sixth century. By 314 – only two years after the conversion to Christianity of the Emperor Constantine – Britain was able to send three bishops to a council at Arles to discuss matters of doctrine. Impossible though it is to determine the full extent of Christian allegiance in the following decades, it is certainly clear that the new religion had powerful adherents, including those wealthy enough to adorn their villas (as at Lullingstone, in Kent) with Christian symbols and to enjoy fine silver decorated with Christian iconography.[3] That the departure of the Roman army in 410 did not bring such Christian worship to an abrupt end in the English heartlands is well illustrated from the account in the *Life of Germanus* of the mission undertaken by this bishop of Auxerrre in 429 to eradicate the Pelagian heresy (see Chapter 1), and of Germanus' visit to the tomb of St Alban, near Verulamium. St Alban had suffered martyrdom during the third century for sheltering a Christian fugitive, making matters worse by espousing Christianity himself. The attention paid to his cult by Germanus and later by both Gildas and Bede strongly suggests that veneration of Alban may have been maintained throughout the fifth and sixth centuries. And his shrine may be only one among a number that managed to survive. A mysterious saint named St Sixtus (of whom Gregory the Great was highly suspicious) seems to have been known at Canterbury before the arrival of St Augustine. Meanwhile, news of the ever-growing number of saints in Britain, notably in Wales (the sixth century is the floruit of St David), will surely have seeped into regions of England generally classified as 'pagan'.[4]

The Pelagian heresy is itself proof of keen interest shown in matters of doctrine and in the all-important question of salvation. Pelagians did not believe in the doctrine of original sin as propounded by St Augustine of Hippo. It was a heresy, therefore, which had serious implications for the place of the sacraments of the Church and it seems highly probable that the sending of Bishop Palladius to Ireland by Pope Celestine just two years after Germanus' visit of 429 was similarly connected with anxiety about the spread of Pelagian teaching. Palladius' mission has become so overshadowed by the charismatic career of St Patrick that it is hard to estimate the impact of his preaching, but something of his success may be

Fig. 7: St Martin's Church, Canterbury

gauged by the sermon delivered by Pope Leo the Great, some ten years later, in which Leo boasted how much more glorious for Rome than the achievements of Romulus and Remus were those of Peter and Paul. It was no longer military victory on which the power of Rome depended. What mattered now was Rome's ability to spread the Gospel to the ends of the earth and to thus extend the authority of 'Christian peace'.[5]

When Augustine arrived in 597, the concept of a new world order centred on Christian Rome and a 'Christian peace' was by then already old, but Augustine's task was urgent because it was not at all obvious how much longer it would be before God called time and the world came to its end. But King Aethelberht of Kent, Augustine's host, was no stranger to Christianity, since he had long been married to a Christian princess, Bertha, sent to him from Gaul, on the condition that Bertha be allowed to continue to practise her religion. A chaplain, Bishop Liudhard, had accompanied the queen, and the ruined church of St Martin outside the walls of Canterbury had been restored for her use. It is more than probable that the marriage and its terms will have been negotiated not by Aethelberht himself but rather by his father, King Eormenric, whose Frankish name is already suggestive of close cross-channel links. The gold medalet, found at Canterbury and inscribed 'Liudhard, Bishop', gives some indication of the wealth and prestige of Bishop Liudhard and it would be surprising had not Aethelberht, under his influence, made the decision to convert to Christianity even before Augustine and his party of missionaries arrived. Nevertheless, even if Aethelberht himself needed no persuading of the merits of Christianity, it would be both rash and misguided to imagine that the conversion of Pope Gregory's 'angels' would be a simple or straightforward task and it took some 70 years before every English kingdom had finally abandoned its pagan gods in favour of the new faith.

Cautious though we need to be in supposing we can understand Anglo-Saxon pagan beliefs (given that the pagans themselves left no written sources), we nonetheless have certain clues. We can start with the reminder that Christian Easter is named after Eostre, the goddess of spring, and four days of the week still have Germanic pagan names – Tuesday (Tiw), Wednesday (Woden), Thursday (Thor) and Friday (Frig). These gods would come to enjoy so long a life in later Scandinavian literature that it is difficult to avoid reading back their later attributes into the earlier Anglo-Saxon period, but new approaches to the meagre fund of sources that we have are proving fruitful. Thus, while it has long been assumed that natural features – lakes, hills and trees – had cultic significance for Anglo-Saxon pagans, it now seems increasingly likely that paganism was much less bucolic than has hitherto been imagined.[6] Pagan worship took place in groves, but also too in temples. So much has always been known (if not always sufficiently noted) from the thoughts of Pope Gregory on what to do with such temples, particularly those that were 'well-built'. 'After long deliberation', Gregory had decided that, while the idols should be destroyed, such temples should be preserved and transformed into Christian churches. Cleansed by holy water and sanctified by altars containing relics, these buildings would then be fit for Christian worship and the new religion would seem less daunting to the erstwhile pagans. These folk should also, continued Gregory, be allowed to celebrate the feast days of saints in ways not dissimilar from the pagan festivals, to which they had long been accustomed. Beasts could still be killed, to be eaten now with due ceremony in huts constructed from branches gathered from the trees that grew around former pagan shrines.[7]

The smooth transition advocated by Gregory, and seemingly adopted, may nonetheless have at times been stretched to breaking point – witness the case of King Raedwald of East Anglia who evidently maintained two altars, one for Christ and one on which to sacrifice animals. Such behaviour deeply shocked Bede, all the more since Raedwald's temple was still standing when Aldwulf, later king of East Anglia, was a boy, but it may well be that many other temples ceased to be identifiable as such, since, following Pope Gregory's instruction, they were indeed turned into churches. The current church at Goodmanham, for example, sits atop a hill in such a way as to suggest the possibility that it may have been built over the remains of that pagan temple which was so dramatically desecrated and burnt by the pagan priest Coifi, following the decision of the Northumbrian king Edwin to adopt Christianity in 626.[8]

Goodmanham lies in the heart of the Yorkshire wolds, 'not far from York, to the east over the river Derwent', so Bede tells us.[9] The site had long been hallowed; 25 round and two square barrows within the present parish testify to its importance even before the coming of the Romans. Here then, beyond all reasonable doubt, was housed the major shrine of the Deiran royal house in the years before King Edwin's official acceptance of Christianity. This is the place to which the chief priest Coifi rode after the great debate held nearby when paganism was officially abandoned. Present at this debate were, according to Bede, Paulinus, bishop of York, and all of Edwin's close circle.[10] Edwin, who had a Christian wife (a daughter of the Kentish King Aethelberht), had long pondered the possibility of the conversion of his kingdom; now he prepared to take counsel. All in turn were asked to give their views on the proposed new faith. It was on this occasion that one of Edwin's close circle famously compared the life of man to the flight of a sparrow:

> You are sitting feasting with your ealdormen and thegns in winter time; the fire is burning on the hearth in the middle of the hall and all inside is warm, while outside the wintry storms of rain and snow are raging; and a sparrow flies swiftly through the hall. It enters in at one door and quickly flies out through the other. For the few moments it is inside, the storm and wintry tempest cannot touch it, but after the briefest moment of calm, it flits from your sight, out of the wintry storm and into it again.

So this life of man appears but for a moment; what follows or indeed
what went before, we know not at all. If this new doctrine brings us more
certain information, it seems right that we should accept it.[11]

More speeches followed. Finally, the time came for the Christian
Paulinus and the pagan Coifi to bring the debate to a close. According
to Bede, so persuasive was Paulinus that Coifi himself was won over,
declaring that his paganism now seemed 'worthless', in comparison
with a religion that could offer 'the gift of life, salvation and eternal
happiness', whereupon Edwin publicly announced his acceptance
of the new faith. It was now that Coifi volunteered 'to profane the
altars and the shrines of the idols, together with their precincts'. In
flagrant defiance of pagan convention, which expected its priests to
ride only mares and to be unarmed, Coifi asked Edwin to provide
him with weapons and a stallion and off he set to Goodmanham,
duly girded with a sword and with a spear in his hand. To the
amazement of the bystanders, who thought he had gone mad, Coifi
rode up and cast the spear into the shrine, ordering his companions
to destroy and burn the shrine itself 'and all the enclosures' (most
likely fences or hedges).[12]

Coifi's violation of the Goodmanham temple is unparalleled in
the story of the conversion to Christianity in England and seemingly
at odds with Pope Gregory's considered and explicit instruction
to the missionaries not to destroy pagan shrines, but rather only
the idols within them. But Coifi was not, of course, a Christian
missionary; he was a pagan priest, even perhaps a personification
of Woden himself.[13] His spear-hurling may itself draw on ancient
pagan symbolical battle practice. As presented by Bede, here is the
challenge of a defiant and embittered priest to the old gods whom, he
claims, 'have never done nothing much for him'. Will they retaliate
if he throws down the gauntlet? They do not. The conversion of
Northumbria can now proceed apace.

Edwin's adoption of Christianity made possible his triumphant
reclamation of the Roman inheritance of northern England. On
Easter Day 627, Edwin was baptized by Paulinus at York, in a hastily
erected wooden church. At Paulinus' suggestion, plans were made
for the building of a stone church, which would both enclose and
preserve this baptismal church, thus surrounding it with Roman-
style magnificence.[14] For Edwin, as before him for his father-in-law

King Aethelberht, Christianity thus brought an increase of status and power. Both Canterbury and York were former Roman towns; both kings could now rule 'in the Roman manner'. Thus Aethelberht, once a king of an illiterate people, could now promulgate a written law code while Edwin could process through his kingdom preceded by a standard 'which the Romans call a *tufa*'.[15] And glory not only now, but also hereafter, was promised to these new Christian kings. Thus, Pope Honorius exhorted King Edwin to constantly read the works of Gregory, the apostle of the English, in the assurance that his prayers would 'exalt both your kingdom and your people and present you faultless before Almighty God'.[16] And yet, despite such promises, and despite their early successes, the progress of the missionaries was extremely uneven. During the course of the seventh century, every kingdom at some point experienced a pagan reaction.

The faltering progress of the Christian mission was complicated by the existence of two branches of Christianity. In those parts of the British Isles unconquered by the Romans, Christianity had been introduced by various means: in Ireland, through the papal emissary Palladius and by St Patrick; in Scotland, through a succession of charismatic exiles from Ireland (and notably, in Iona, by St Columba). Added to these was the caucus of British Christians firmly established in parts of Northern Britain, Wales and the South-West of England. The relations between these two sets of Christians, the so-called 'Roman' and 'Celtic' or 'British', were not necessarily inimical, but political tensions made them so, in such a way that the conflict between the two got caught up both in the struggle for the domination of the northern territories of Britain and in the emergence and consolidation of new kingdoms further south.

In the highly fluid and volatile situation of the seventh century, the success of any king necessarily depended on his ability to attract and reward followers, with whose help he could then further expand his lands. The appeal of the Christian deity was indeed precisely that, as 'a God of Hosts', he might be better able to secure victories for his adherents than did those pagan gods now declared to be nothing more than useless man-made idols. But on the one hand, the pagan gods, despite the battering they were receiving, still had their adherents; and on the other, there were Christian kings and prelates who were not so sure that bloody battles were a part of God's plan, and others such for whom allegiance to a particular saint counted for more than did political allegiance. Thus, while the conversion of England clearly underpins the story of kingdom formation, it is a story full of messy alliances and unexpected twists and turns. A closer look at the conversion of King Edwin will bring to the fore some of these numerous strands.

Edwin's father was Aelle, king of the Northumbrian kingdom of Deira. When his father died, Edwin was still too young to press his claim to his inheritance and Deira soon fell into the hands of Aethelfrith, king of neighbouring Bernicia. Aethelfrith strengthened this newly won position by marrying Edwin's sister and by sending Edwin himself into exile. Where Edwin initially found refuge is far from clear, but some traditions place him among the British Christians of Wales and even suggest that he was fostered by Cadfan, king of Gwynedd, and then baptized at the court of King Rhun of Rheged.[17] Thereafter (and here Bede picks up the story), Edwin moved on to Mercia, where he married Cwenburh, daughter of the Mercian King Ceorl, by whom he had two sons, Osfrith and Eadfrith.[18] But Edwin then moved again, this time to East Anglia, where he gained the support of Raedwald (the king with two altars). On Edwin's behalf, Raedwald took the field against Aethelfrith, killing him at the Battle of the Idle. Edwin was thus able to return to Northumbria, and, in 616, to become its king and to marry again, this time a Christian princess from Kent. However, according to Bede's account, it then took another ten years before Edwin, too, finally became a Christian.

It is possible that Bede did not know of Edwin's baptism at Rhun's court or did not recognize the rite used or that the event never happened. But the probability is that it did. Consider what happened when Edwin became king: it was then the turn of Aethelfrith's sons to seek exile and, accordingly, they fled to the Scots and to the Picts. When Edwin died (killed in the Battle of Hatfield Chase by an alliance between Penda of Mercia and Cadwallon of Gwynedd), Northumbria was again divided. The southern kingdom of Deira was inherited by Osric, one of Edwin's kin who had been baptized by Paulinus, while Bernicia was successfully claimed by Aethelfrith's son Eanfred, who was baptized, so Bede tells us, along with his brother Oswald during his years in exile. However, both Osric and Eanfred, once they became kings, gave up their new-found faith. What happened next reveals very clearly how local traditions and sentiment could sometimes confuse Bede's narrative: Osric and

Eanfred, Bede reports, were punished for their apostasy by King Cadwallon, who invaded Northumbria, but Bede is refusing here to acknowledge that Cadwallon was himself a Christian; instead, he is described as 'godless' and Bede goes on to rejoice at his downfall and destruction at the hands of Eanfred's brother Oswald. Furthermore, Bede attributes Oswald's victory over Cadwallon to Oswald's erection of a wooden cross before which his soldiers prayed before engaging in battle at Heavenfield, whereas in Adomnan's *Life of Columba*, written some 30 years earlier, it is St Columba of Iona who secures Oswald's victory. But for Bede's purposes, Oswald needs to be, and so becomes, a Roman, Constantine-like, figure.

In his preface to his *Ecclesiastical History*, Bede never promised that what he was about to relate would necessarily be 'the whole truth':

> I humbly beg the reader, if he finds anything other than the truth set down in what I have written, not to impute it to me. For, in accordance with the principles of true history, I have simply sought to commit to writing what I have collected from common report, for the instruction of posterity.[19]

'Common report' in Bede's England had little to say about British Christians, or at least little that was good. To be sure, such folk had originally been included in Pope Gregory's plan for the conversion of England. But the account that reached Bede suggested that when they met St Augustine, they had been extremely recalcitrant, refusing to change their customs. Moreover, and this was the last straw, they had refused to preach to the English. All negotiations having failed, Augustine allegedly prophesied that God would punish them for their obduracy. It came therefore as no surprise when the mighty (pagan) Aethelfrith, at war near Chester against the Britons of North Wales, ordered the massacre of a great company of monks at prayer, on the grounds that their prayer counted as fighting. Thereafter, concluded Bede, the battle was won and in this way was Augustine's prophecy fulfilled.

One of the major problems Bede had both with the British and Irish was with their dating of Easter. In any discussion of the conversion of Anglo-Saxon England, this vexed dating question frequently takes up what may seem a disproportionate amount of space. The calculations, depending as they did on the phases of the moon, were indeed complex and were widely discussed not just in England but also across Europe, but it was not every year that the dates given by the various methods of computation varied greatly, nor everywhere was Easter as prickly an issue as it was in England. In Northumbria, where the details of the debate are particularly well known, the opponents were, on the one side, Wilfrid, abbot of Ripon, keen to introduce a dating method he had learnt in Rome, and, on the other, the monks of Lindisfarne who wished to remain loyal to the customs they had inherited from Columba of Iona. In 664, after heated debates at the Synod of Whitby, it was Wilfrid, with the support of King Oswiu, who won the day. Thereafter, the way was clear for Wilfrid to advance claims over northern territories previously administered by British clergy and even to suggest that his jurisdiction might extend as far as Ireland. Pope Vitalian's letter to King Oswiu, written soon after the synod, suggests that a Northumbrian *imperium* comprising modern Scotland and stretching across the Irish Sea was indeed a serious possibility. Some 20 years later, in 685, at the Battle of Nechtansmere, fought in Pictish territory, such ambitions received a bitter blow: King Ecgfrith's force was annihilated and Ecgfrith himself killed. 'From this time', reported Bede (quoting Virgil), 'the hopes and strengths of the English Kingdom began to "ebb and fall away".'[20] Bede was unhesitatingly critical of Ecgfrith's political ambitions. Just the year before Nechtansmere, Ecgfrith had sent an expedition to the eastern shores of Ireland that clearly shocked Bede to the core, devastating, as it did, 'a harmless race that had always been most friendly to the English' and sparing 'neither churches nor monasteries'.[21]

There can be no doubt that staunch though Bede was in his espousal of the 'Roman' dating of Easter, his heroes were the Irish missionaries whom Oswald had invited to his kingdom after his victory at Heavenfield. Whether Oswald himself understood that victory as mediated by Columba or not cannot be known, but since Iona was at the time Scotland's chief monastery it need cause no surprise that it was a monk from Iona, Aidan, who came to help Oswald evangelize his new kingdom. Bede's portrayal of Aidan and of his close relationship with Oswald (he had learnt Irish during his years of exile and acted initially as Aidan's interpreter) is likely to have been written with Bede's own king, Ceolwulf, in mind. Bede was convinced that, in his own day, there were not enough bishops and that, of those there were, few took sufficiently seriously their duties of preaching. Thus he urged Egbert, bishop of York, to seek remedies, impressing on him that in King Ceolwulf he would find a 'very ready helper'.[22] Bede, who was a great believer in models, will have hoped that Ceolwulf, to whom he dedicated his *History*, would take careful note of the relationship between Aidan and Oswald.

Bede's determination (stated in his preface) 'to eschew anything harmful or perverse' and to present Ceolwulf and his other readers only with tales of 'good men and their good estate' did not, however, preclude plenty of stories illustrating the tensions of the first century of Anglo-Saxon Christianity. There had been only six years between Edwin's baptism at York and his death in 633; some sense of the turmoil surrounding this death can be gauged by Bede's determination to expunge the year from the historical record – the year was to be assigned instead to Oswald's reign – and by the flight of Edwin's queen, together with her children and with Paulinus, back to Kent. Of the Roman mission, only the doughty deacon James stayed behind in York, where he continued to teach the singing of Roman-style chant. With the accession of Oswald, however, the centre of the Christian mission decisively shifted north.

The differences between the Roman mission initiated by Paulinus and James, and the Ionan mission led by Aidan, may often have been exaggerated, but differences there surely were. Paulinus had envisaged a city-based Christianity, starting with York, on the model of Augustine's church at Canterbury. This too had been the vision of Pope Gregory (though he had at first imagined London rather than Canterbury would be England's chief see). But the Irish had no experience of towns and Aidan's decision to live on Lindisfarne, and thus near to, but not in, the royal city of Bamburgh, gave Aidan the chance both to co-operate with his king but also (literally and figuratively) to place clear water between his monastery and the palace. For despite his close relationship with Oswald, Aidan is described by Bede in terms that make it clear he was no palace creature. He went to feasts but rarely, he preferred to go about on foot rather than on horseback and he did not hold back from criticizing the rich. This characterization of Aidan as a prelate with a mind of his own is further illustrated by the friendship Aidan subsequently developed with Oswine, who had become king of Deira on Oswald's death – Northumbria having again split into two – while Oswald's brother King Oswiu took Bernicia. On one occasion, Oswine gave Aidan a particularly fine horse which Aidan promptly gave away to the nearest beggar. Oswine's anger at this act of generosity was assuaged by Aidan's rebuke: 'Surely this son of a mare is not dearer to you than that son of God.' The king thereupon sought Aidan's pardon for his outburst, promising he would never again question any almsgiving from the royal purse. Aidan in turn became unexpectedly gloomy. And why? Because, he said, 'he had never before seen a humble king', and he could not believe that Oswine would live much longer.[23]

Nor did he. The story of how Oswine died bears close examination, because it raises so many questions about the paradoxes of Christian kingship. Oswine is a new kind of hero. He knows his brother is gathering an army to fight him, but he has limited resources so he decides that he will hide, rather than risk battle. He is betrayed and killed, but no one suggests that Oswine had acted in a cowardly manner and no one avenges the treacherous behaviour of the servant Oswine who had revealed the king's hiding place. Instead, a monastery is erected to Oswine's memory at Gilling, where both the murdered king and his murderous brother are to have prayers said for their souls. And Oswine will be long revered and remembered for his humility. Bede's unusual interjections in the story – *heu*! *pro dolor*! (alas! what grief!) – suggest Oswine's story was widely known, possibly even the subject of a vernacular lay.[24]

There is, nonetheless, something distinctly strange about Oswine's behaviour. Germanic heroes, whether Christian or pagan, fictional or 'real', surely seek revenge and fight even against the odds. Thus, Beowulf takes on the dragon, knowing very well he may die, but he is determined to 'seek out the feud, achieve a deed of glory … display heroism'.[25] One of the reasons given for Edwin's delay in becoming a Christian (at the same time as expecting the Christian God to help him) was that he had first to take revenge against Cwichelm of Wessex for attempting to have him assassinated. Oswald at Heavenfield may have a tiny army but by the strength of his faith he wins the day. Much was at stake between Oswine and his brother. After Oswine's death, there would never again be an independent

Deira, yet Oswine is venerated rather than despised for his actions in avoiding battle.

Oswine is not the only Anglo-Saxon king whose life and death illustrate the paradoxes, tensions and complications which Christianity was bringing in its wake. Sigeberht, king of Essex, was converted to Christianity by King Oswiu. He was baptized by Finan (bishop of Northumbria in succession to Aidan) and, through the preaching of Cedd of Lindisfarne, his kingdom accepted the new faith. But one day (as Bede tells the story), Cedd happened to spot Sigeberht coming away from having had dinner at the house of someone whom Cedd had excommunicated for his marital irregularities. Sigeberht's terror at being caught out and Cedd's anger at the king's disregard for his command make intriguing reading:

> When the king saw [Cedd], he leapt from his horse and fell trembling at the bishop's feet, asking his pardon. The bishop, who was also on horseback, alighted too. In his anger he touched the prostrate king with his staff which he was holding in his hand, and exercising his episcopal authority, he uttered these words, 'I declare to you that because you were unwilling to avoid the house of this man who is lost and damned, you will meet your death in this very house.[26]

The follow-up is just as arresting: Sigeberht indeed dies, murdered by his dinner host and his brother. When questioned as to their motive, the brothers reply that Sigeberht has been too willing to forgive his enemies. Bede concludes the story by assuring his readers that through his death and obedience to Christ's commands, the king will have atoned for his earlier disobedience to Cedd. (There are interesting parallels to be drawn between the conflict of values this story illustrates and the Irish tale *Sweeney Astray*, translated by Seamus Heaney, which may already date from oral traditions of the seventh century: Sweeney is an Irish king cursed and made mad by the priest and missionary Ronan Finn. Sweeney is infuriated both by Finn's bell – and the claims he is making to land – and by the priest's blessing of his army before battle through the sprinkling of holy water, which Sweeney interprets as mockery.)

The Christian God was indeed expected to bring victory in battle; Pope Honorius had promised no less. But the record was, to say the least, patchy. Sigeberht, son of Raedwald of East Anglia, had gone into exile in Gaul. While abroad, he had become a Christian and

Fig. 8: St Luke from St Augustine's Gospels

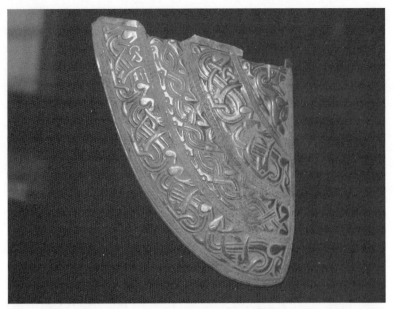

Fig. 9: Fragments from a helmet (Staffordshire Hoard)

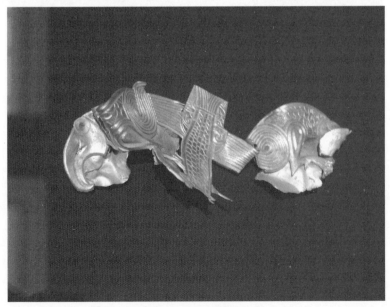

Fig. 10: Sheet gold plaque (Staffordshire Hoard)

Fig. 11: Sword hilt fitting (Staffordshire Hoard)

when, on his brother's death, he returned to East Anglia to take up the kingship, he brought his faith with him. Having established Christianity throughout his kingdom, Sigeberht then handed the kingship over to Ecgric (who was already acting as co-king) and became a monk. Not long after, East Anglia was invaded by the pagan king of Mercia, Penda. The terrified East Anglians insisted Sigeberht leave his monastery to join Ecgric in the fight. Both kings were killed, Sigeberht with nothing in his hands but a staff. The next king of East Anglia, Anna, despite fathering four daughters, all of whom became saints, and despite converting the king of Wessex, was to also die at Penda's hands.

Penda's days were, however, numbered and in 655, at the Battle of the Winwaed, he met his match. The battle was recorded by Bede as a victory won on behalf of Oswiu of Northumbria by God. Thus, to secure the victory Oswiu had promised land on which to build monasteries and he had offered his daughter Aelfflaed – later abbess of Whitby but at the time of the battle barely a year old – to the religious life.[27] Initially, or so Bede tells us, Oswiu had in fact hoped to avoid battle and had attempted to buy off Penda with 'an incalculable and incredible store of royal treasure and gifts'.[28] These Penda had apparently refused, but there has been considerable speculation as to whether the Staffordshire Hoard, discovered by metal detectors in 2009 in a field near Lichfield, might not be this treasure. This remains speculation, as there is still much work to be done on the hoard. But whatever conclusions it becomes possible to draw, the outstanding quantity of gold found there and its overwhelmingly military character – at first count 92 pommels from swords and 354 hilt fittings, and the number since then has risen – throw remarkable light on the nature of warfare in eighth-century England.[29]

Oswiu's victory at the Battle of the Winwaed ushered in the final conversion of Mercia, but the battle should not be seen as some final triumph of Christian forces over a pagan remnant. One of Penda's allies at the battle was none other than the Christian Aethelhere, king of East Anglia, in succession to Anna. This was not of course the first time Penda had allied with a Christian king. The strength of Mercia had been built up by swallowing up a patchwork of kingdoms, some of which belonged to British Christians; the tolerance Penda showed towards the Christianity of his own son (married to a daughter of Oswiu's and ruler of a Mercian sub-kingdom) and his objection only to those 'who, after they had accepted the Christian faith, were clearly lacking in the works of faith' need to be understood within this context.[30]

Penda has often been seen as the greatest of all the Anglo-Saxon pagan kings but he was not the last. That accolade (even though he died a Christian) surely belongs to Caedwalla, king first of Wessex and then of Sussex, and it is to conversion stories of these kingdoms that we should now turn.

In Wessex, the course of the conversion had been anything but smooth. Its first Christian king of Wessex, according to Bede, was Cynegils, converted by the Italian bishop, Birinus, whom Pope Honorius (625–38) had sent to England to further the mission. At Cynegil's baptism, his godfather was none other than King Oswald of Northumbria. Cynegils in this way became Oswald's spiritual son and he would have been expected to act with appropriate filial loyalty. Some sort of treaty between the two kingdoms is further suggested by the marriage, proposed at the time of the baptism, between Oswald and Cynegils' daughter; given the threat Penda of Mercia was already presenting to both Wessex and Northumbria, an alliance between them would have made sense. Wessex, nonetheless, remained fragile as a kingdom, under constant threat from Mercia and unsteady in its adherence to Christianity. In 685 it was conquered by the pagan Caedwalla; not content with Wessex, Caedwalla, as we shall see, then advanced towards Sussex, the kingdom of the South Saxons.

Aelle, king of the South Saxons (or Sussex), had been named by Bede as the first in his list of super-kings or 'bretwaldas'.[31] Nothing certain is known of this Aelle, though an Aelle indeed appears in the *Anglo-Saxon Chronicle*, landing in England with three sons in 477, the successful victor of a series of battles against the native Britons. But what happens thereafter to his supposed kingdom is something of a mystery and it is not until many chapters later in Bede's *History* and in Stephen's *Life of St Wilfrid* that the kingdom again comes into focus. It then emerges that but for a tiny community of Irish monks at Bosham whom the locals, apparently, had all chosen to ignore, the kingdom had remained pagan. How this paganism is finally overcome varies significantly between Bede and Stephen's accounts, yet both are equally compelling, as much for the light they throw on the partisan nature of our sources as on the enduring strength of paganism.

In Stephen's *Life*, Wilfrid's encounter with the South Saxons begins by chance.[32] The tale reads like an episode from a heroic saga: it is 666, so just two years after Wilfrid's triumph at the Synod of Whitby. Wilfrid has been to Gaul where he has been consecrated bishop of York in a ceremony of spectacular splendour. He is nearly home when his flotilla is caught in a storm. The wind howls, waves lash the boats – it is, says Stephen, just like being on the Lake of Galilee. The shore comes closer. Assembled along the beach are hordes of pagans, eager for booty. But Christian magic and militancy outwit all pagan curses. A stone, blessed by a Christian and hurled from a sling, kills the pagan priest. Battle is joined. The pagans flee, regroup, flee again and yet again but, before their king has the chance to join them, the tide has turned (miraculously early), whereupon Wilfrid can sail off for Kent. Despite the drama of the tale, Stephen makes no attempt to link it with Wilfrid's return to Sussex some 15 years later, when he is this time living in exile from Northumbria (with whose king he had quarrelled). On this occasion, as Stephen tells the story, Wilfrid

Fig. 12: Pictish stone from Aberlemno, possibly commemorating the Battle of
Nechtansmere, 685

is welcomed into Sussex by the king, Aethelwealh, whom (along with his queen) he duly converts. Thereafter, he preaches to 'hosts of pagans' and by his eloquence he converts them by the thousand. In gratitude, the king gives him land at Selsey. Stephen, without missing a beat, goes on to report how next Wilfrid allies with Caedwalla, a royal exile from Wessex, as yet still a pagan, whom he supports in his efforts first to conquer Wessex and next Sussex. What happens to Aethelwealh, Stephen does not care to tell us.

Bede's story is markedly different. According to Bede, before Wilfrid's arrival the whole kingdom of Sussex was still in the grip of paganism, except for its king, Aethelwealh, who had been baptized at the instigation of Wulfhere of Mercia. Wulfhere had acted as Aethelwealh's godfather and he had given him as a baptismal present the Isle of Wight (recently conquered by Wulfhere), together with a sub-kingdom (Bede calls it a province) in Hampshire. In Bede's account, the Mercian dimension of Aethelwealh's conversion is further underlined by his marriage to a Christian princess from the Hwicce, a kingdom by now dependent on Mercia. Only then does Wilfrid arrive. Wilfrid does indeed preach to great effect to the South Saxons. And it is not just his preaching; it is also his fishing lessons which are hugely successful.[33] But then onto the scene comes the exile, the pagan Caedwalla, who invades Sussex, kills King Aethelwealh and moves on to capture the Isle of Wight, handing over a quarter of it to Wilfrid to Christianize. Particularly shocking to present sensibilities is Caedwalla's ethnic cleansing programme, his clearly expressed plan 'to wipe out all the natives [of the Isle of Wight] by merciless slaughter and to replace them with inhabitants of his own kingdom'.[34] Bede's blithe tale of the baptism of two Isle of Wight princes prior to their execution will do little to cheer the modern reader. But it is on this sombre note that Bede notes that the conversion of all England's kingdoms, including the Isle of Wight, is now complete. Did Bede himself feel something else was needed? Just possibly. He returns to Caedwalla much later in his *History* to tell how in 689 he died in Rome, where, after abdicating his throne he had gone to be baptized, and where an epitaph recorded how he 'had laid aside his barbarous rage and shame/and with changed heart to Peter changed his name'.[35]

In the final chapter of his *History*, Bede supplied a list of the dates he thought would 'assist the memory' of the reader. Caedwalla's journey to Rome is included. The next entry, just two years later, records the death of Theodore, archbishop of Canterbury. By any standards, Theodore's achievements as archbishop had been considerable. Given the fragility of Christianity in England during his time in office, they can be reckoned as astounding.

Theodore had arrived in England in 668. How and why he had been chosen for the job will always be something of a mystery. Here was an eminent Greek scholar, already 66 when the pope chose him, and 67 by the time when he reached England, his hair having meanwhile grown long enough for him to be tonsured appropriately (arguments about the correct tonsure had been on the agenda at the Synod of Whitby, so this mattered). With Theodore came Hadrian, a monk of North African origin. They had been accompanied on their journey by Benedict Biscop, who went on to found the monasteries of Wearmouth and Jarrow. Before crossing the channel, Theodore spent some time with Agilbert, one of the former spokesmen for the 'Roman' party at the Synod of Whitby but now bishop of Paris. Despite their background, it cannot therefore be said that Theodore and Hadrian were entirely unprepared for what they found on their arrival in England. They may, nonetheless, have been shocked. Scars caused by the Synod of Whitby had yet to heal; an outbreak of plague had weakened religious communities and encouraged a return to paganism; only three bishops were in post and of these one, Wini of London, was accused of having paid money for the job.

Theodore's response to the problems he faced was swift and decisive. He toured the whole country, filled vacancies and set about attempting to create a clear diocesan structure.[36] At the Synod of Hertford, summoned in 672/3, his proposal to create more bishoprics 'as the number of the faithful increases' was controversial and no decision was taken, but Theodore was not to be deterred. He had already created a new see for Mercia, where he had installed Chad, a former pupil of Bishop Aidan (in his insistence that Chad abandon Aidan's habit of going about on foot, Theodore personally set Chad on a horse). In 677 he went further: a quarrel between Bishop Wilfrid and his king provided Theodore with the opportunity to depose Wilfrid and to divide the Northumbrian see into three. Wilfrid, in consequence, withdrew for some years to Sussex (where, as we have seen, he worked towards its conversion). Attempts thereafter both to placate Wilfrid and to create more – and smaller

– dioceses continued throughout Theodore's episcopacy. By the time of his death in 690, he had been able to establish at least half of the 24 bishoprics Gregory the Great had envisaged.

Theodore's companion, Hadrian, had meanwhile been installed at Canterbury in the abbey of Saints Peter and Paul. There, working in collaboration with Theodore, he established a school of exceptional brilliance. Canterbury already had some sort of school, since when the missionaries first arrived in 597 the Anglo-Saxons (unlike the Irish and the British) knew no Latin and wrote only in runes. Lessons in basic skills of literacy and numeracy and some rudimentary theological training may have been all that was provided at this stage, but by the 630s the Canterbury school was sufficiently well-established to act as a model for King Sigeberht of East Anglia. Impressed by what he had seen of education in Gaul, Sigeberht had returned home and, so Bede tells us, 'he established a school where boys could be taught letters, with the help of Bishop Felix, who had come to him from Kent and who provided him with masters and teachers as in the Kentish school'.[37] But under Hadrian and Theodore, the school at Canterbury went far beyond elementary education. 'Letters' now included Greek as well as Latin, together with the study of law, computus and astronomy. All these were considered necessary if students were to be able to compare and comment both on the Latin Bible, the Greek Septuagint and on early biblical commentaries. Bede's own learning, of course, bears witness to these extraordinary intellectual challenges and changes which Christianity had brought to Anglo-Saxon England, but for Canterbury itself we also have the firsthand testimony of Aldhelm (later abbot of Malmesbury and bishop of Sherborne), a pupil there in its heyday and by his own estimate one of the foremost scholars of his generation. Writing to Aldfrith, king of Northumbria (685–705), Aldhelm claims that he is the first of those 'nourished in the cradles of a Germanic people' to have 'toiled so mightily' at literary accomplishments. And his publications, both in poetry and prose, do indeed exhibit a dazzling command of Latin. Aldhelm is unstinting in his praise of the extraordinary talents of Theodore and Hadrian and of their capacity to 'unlock and unravel the murky mysteries of the heavenly library' (as well as complaining of the difficulties of the mathematical skills he was expected, as a Canterbury pupil, to master).[38]

This education of a new Christian elite, which Canterbury provided, may have been startlingly successful, but what did the new religion mean to 'the people'? What form of education did they receive? A later tradition (reported by the twelfth-century chronicler William of Malmesbury) depicts Aldhelm the scholar as being also a great popularizer. When he was abbot of Malmesbury, Aldhelm would apparently stand by the bridge over the River Avon just at the time when it was crowded with people coming away from mass. And there:

> The holy man took his stand ... and barred the way, playing the part of the professional minstrel. After he had done this more than once, the common people were won over and flocked to listen to him. Exploiting this device, he gradually started to smuggle words from Scripture into the less serious matter, and so brought the inhabitants round to sound sentiments. If he had thought fit to deal in stern words and excommunication, he would assuredly have achieved nothing.[39]

This story William of Malmesbury claims he got from a book of King Alfred's. There would seem no reason to doubt it, all the more because it chimes in with the better-known story, recorded by Bede, of Caedmon, the cow herd of the Whitby minster, who with divine help overcomes his natural shyness to become the poet and minstrel who puts into the vernacular 'the story of the creation of the world and of mankind, the whole history of Genesis, and the departure of the Israelites from Egypt'.[40] Bede's advocacy of the vernacular is further displayed in his letter to Egbert, bishop of York, in which he urges the teaching in translation of the Apostles Creed and the Lord's Prayer throughout Egbert's diocese, even down to 'every hamlet and field'.[41] Everyone is to know these texts by heart and to 'chant them carefully'. Significantly, in the scene described by Cuthbert (later abbot of Wearmouth) of Bede's death, both the vernacular and the practice of chanting play a role. In these last days, Bede was still hard at work translating into the vernacular chapters from the Gospel of St John. He also recited an English poem concerning 'the soul's dread departure from the body' and he died with chant on his lips.[42]

Although no chant book earlier than the tenth century has survived, there can be little doubt of the widespread role played by chanting in spreading the tenets of the new religion. St Augustine, when he entered Canterbury for the first time, did so while chanting; James the Deacon, who alone of the Roman missionaries had stayed in Northumbria after the defeat of King Edwin in 633, is described by Bede as being 'very skilful in church music' and as teaching many how to sing 'in the manner of Rome and the Kentish people';[43] Putta, bishop of Rochester, when his see was devastated during one of the numerous outbreaks of seventh-century warfare, decided the moment had come for him to retire. He was given land in Mercia and there, according to Bede, 'he went round wherever he was invited, teaching church music'.[44] Such singing was of course both didactic and devotional in intent. It was a way of joining heaven and earth. Angels sang in perpetual praise of God; so, too, could the new people of God, the English.

Today, within mainstream Christianity, the role of angels has been marginalized. Even if the Archangel Gabriel still has a role at Christmas, angels in general are considered somewhat risible, fit company for fairies and hobgoblins but not to be taken too seriously within the economy of salvation. But in the period of the conversion, and indeed throughout the Middle Ages, angels were central to any understanding of God's intervention in the world and of the fate of each and every Christian. The sparrow who had flown somewhat randomly through the hall at the court of King Edwin was replaced now by angelic beings, who flew to and fro from the court of heaven. At times, such beings might themselves take the shape of birds: when the bones of the Northumbrian scribe Ultan were being washed prior to being re-buried in a new tomb, two birds suddenly appeared. They arrived on beams of sunlight; they glistened, 'various colours mingled in them'. They covered Ultan's skull with their wings and then they began to sing. They sang all day until the bones were dry. Once the bones had been re-interred, then these 'musical birds mingled with the lofty clouds' and vanished from sight.[45]

But if angels could assume the shape of birds, so, alarmingly, could devils. And devils might of course assume other forms. They might turn themselves into snakes or wolves or perhaps, even more treacherously, into abstract forms such as darkness or nightmares.[46] Help was, however, always at hand for every Christian. Although constantly beset by the devil, every Christian always had protection, above all in the form of prayer – not just the prayer of the individual sinner, but also collective prayer, in particular the prayers offered on his behalf by those expert practitioners of prayer: monks. And it is to monks, monasteries or minsters that we must now turn.

3

MONKS AND MISSION

But because you, brother, are conversant with monastic rules, and ought not to live apart from your clergy in the English Church, which, by the guidance of God, has lately been converted to the faith, you ought to institute that manner of life which our fathers followed in the earliest beginnings of the Church: none of them said that anything he possessed was his own, but they had all things in common.

(Bede, *Ecclesiastical History*, i, 27)

Not long after his arrival in Canterbury, Augustine (assured by now that his mission was set to prosper) had written to Pope Gregory with a number of questions as to how he should exercise his ministry. He began by asking about bishops: 'how', he asked, 'should bishops live with their clergy? How are the offerings which the faithful bring to the altar to be apportioned and how ought a bishop to act in his church?' The Pope replied 'without delay': Augustine, because he was first and foremost a monk, must live with his clergy, holding with them all property in common even if provision (in other words stipends) had also to be made for those married clergy in minor orders, upon whom would fall the duty of 'attending to the chanting of psalms' within the cathedral.[1] The main burden of conversion, however, clearly fell on Augustine and his monks. This recognition that it was monks, rather than secular clergy, who initially organized and undertook the preaching of the new faith has led many historians of the conversion to describe the establishments they set up as 'minsters' rather than 'monasteries', since monasteries are not normally associated with pastoral care.

A minster was then both a centre of royal authority and of mission, since the consolidation of kingdoms and conversion went hand in hand. Each minster had its own rule (which at this stage might, or might not, include some of the provisions from the sixth-century *Rule of Benedict*, a rule which only gradually become mandatory for communities across Europe). In the seventh century, the inmates of any minster might number men or women, and sometimes both. Such communities have long been known as 'double monasteries'. In these cases, it was an abbess of aristocratic birth who would be expected to rule the community. Such women were used to holding positions of authority within their households. Frequently married into rival kin-groups, their inherited role was to act as 'peace-weavers', to help to break, if they could, the cycle of violence which threatened the lives of their kin. Thus, in the Old English poem *Beowulf*, Queen Wealhtheow presides as a resplendent hostess over the feasting, but her role is not simply ceremonial: she is there to speak in defence of the rights of her sons. But time and again, the audience are reminded of how often a woman's role is as chief mourner; thus, the Danish Hildeburg 'mourned, chanted a dirge' beside a funeral pyre that was consuming the bones both of her brother and of the son(s) against whom he was fighting.[2]

Christianity offered women new ways to continue their role as peace-weavers; across England, women of high birth supported the process of the conversion both through earthly and spiritual marriages.[3] Trouble indeed arose only if queens failed to procreate before joining a community, as did Aethelthryth, wife of King Ecgfrith of Northumbria, who refused to consummate her marriage. After 11 necessarily barren years, Aethelthryth finally left Northumbria, returning to her native East Anglia (she was the daughter of King Anna) where she founded Ely. But Aethelthryth's persistent virginity is the exception rather than the rule. In general, royal women served both God and king; judicious marriages brought together rival royal families, produced heirs and fostered memorialization. As we have seen (see previous chapter), in 651 King Oswine of Deira was murdered by King Oswiu of Bernicia (who thereby successfully reunited Northumbria's two halves). A cycle of revenge might well have been expected, but Oswiu's queen, Eanflaed, instead persuaded the king, as Bede tells the story:

> to expiate Oswine's unjust death by granting God's servant Trumhere, also a near relative of the murdered king, a site at Gilling to build a monastery where prayer was continually to be said for the eternal welfare of both kings, for the one who planned the murder and for his victim.[4]

Eanflaed herself, after Oswiu's death, joined the minster at Whitby, a house founded by the Deiran princess, Hilda. Hilda's father had been assassinated and Hilda had been brought up at the court of her great-uncle King Edwin of Northumbria. Along with the king, Hilda had been converted to Christianity through the preaching of Bishop Paulinus (see previous chapter) in 626. However, the anarchy in Northumbria, following the Battle of Hatfield Chase in 633 (in which Edwin was killed), led Hilda to leave Northumbria, and to take refuge at the court of her brother-in-law, Anna, king of the East Angles. She re-appears only in 647, when, on the eve of setting off to Gaul to become a nun, she returns instead to Northumbria at the invitation of Aidan, bishop of Lindisfarne. After what looks like a probationary year, living the monastic life in a small community by the river Wear, Hilda became firstly abbess of Hartlepool (the house founded by Oswiu after his victory at the Battle of the Winwaed in 655 over the pagan king Penda of Mercia) and next, abbess of a new community at Whitby.

Hilda's achievements, as chronicled by Bede, are remarkable: five men educated at Whitby under her tutelage became bishops (six if you count a certain Tatfrith, appointed to a see but dead before he could be consecrated) and as already mentioned it was through her encouragement that the cowherd Caedmon was led to put into vernacular song the story of the new faith. Caedmon's compositions have not survived (as was once supposed), but since Anglo-Saxon is not a romance language, Latin was unusually difficult for Germanic-speaking Anglo-Saxons to learn or to understand. Caedmon's story therefore underlines the exceptional importance attached to the vernacular in spreading the Christian message in England – an importance it maintained throughout the Anglo-Saxon period. But Hilda's success with the men under her care – from bishops-in-waiting to the cowherd – relied heavily on her own aristocratic birth:

first and foremost, she was royal, a representative of the line of her uncle King Edwin, and thus a fit guardian for Aelfflaed, Edwin's granddaughter, given into Hilda's care by her father in thanksgiving after his victory at the Winwaed. When Oswiu died in 670, his queen Eanflaed joined Aelfflaed. Thereafter, mother and daughter seem to have acted as joint abbesses, intent on memorializing King Edwin, whose relics they had translated to Whitby together with Pope Gregory, whose missionaries had first brought Christianity to Northumbria. The *Life of Gregory*, written at Whitby under their aegis – very possibly by one of the nuns – is considered the first major work of hagiography to be written in England.

In contrast to Hilda and Aelfflaed and to the other abbesses of whom we have records, Anglo-Saxon churchmen of note are not always of noble birth. In the century of the conversion it is clear that the church often bought up slave boys to train them for the ministry and it may well be that monasteries provided havens for boys orphaned through wars or through plague: Barking, a house founded by a bishop of London for his sister and famed for the learning of its nuns (as well as castigated for the aristocratic style of their living), evidently took care of quite young children. This was a community for both sexes and at one of those times when the plague was raging its victims included a boy of 'not more than three years of age who ... was being looked after and was learning his lessons in the dwelling of the maidens dedicated to God'.[5] The possibility, recently suggested, that tensions existed between such oblates and those who joined communities as adults is an important consideration and well worth further study.[6] Certainly, it is clear that within any community successful leadership depended on the capacity of the abbot to meld together various factions, possibly even to compose the rule under which the community was to live. Benedict Biscop boasted that the rule he himself introduced at Wearmouth was ecletic, based on all he had learned from the 17 monasteries he had visited during his travels on the continent.

In such an ambiance, personal loyalties could trump all other considerations. The position taken by the Lindisfarne party over the correct dating of Easter is couched in just such terms. The first bishop of Lindisfarne, Aidan, had been allowed to keep the dating method he had brought with him from Iona, since it was 'clearly understood that ... he could not keep Easter otherwise than according to the manner of those who had sent him'.[7] After the Synod of Whitby, when the Lindisfarne dating system had been rejected in favour of the so-called 'Roman' method, Aidan's successor, Bishop Colman of Lindisfarne, abdicated and returned to Iona, taking with him some of Aidan's bones. For Colman to have abandoned customs initiated by Columba of Iona, and then followed by Aidan, would have been a form of betrayal he could not contemplate.

Colman was not alone in returning to Iona, though Bede fails to mention how many monks accompanied him. But when Bede's own abbot, Ceolfrith, abdicated to go to Rome, where he hoped to end his days, 80 monks went with him. Bede's *History of the Abbots* and the anonymous *Life of Ceolfrith* give us graphic accounts. Here is the departure as described in the *Life*:

> When he [Ceolfrith] had finished speaking, they resumed the [singing] of the antiphon and the psalm ... and went out to the river, leading with a mournful song their father ... a prayer was said on the shore, [Ceolfrith] went on board the ship, and sat in the bows; the deacons sat next to him, one holding the golden cross he had made, the other holding lighted candles. As the ship sailed swiftly across the river, he looked across at the brothers mourning his departure, and heard the glorious sound of their song mingled with their grief, and he could not prevent himself from giving way to sobs and tears.[8]

It is impossible not to compare this with the funeral scene of Scyld Shefing in the poem *Beowulf*, in which the body of Scyld is carried out to sea in a boat with a gold banner fixed to its mast; Scyld's breast is laden with treasure. His followers watch as the sea carries him: 'Their spirits were sad, their hearts sorrowful. Men cannot say for certain, neither councillors in the hall, nor warriors beneath the skies, who received that cargo.'[9] Ceolfrith's boat, by contrast, was equipped both with provisions for the journey and with gifts intended for Rome. One such gift was the *Codex Amiatinus*, one of the three single-volume Bibles which Ceolfrith had had made at the Wearmouth-Jarrow scriptorium (copied from a text Benedict Biscop had acquired from Rome during one of his expeditions in search of just such treasures with which to enrich his foundations). Of these three volumes, only one has survived intact; its provenance remained unrecognized for centuries because it seemed in style so Mediterranean rather than 'Anglo-Saxon'. But it was indeed

Fig. 13: Jarrow Church dedication, 685

Anglo-Saxon scribes – and the hides of many a Northumbrian sheep – which produced this book.

Ceolfrith never reached his destination. He died, after a short illness, at Langres. Some of his followers returned home to relay the news; others continued the journey on to Rome and yet a third contingent stayed in Langres 'because of their love for their parent, buried there'.[10]

The journey from Northumbria to Rome, even for a crow, is over 1,000 miles. In the seventh century, a pilgrim could expect to take many months to cover around 1,500 miles, facing en route both physical challenges as well as the dangerous political uncertainties of the countries through which he had to pass. Yet this was a journey many Anglo-Saxons, both men and women, undertook with relish. Indeed, so many there were that by the late eighth century a 'hostel for the English' had been established in Rome. (In 816, it burnt down, but with papal support it was rebuilt).[11] Rome was a magnet. It represented the old world order, a world of literacy, of cultural achievements and monuments, and it represented now a new order

Fig. 14: Ezra the scribe from the *Codex Amiatinus*

destined to last until the end of time, with a mission – the bringing of the Christian message to the ends of the earth – in which the Anglo-Saxons, the self-professed heirs of a far-flung corner of old Rome, could now partake. Let us look more closely, then, at the lives of Benedict Biscop (a pilgrim to Rome six times) and St Wilfrid (who went thrice). Let their stories start in each other's company, on their first expedition (though it should be pointed out that Bede, in his *History of the Abbots*, gives no account of Wilfrid's part in the journey; it is only Stephen who, in his *Life of Wilfrid*, tells us that Wilfrid and Biscop set off together).[12]

In 653, Biscop and Wilfrid (both already enriched through royal service) decided to leave England to make the pilgrimage to Rome. Biscop was about 25 at the time, Wilfrid some five years his junior. Neither of them was at the time a monk, although Wilfrid had spent a year at Lindisfarne acting as companion to a certain nobleman who had retired there from court. All seemingly went well between them until they reached Lyons, where Wilfrid decided to stay under the protection of the bishop, while Biscop continued on to Rome. How long Biscop then stayed in Rome is not clear but, having returned to Northumbria, he crossed the channel again around 665, this time, after a stay in Rome, going on to the renowned monastery of Lerins in Southern Gaul, where indeed he became a monk. But, having taken his vows, rather than staying at Lerins, Biscop, after two years, made another journey to Rome, his visit coinciding this time with the surprise appointment of Theodore of Tarsus as archbishop of Canterbury and of his assistant Hadrian. (The nominated candidate Wigheard of Kent, who had journeyed out from England, had died before he could be consecrated.) In response to this emergency, Biscop agreed to forsake Lerins and to go back to England as Theodore and Hadrian's interpreter and supporter of their plans. The next two years he therefore spent at Canterbury, as abbot, before setting out once more for Rome, this time in search of books. This trip was short; perhaps by then Biscop had already set his mind on founding his own community in England, in Wessex, because of his friendship with its king, Coynwalh. But the chance death of Coynwalh returned Biscop to Northumbria, where, with the help of King Ecgfrith, he founded, in 674, the minster of St Peter's at Wearmouth.

St Peter's, from the start, was always intended to be a showcase. It was the work of a connoisseur, of a patron determined to bring the sophistication of Gaul and of Rome to his native Northumbria: thus, stone masons and glaziers came from Gaul, books from Rome and Vienna. In 679, Biscop was again on the road to Rome, taking with him this time Ceolfrith, whom he had appointed as the prior of his foundation. The two collected, besides more books, relics, pictures and a calendar, and they persuaded the arch-chanter John to return with them so that English monks could be properly instructed in the singing of the liturgy – always a matter of considerable concern.[13] So dazzled was King Ecgfrith by this influx of Mediterranean culture into his kingdom (all the more, it may be imagined, since in this case it had nothing to do with Wilfrid, to whom we will shortly return) that he planned a further foundation: Jarrow, founded in c.681. Before long, the two communities of Jarrow and Wearmouth became one, but it is not clear that this was always intended to be the case. Recent scholarship suggests, rather, that Jarrow was initially planned as a royal house, where, but for his death in 685, Ecgrith (who himself marked out the site for the altar) could have expected particular veneration, honour and glory.[14]

Meanwhile, Biscop, in the mid 680s, was again on the road to Rome, bringing back with him this time more books, a series of pictures specially chosen to illustrate the congruence of certain Old and New Testament stories and silk cloaks to be used in exchange for more land for his foundation. But when he returned, it was to be greeted with the news that Ecgfrith had been killed in battle at Nechtansmere in 685. Four years later, Biscop, too, was dead.

And what, meanwhile, of Wilfrid? Historians have long suspected that when Wilfrid and Biscop parted ways on their first journey abroad there had been some sort of quarrel. Speculative though this is, it seems highly probable, and it may well be that relations between the two men always remained at best strained; it is even possible that they never met thereafter. Nonetheless, when, after his sojourn in Lyons, Wilfrid finally reached Rome, he, like Biscop, was overwhelmed: despite the best efforts of the masons of Canterbury to use Roman models for their work there (and Canterbury was a city Wilfrid knew well, for he had spent a year at Canterbury before setting off for Rome) there was, as yet, nothing in England that could have prepared him for the grandeur he now met. And it was not just a question of buildings – Rome, especially after the Muslim capture of Jerusalem in 637, had become an unrivalled place of pilgrimage and possessed an exceptional collection of relics (St Andrew's in particular evoked Wilfrid's devotion) and with liturgies of striking richness and complexity. After some months, Wilfrid returned to Lyons before finally returning to England, where, in *c*.663, he was ordained a priest.[15]

Wilfrid's patron was now Alhfrith, son of King Oswiu and sub-ruler of Northumbria. Alhfrith gave Wilfrid the monastery of Ripon, where he installed his own company of monks, thereby expelling the future St Cuthbert who was forced to move elsewhere. In 664, as we have seen, Wilfrid, together with Alhfrith, led the party at the Synod of Whitby that favoured the so-called Roman system for calculating the date of Easter over the 'Irish' method. King Oswiu's decision to give his support to Wilfrid was startling, unexpected and momentous. Bishop Colman of Lindisfarne, finding this rejection of traditional ways totally unacceptable, returned to Iona, taking many of his community (and its relics) with him. His departure paved the way for the removal shortly afterwards of the episcopal see from Lindisfarne to York and for the appointment to the see at York of Wilfrid.

It is not hard to see the appeal of York to Wilfrid: Pope Gregory, in his plans for the conversion of England, had always envisaged that this former Roman city – the very city where Constantine the Great had been proclaimed emperor just six years before his official adoption of Christianity in 312 – would become the site of England's northern metropolitan see. And it was indeed to York (p. 36) that King Edwin hastened after his conversion in 627, so as to be baptized by Bishop Paulinus in a 'speedily' erected wooden chapel. Even after Edwin's death, when Paulinus had retreated South, a Roman missionary presence had been maintained at York by James, a deacon of Paulinus' who had stayed behind teaching not only liturgical singing but also the correct way (in Bede's eyes) of calculating the date of Easter. But for the rigorist Wilfrid such a legacy could only be inherited when he was properly consecrated: to have made do with the bishops available in England at the time (there were only three, none of whom, given their 'Irishness', Wilfrid considered canonically appointed) would have been unacceptable. Nor, it might be added, could they have provided a ceremony as grand and lavish as that which Stephen tells us was accorded to Wilfrid in his chosen city of Compiègne, borne aloft, as he allegedly was, on a golden throne with 12 bishops in attendance.

Wilfrid's rather tardy return to England after such a ceremony is hard to explain unless it is that his position there was in some way compromised by the disappearance from the scene of his earlier patron, Prince Alhfrith, sidelined, or so it would seem, by King Oswiu. By the time Wilfrid re-appeared in Northumbria, his see at York had a new occupant, Chad, installed there by Oswiu. At this juncture, Wilfrid retreated to his monastery at Ripon, all the while cultivating friendships with the kings of both Mercia and Kent until 669, when the newly arrived archbishop of Canterbury, Theodore, gave him back his see. Once re-established in York, Wilfrid lost no time in restoring its buildings.[16] Quite what this may have entailed is impossible now to know – Stephen tells us what a mess birds had made in the building and how Wilfrid had the walls washed and glass put in the windows to help prevent any further bird droppings but he gives few further details.[17] However, his ecstatic descriptions of Wilfrid's buildings at Ripon and Hexham, where land was given to him by Northumbria's new queen Aethelthryth, make it clear that Wilfrid was erecting in Northumbria great stone buildings of Mediterranean grandeur, lavishly furnished with dazzling splendour and whose completion was celebrated in a style to match. When the church at Ripon was finished (it included, as at Hexham, a highly complex crypt) the feasting lasted for three days, the altar on this occasion being draped in 'purple woven with gold' – a match for the gospels Wilfrid had commissioned for his new church written as they were 'in letters of purest gold on purpled parchment and illuminated', with a case to match 'all made of the purest gold and set with the most precious gems'.[18]

Wilfrid's foundations at York, Ripon and at Hexham were then magnificent manifestations of the new religion, but they were much more besides – they provided not only the liturgical services, but also the education necessary to keep the Church supplied with a literate priesthood. As monastic foundations, all three had schools attached, in the case of York with a school that already by the mid-eighth century had won international fame. And, as mission centres, they stood for the power and authority of both king and Church. The dedication of Ripon had been attended by Ecgfrith, king of the Northumbrians, together with his sub-king Aelfwine.

Both gave Wilfrid large estates. 'It was', claimed Wilfrid's biographer Stephen, 'truly a gift well pleasing to God that the pious kings had assigned so many lands to our bishop for the service of God.'[19] Monastic expansion now went hand in hand with the extension of Northumbrian power; the operation was seamless. British clergy fled; Wilfrid moved in.

> Thus that most pious king, Ecgfrith, found his kingdom extending both north and south by his triumphs, while at the same time the ecclesiastical kingdom of St Wilfrid of blessed memory increased to the south among the Saxons and to the north among the British, the Picts and the Scots.[20]

But then came trouble: Ecgfrith's queen, and Wilfrid's patron, Aethelthryth, having failed to produce an heir – and even, or so it was said, to have consummated the marriage – left Ecgfrith in order to take the veil (ultimately to return to her native kingdom where she founded the minster at Ely). The new queen disliked Wilfrid. (She was, said Stephen, a 'Jezebel'.)[21] Added to this personal animosity, soon shared by King Ecgfrith, was the long-standing fact that Wilfrid's empire conflicted sharply with Archbishop Theodore's vision (as adumbrated at the Synod of Hertford, in 672) of a Church governed by dioceses of moderate size. The conflict that followed was both protracted and bitter. In 678, Wilfrid was removed from his see and when three new bishops were consecrated in his place Wilfrid duly set off to Rome to lodge a complaint to the pope. It took some time for Wilfrid to reach Rome, but when finally he arrived it may well be that he found he had to share the city with none other than Biscop and Ceolfrith, since all three were undoubtedly at some point in Rome in 679. But if they did meet, we have no record of the event. Captivated though each was by Rome, by its liturgy and by its saints, and comparable in their *romanitas* as were Ripon and Hexham with Wearmouth and Jarrow, the scale and scope of their ambitions set Biscop and Wilfrid so far apart that it would be no surprise to learn that they had deliberately cold-shouldered each other. For Wilfrid, the world was his oyster. Biscop's aims were no less resplendent but they were limited: he would bring to his two foundations in Northumbria the best of Rome, the best of his monastic experience. In his last days he enjoined that the library he had amassed was to be 'carefully ... preserved intact ... and not divided up all over the place'. His rule, too, was to be observed. It also was, in a sense, a gathered treasure and as such was to be carefully guarded: 'you see', explained Benedict, 'I have taught you all the best things I have found from seventeen monasteries during the long absences of my frequent pilgrimages, and passed them onto you for your good.'[22]

Biscop and Wilfrid's last days, as described in their *Lives*, provide interesting contrasts. Both men are concerned with their legacy, but Benedict, having assured himself of the 'peace, unity and harmony' of his communities, dies while his monks sing the night office, reassured by the psalm (Psalm 82/3) they have reached at the moment of his death that he will safely reach heaven, despite the sombre notes the psalm otherwise strikes. Here is an exemplary monastic death. Wilfrid, on the other hand, dies as an Anglo-Saxon nobleman and Old Testament prophet. He has treasure to give away – gold, silver and precious stones – and it is to be divided up. His treasurer at Ripon puts these riches on display. Wilfrid announces that a quarter are to go to Rome, a quarter to the poor, a quarter for Ripon and Hexham. The final share is reserved for his loyal followers: 'those [to whom] I have given no lands or estates ... so that they may have the means to maintain themselves after I have departed'.[23] Wilfrid then journeys southward, where, surrounded by 'his abbots', he repeats his will, 'and for each of them in due proportion, he either increased the livelihood of their monks by gifts of land, or rejoiced their hearts with money'.[24] At last, he reaches Oundle, repeats his behests, announces that his monastery at Hexham is to go to Acca and then 'after speaking a few words he blessed them, just as Jacob blessed his sons'. As Wilfrid dies, his community is singing Psalm 103/4, a psalm of untroubled triumph.[25]

Wilfrid was, and remains, a controversial figure, but it is as well to remember how much had yet to be decided following the arrival of St Augustine and his monks in 597.[26] The work of the mission was still necessarily precarious, experimental and ad hoc. The controversies surrounding Wilfrid in Northumbria were, moreover, exacerbated by his ability to find allies both from other Anglo-Saxon kingdoms (notably Mercia) and from Rome. And Wilfrid had his models. In nascent Europe his was not an unrecognizable form of sanctity. Had he stayed in Gaul (as he was more than once invited to do), it is doubtful whether the munificence and magnificence of his way of living would have caused a ripple (though in that politically volatile environment he might well have lost his life, as Stephen's narrative complete with assassination plots makes plain).

How far Bede disapproved of aspects of Wilfrid's career is a matter of some controversy.[27] In his obituary notice for Wilfrid, Bede gives no hint of those gifts bestowed by Wilfrid during his last days which figure so prominently in Stephen's account; undoubtedly to Bede, Ceolfrith's death was the more edifying.[28] Nonetheless, it is worth remembering that while there was much about the Church of his day that upset Bede, it is not clear that ostentation as such was high on the list. It would be hard, living among the treasures Biscop had secured for his foundations, had this been so. What upset Bede was frivolity, indolence and hypocrisy: bishops who did not fulfil their pastoral duties; imposters who used the pretence of a monastic calling to gain plots of land which they turned into hereditary estates. What Bede cared about above all was mission and in this respect, at least, Wilfrid could not be faulted. Or could he?

As we have seen, Bede and Stephen give very different accounts of Wilfrid's activities in Sussex; but what is striking is that both accounts suggest that Wilfrid's missionary activities are matters of chance – it is firstly a storm and then a period of exile from Northumbria that brings Wilfrid to Sussex, rather than some long-nourished plan. Similarly, when Wilfrid sets out for Rome in 678/9, it is weather – and a lucky escape from an assassination attempt, in which an unfortunate bishop called Winfrid nearly gets murdered instead – not missionary zeal, that leads Wilfrid to winter, and thus to preach, in Frisia. The contrast with Egbert, arguably the greatest of Bede's heroes in his *Ecclesiastical History*, could hardly be starker.

Egbert first appears, at any length, in a chapter of the *Ecclesiastical History* immediately after Wilfrid's triumph at the Synod of Whitby of 664, when the so-called Roman method of dating Easter had been chosen over the system in use at Lindisfarne up to then. Bede follows up the verdict with a carefully written panegyric of the former bishops of Lindisfarne (Aidan and Colman). Before continuing Wilfrid's story (his departure to Gaul for consecration as the new Northumbrian bishop) Bede notes the portents of 664 – an eclipse and the outbreak of plague – and thereafter comes an account of how before 664 there were many in England 'both nobles and

Fig. 15: St Wilfrid's crypt, Ripon Cathedral

commons, who ... had left their own country and retired to Ireland either for the sake of religious studies or to live a more ascetic life'. It is a passage that needs to be quoted in full:

> In course of time some of these devoted themselves faithfully to the monastic life, while others preferred to travel round to the cells of various teachers and apply themselves to study. The Irish welcomed them all gladly, gave them daily food, and also provided them with books to read and with instruction, without asking for any payment.[29]

The panegyric here contains an inherent rebuke to the sinners of his own day. In recent years, increasing emphasis has indeed been placed on Bede's concern with the abuses he felt were threatening the new Church. The 'gallery of good examples' Bede musters in his *History*, in the hope that they may spur on the listener to 'imitate the good', serves to introduce us to one of the undoubted heroes of the *History*: Egbert.[30]

Egbert and his friend Aethelhun were, Bede tells us, two of the Englishmen who had gone to Ireland in search of mentors. While there, the country was hit with a severe outbreak of plague. Both Egbert and Aethelhun contracted the disease; Aethelhun died, but Egbert, having vowed that if he recovered he would never again return to England, overcame the illness, living to the age of 90; he died in 729, while Bede was still at work on his *History*. Egbert's virtues were, to Bede, exemplary: humility, gentleness, temperance, simplicity and righteousness; the contrast to Wilfrid hardly needs stressing but Bede leaves nothing to chance. Having reported Egbert's recovery from plague, Bede closes the description with a detailed account of Egbert's fasting practices (in particular how he skimmed his milk) before moving straight on to a report of Wilfrid's consecration as bishop in Gaul 'in great splendour'.[31] Bede does not then return to Egbert until 684, some 20 years after the Synod of Whitby, but when he does, it is in the chapter in which Bede reports the disastrous expedition led by King Ecgfrith against the Picts culminating in the Battle of Nechtansmere of 685. The prelude to the battle should indeed have been a warning: Ecgfrith had in 684 sent an army to Ireland which had 'wretchedly devastated a harmless race that had always been most friendly to the English, and his hostile bands spared neither churches nor monasteries'.[32] Ecgfrith's defeat and death in the following year finally put paid to the grandiose ambition seemingly long harboured by Wilfrid of holding authority over 'all the northern part of Britain and Ireland and the islands which are inhabited by the races of Angles and Britons as well as Scots and Picts'.[33] But what was still both possible and desirable was ecclesiastical communion with such peoples, if they could only be persuaded to celebrate Easter in accordance with Roman rules accepted at the Synod of Whitby in 664. As far as Iona was concerned, this was the mission which fell to Egbert.

Egbert's original aim was to preach on the continent but, as Bede tells the story, Egbert is forestalled by a vision of Boisil, the former prior of Melrose (and mentor of St Cuthbert), in which Boisil insists Egbert instead go to Iona: 'whether he likes it or not, he must go to Columba's monasteries for they are cutting a crooked furrow and he must call them back to the true line'.[34] Thus instructed, Egbert moves to Iona, where he indeed persuades the community to accept the required dating rules. Meanwhile, Bede's abbot Ceolfrith is teaching the Picts to do the same. Miraculously, Egbert then dies on Easter Sunday 729, on a date which by the 'old' rules of Iona would have lain outside their liturgical calendar for the feast. And it is with this death that Bede closes the penultimate chapter of his *History*.

The conversion of Iona to the 'correct' dating of Easter, together with the conversion of the Picts to the same system, was not, of course, a pedantic detail. It was to Bede an essential part of his story of conversion; it mattered quite as much as missionary endeavour overseas. Not that this was of indifference to Bede. Quite the contrary: just as his story of the mission to England begins with an anecdote about the 'English' ('not Angles but Angels'), so does his book close with stories of the conversion of various peoples. Strikingly, Bede attributes to Egbert the knowledge that:

> there were very many peoples in Germany from whom the Angles and the Saxons, who now live in Britain, derive their origin; hence even to this day they are by a corruption called *Garmani* by their neighbours the Britons. Now these people are the Frisians, Rugians, Danes, Huns, Old Saxons and *Boruhtware* (Bructerii).[35]

Egbert himself may not be allowed to go to these people, but he organizes, with considerable success, the sending of others, including

Willibrord, a Northumbrian who had been living with Egbert in Ireland in 678. Willibrord's mission prospers to such an extent that in 696 he becomes 'archbishop of the Frisians'; two years later, he founds the monastery of Echternach (near Trier), a house that was to become one of the great centres of manuscript production in the eighth century, and where, thanks to Willibrord, the cult of St Oswald of Northumbria was established.

Bede's knowledge of the work of Anglo-Saxon missionaries abroad remains, nonetheless, unusually hazy. He has heard something of its dangers, such as the brutal murder of two other English missionaries who had come from Ireland and who, distinguished by the colour of their hair, were known as Black Hewald and White Hewald, but there seem, nonetheless, to be notable gaps in his knowledge. Thus we hear nothing from him of the missionaries who went to Germany from southern England; not even Boniface, already a prominent figure in Bede's day, gets a mention.

Boniface (his chosen name as a missionary) had been born in South-West England sometime around 675–80.[36] In 716, he left his community at Nursling, in Hampshire, to join Willibrord's mission in Frisia; it was not a propitious moment – civil wars in Gaul made the trip difficult, so Boniface returned home, but he was not deterred; by 720 he was back again in Frisia, working once more with Willibrord, who had hopes of continuing the partnership. But in 722 Boniface set off for Rome, where he was consecrated as a missionary bishop, with a brief to work in Hesse and Thuringia. Popes would continue to back Boniface throughout his career – it was with their authority behind him that he could preach so widely in territories east of the Rhine. Reputedly, it was the Saxons whom Boniface most wished to convert: 'have pity on them', he wrote back to his English colleagues, 'have pity on them, because their repeated cry is "We are of one and the same blood and bone"'.[37] Such, too, as we have seen, was Egbert's reasoning and it may go some way to explain how eager monks and nuns were in England to rally to Boniface's cries for help. Not only did nuns make him books ('I beg you to continue', he wrote to one, 'the good work you have begun by copying out for me in letters of gold the epistles of my lord, St Peter, that a reverence and love of the Holy Scriptures may be impressed on the minds of the heathen to whom I preach') – they were also ready to join him.[38] Thus, Leoba (probably a kinswoman) left her community of Wimborne, in Dorset, to join Boniface, becoming abbess of Bischofsheim, in the diocese of Mainz; a further relative became abbess of Kitzingen am Main.

Boniface was succeeded at Mainz by another Anglo-Saxon, Lul. A monk of Malmesbury, Lul had met Boniface while he was on a pilgrimage to Rome and had been persuaded by him to leave England and join the mission field. The survival of his letters, together with a number from Boniface, provides a vivid sense of the network that existed between the missionaries and their English supporters.[39] Kings and archbishops, moreover, sought advice and support; practical help was expected as well as the consolation and communion offered by prayer. And it is Lul who makes good the curious gap between the worlds of Bede and Boniface created by Bede's silence. Thus Lul sent presents to Bede's tomb at Jarrow and himself possessed a number of Bede's works including *The Ecclesiastical History of the English People*.

The wide dissemination of Bede's *History* after his death should not allow us to forget that it was a work written in Northumbria, for a Northumbrian king, and that it was deeply coloured by Bede's particular concerns about the state of the Church in his day. Supposing instead that Bede had been writing in Wessex, how different might his work then have been? Fanciful though the idea may seem, it is not wholly preposterous. As a child, Bede was in some sense Benedict Biscop's ward – Bede's kinsmen had placed him into his care – and it is from Bede himself that we know that Biscop had originally intended his foundation to be in Wessex, not Northumbria; it was only the death of King Coynwalh of Wessex, whom he regarded as his friend, that caused Biscop to return North.[40] But deprived though it thus was of Benedict Biscop's munificence, it is worth remembering that Wessex could, nonetheless, boast fine libraries both at Malmesbury and at Nursling (the latter much used by Boniface, both before he became a missionary and as a resource thereafter: copies of books from its holdings were made at his request).[41] And it now seems from recent excavations as if the ancient cultic site of Glastonbury was being transformed already under King Ine (died c.726), even to the extent that it may well have had stained glass in its windows before Bede's monastery of Jarrow had any such luxury.[42] To imagine, then, as the evidence might at first suggest, that power and glory moved from Aethelbert's Kent to Bede's Northumbria and thence to Mercia (under Offa, to be met in Chapter 4) and that it is only with King Alfred that Wessex emerges as a force in the land is a serious misjudgement. Though royal authority in Anglo-Saxon England was always precarious, some kings achieved greater stability than others and one such was Ine of Wessex.[43]

Ine had succeeded Caedwalla, England's last pagan king (though Caedwalla died as a Christian, ten days after his baptism in Rome; see Chapter 1). Caedwalla's reign had been both brutish and short, whereas Ine, who also abdicated to go to Rome, did so only after a relatively long reign, from 688 until *c.*726, when he resigned to make way for the succession of his kinsman Aethelheard. The problems Ine faced would have been familiar to any Northumbrian or Mercian king – competition with neighbours, both British and Anglo-Saxon, the need for resources other than the spoils of war, accommodation with the growing power of the Church and the uncertain rules of succession. But Wessex under Ine had a period of relative peace, not least since Ine had the support of Abbot (later Bishop) Aldhelm (and of two sisters, both recognized as saints). Holy power in Wessex, as in Northumbria, mediated through royal women, could do much to consolidate any dynasty.

We have met Aldhelm already on the bridge at Malmesbury, but Aldhelm was, in fact, a towering figure across Anglo-Saxon England; that much is certain, even if many of the details and dates of his life are not. Born probably in Wessex soon after its conversion to Christianity, possibly with royal blood in his veins, Aldhelm was one of Archbishop Theodore's first pupils at his Canterbury school (having, perhaps, first received some education at Malmesbury from an Irish master). Thereafter, by 680, if not before, Aldhelm became abbot of Malmesbury, thereby, seemingly, turning a British monastic community into a key Anglo-Saxon foundation. What then becomes certain is that, as abbot, Aldhelm utilized to the full the resources of one of the great libraries of Anglo-Saxon England. Possessed of a towering intellect, Aldhelm wrote in both prose and verse – his treatise *On Virginity* appears in both forms but his mastery of words shines through other genres too, from letter writing to the composition of riddles.[44]

In a letter to Acirius (a pen name for Aldfrith, king of Northumbria, probably Aldhelm's godson), Aldhelm laments the 'loud tumultuous uproars in secular affairs', together with 'the ecclesiastical concerns of the pastoral care by which the meticulous and scrupulous mind is constrained as though by the tightest sort of bolt and chains'.[45] There can be no doubt that Aldhelm did indeed expend much energy in the fulfilment of his duties, first in his role as abbot and then in his last years, from 706, as bishop of the new see of Sherborne. He was an enthusiastic builder of churches, not only at Malmesbury and Sherborne, but also at Frome, Wareham and Bradford on Avon. He was also, as we have seen, as committed as was Bede to expressing Christian truths in the vernacular. Like Bede, too (and for this he elicited Bede's praise), he was anxious to persuade his British neighbours of the need to comply with the 'orthodox' calculations for the dating of Easter, but this never seems to have become as bitter an issue in Wessex as it did in Northumbria. British foundations were gradually absorbed, their traditions appropriated, rather than expunged. And if Wessex was in this way spared the divisiveness of the Synod of Whitby, so too was it spared the destructiveness of Nechtansmere. Thus, Ine, after his victory in 710 over King Geraint of Dumnonia, showed no ambition to extend his territory beyond the boundary set by the river Tamar; perhaps his victory had already given him a sufficient supply of salt and of slaves, essentials for any Dark Age king.

Ine was the first king of Wessex to issue a lawcode.[46] It is manifestly a code for a Christian people, issued for both 'the salvation of our souls and the security of our kingdom'. Babies must now be baptized within 30 days of their birth; slaves forced to work on a Sunday can claim their freedom; anyone condemned to death who can reach a church can commute the sentence. Every year at Michaelmas, churchscot (a render of grain) is due. It remains, however, worse to fight in the king's house (the culprit may lose his life) than it does in a minster (where the compensation is just 120 shillings). Good order remained the responsibility of earthly kings.

4

A MERCIAN CENTURY

You have written to us also about merchants, and by our mandate
we allow that they shall have protection and support in our kingdom,
lawfully, according to the ancient custom of trading. And if in any place
they are afflicted by wrongful oppression, they may appeal to us or to
our judges, and we will then order justice to be done. Similarly, our
men, if they suffer any injustice in your dominion, are to appeal to the
judgement of your equity, lest any disturbance should arise anywhere
between our men.

(Letter from Charlemagne to Offa, 796)[1]

Whereas it is possible to tell a story of the seventh century from the
vantage point of its minsters, in the eighth century, mints, markets
and new commercial settlements must vie now for our attention.
England in this century has even been said to have experienced its
first 'industrial revolution'. But it is vital to remember that minsters,
mints and markets do not belong to separate, disconnected worlds,
since it was the minsters themselves which were at the forefront
of the new prosperity that blossomed around the year 700. It may
then be worth recalling the luxuries introduced during the period of
the conversion before considering the economic prosperity that so
swiftly followed.[2]

Early medieval Christians, even the most ascetic, were singularly
devoid of puritanical impulses. Their God had lived and died in the
Mediterranean; Christians, accordingly, had every right to expect

'fertile lands, and provinces rich in wine and oil and abounding in other riches'.[3] Garnets and gold, whalebone and ivory, fabrics of silk and purple – all these and much more were imported in the service of the new religion. Even the staples of daily services required exotic goods: wine for communion, for example, balsam for incense, olive oil for chrism. (The *Life* of the Anglo-Saxon missionary Willibald reports with glee the exploits of that saint as a smuggler of balsam.) And then of course there were books. The making of books required, for a start, calves (in their hundreds) for the vellum. Every major minster was thus, necessarily, both a centre of prayer and a hive of industry. A glance at where many minsters were built makes plain how closely involved they were in trade. Rivers and coastal sites were especially favoured.[4] Even sites which might seem sheltered and isolated turn out on closer inspection to have bustled with commercial activity.

Take Flixborough in Lincolnshire. Flixborough lies eight kilometres south of the Humber estuary.[5] For long, its Anglo-Saxon past lay buried beneath thick layers of windblown sand, but recent excavations have uncovered portions of a substantial settlement dating from the late seventh century. From its earliest days, Flixborough seems to have had close trading links with the continent – seventh-century finds include silver coins from Frisia and wheel-thrown pottery from the Rhineland. Extensive workshops provide evidence of specialized skills in metal and textiles from the same period. Meanwhile, the cattle slaughtered at Flixborough suggest that here was a prosperous settlement accustomed to a lavish standard of living, since the beasts were larger than any that have yet been found elsewhere in England. Nor was beef the only fare available on the Flixborough menu; from time to time, cranes and dolphins made their appearance there too. Such 'conspicuous consumption' has led to the suggestion that initially at least Flixborough was a secular rather than an ecclesiastical site and accordingly that the wax tablets and *styli* (writing implements) found in the course of the excavations might have no relation to sacred texts, but rather were only needed for the documents necessary for estate management. While it may be impossible to disprove such an argument, it remains hard to understand the logic behind it. Given the readily expressed pleasure exhibited by monks and clerics in every form of architectural and liturgical display, it is difficult to believe that they would not also have known how to put on a good dinner. In any case, the rigours of the cold from the North Sea made plentiful rations necessary simply for survival and if monks and nuns knew how and when to fast, it was because they also knew how and when to feast. When Abbot Ceolfrith of Wearmouth-Jarrow abdicated to go to Rome, he made it plain to the community that on the day of his departure there was to be no fasting 'but rather all were to hold a great feast'.[6] An additional attraction of feasts, as Ceolfrith's own father had taught him, was that they provided excellent opportunities for giving alms to the poor.[7]

There is every reason to think that by the late seventh century, as society became more hierarchical, so the rich became correspondingly richer and the poor poorer. The wealth of Flixborough, as of other contemporary minsters, was both a sign and an instrument of this prosperity of the middle Saxon period. The development of North Sea trade and with it the emergence of a new Frankish polity created an explosive period of economic activity on both sides of the English Channel. Excavations at London, Southampton and Ipswich have provided some idea of the extent of the new trade within each of these so-called 'wics' (derived from the Latin *vicus*) or *emporia*; so intense was it that during the first half of the eighth century each of these 'wics' trebled in size. Nor were all goods made for export. From *c*.720, Ipswich potters, having rediscovered the art of wheel-thrown pottery, were set to supply pots and pitchers over the next hundred years or so, not only for East Anglia, but also for customers as far afield as Kent and Yorkshire.

The work of archaeologists has been supplemented to a remarkable degree over recent decades by the use of metal detectors and, principally, by their coin finds. Places where large quantities have been found (excluding hoards) have come to be known as 'productive sites', following the inference that some form of commercial activity must have been taking place in the region to explain the density of finds. The evidence of these coin finds fully substantiates the story of the new economic world of the late seventh and eighth centuries. Thus, the gold coinage of the conversion period has, by the 660s, been replaced now by more utilitarian silver 'pennies': these coins are no longer status symbols, but intended for use in trade and it indeed seems clear that the silver coins of England, Frisia and Denmark were used interchangeably. The coins did not, as yet, bear the names of rulers, but sometimes they can be traced to the mints of particular towns and it is possible that a number of the issues can be attributed to minsters, both because so many coins are founds on such sites (not least along the Thames where 33 known minsters were sited) and because of the explicitly religious iconography to be found on many of the coins, with some coins even inscribed with the words MONITA SCORUM, meaning (it is suggested) 'money of the saints'.[8]

From the mid-eighth century, coins become much easier to place: now they regularly carry the name of the ruler, as well as the name of the moneyer. Significantly too, from this point on, Northumbrian coins diverge from southern issues: the Northumbrian coins are more conservative in design, an indication that Northumbria's period of ascendancy has finally passed and that power has by now shifted decisively to Mercia. Throughout the eighth century, it is indeed Mercian coins which are by far the most innovative – and bombastic – as well as the most common. How was it that Mercia had been able to achieve this supremacy?[9]

Mercia was originally made up of a conglomeration of lands that successful rulers managed to weld together to form a kingdom. Much the same could, of course, be said of the other major Anglo-Saxon kingdoms, but in the case of Mercia we are particularly well informed because of the chance survival of the document known as the Tribal Hidage (a 'hide', as defined by Bede, being the land needed to support one family). Controversial though interpretations of the Tribal Hidage have always been, what clearly emerges from it is some sense of the vastly different sizes of kingdoms or principalities when the document was first compiled.[10] In all, 34 different peoples are listed as living south of the Humber and whereas Mercia itself has a hidage of 30,000, the 'Hicca' of Hertfordshire (destined to give their name to Hitchin) can muster only 300. Middle-size areas of 7,000 hides include the 'Hwinca' and 'Westerna', generally identified as the former kingdoms of the Hwicce and the Magonsaetan. The stages whereby even these two reasonably substantial kingdoms lost their status to become incorporated into Mercia may not be fully recoverable, but the outlines suggest much about the origins and stages of Mercia's success.

In the seventh century, the Hwicce occupied the area that would later become the diocese of Worcester. The Hwicce had themselves absorbed a number of other peoples, not least the *Weogoran* from whom Worcester derives its name. And they had a king, Osric, who appears in the pages of Bede. But by the time of Offa (757–96), the Hwicce are ruled first by 'sub-kings' and then, before the eighth century is out, just by ealdormen, in other words by officials who owed their status to royal favour. The Magonsaetan, meanwhile, seem to have been based in and around Hereford. Their first recorded king is Merewalh, Christian son of the powerful pagan Mercian King Penda. Merewalh's appearance may indeed provide a clue as to the likely scenario in the kingdom of the Hwicce as well as of the Magonsaetan: each kingdom, as it expanded, may have taken the initiative in seeking the support of its powerful Mercian neighbours, only to end up being engulfed by them. Mercia would in this way have gained access firstly to the great wealth offered by the salt mines of Worcester (in particular those of Droitwich) and then, through the conversion and kingship of Merewalh, a place in the new Christian economy, even if Penda all the while continued to reap the advantages of himself remaining a professed pagan, periodically at odds with his Christian neighbours of Northumbria, but never hesitating to make alliances with the British Christians of Wales, as need arose.

Mercia's final embrace of Christianity would be sealed, at least in legend, by the eventual adoption of two of Penda's daughters, Cyneburg and Cyneswith, as saints of the minster at Peterborough and, strikingly, when the time had come for a change of dynasty, it was achieved through the help of a holy man. During the reign of the last of Penda's descendants, King Ceolred, his rival Aethelbald was driven into exile. In his despair, he had visited Guthlac, aristocratic hermit and former brigand, who gave him every assurance that, despite all the sins he, Aethelbald, had committed, nonetheless the Mercian crown would soon be his: 'O my child', said Guthlac:

> I am not without knowledge of your afflictions ... [and] I have asked the Lord to help you in his pitifulness; and he has heard me; and granted you to rule over your race and has made you chief over the peoples; and he will bow down the necks of your enemies beneath your heel and you shall own their possessions.[11]

A year after Guthlac's death, Aethelbald indeed became king. It has been suggested (and it is indeed an intriguing possibility) that

Guthlac had himself once been a contender for the throne and that in the depths of the Mercian fens he and Aethelbald had perhaps reached some forms of agreement whereby it was understood that whereas Aethelbald would be king, Guthlac would by association confer holiness on his rule. In this way, they would together vanquish the reprobate Ceolred (who even before his death had been spotted in a vision suffering terrible torments in Hell).[12] Even if no such explicit pact was ever made, Aethelbald indeed did much to ensure and to appropriate the cult of Guthlac, building a splendid shrine for him at his hermitage at Crowland and it would be at Repton, where Guthlac had himself made public his conversion and had become a monk, that Aethelbald was buried.

Mercian kings had every reason to know the trouble a dissident holy man could cause to any ruler, and conversely, the advantages of good relationships with anyone who might have the ability to wield holy power. Both of Penda's successors, King Wulfhere (658–74/5) and King Aethelred (674/5–704), had taken advantage of Bishop Wilfrid's quarrels with his Northumbrian kings by offering Wilfrid shelter. In 679, after the Battle of the Trent in which Aethelred killed a younger brother of the Northumbrian king (the dead man also happened to be Aethelred's brother-in-law), the intervention of Archbishop Theodore was crucial in preventing the eruption of a blood feud between Northumbria and Mercia. Mercia had to pay compensation for the death, but given, as Bede saw it, 'the good reason for fiercer fighting and prolonged hostility' which such a death offered, Theodore's settlement was a remarkable achievement. Ultimately it proved highly beneficial to Mercia. Never again was Northumbria able to claim authority over those lands south of the Humber that hitherto had formed the kingdom of Lindsey.[13]

Lindsey had long been contested territory between Mercia and Northumbria. The resentment towards Northumbria felt in Lindsey is graphically illustrated by Bede's story of the hostility with which the relics of St Oswald were greeted at the monastery of Bardney, when brought there by Osthryth, niece of Oswald and Northumbrian wife of King Aethelred; it took a miraculous shaft of light to persuade the monks of Bardney to accept the proffered bones, since Oswald was in their eyes no saint, but rather a hated conqueror.[14] And it may be that Osthryth was never quite forgiven, since years later, in 697, she was assassinated by her Mercian nobility.[15] The widowed

Aethelred continued as king for another seven years, whereupon he entered Bardney as a monk and later became its abbot. Such devotion to Bardney suggests that perhaps its very foundation should be connected with the Battle of the Trent; it is quite possible that the honour paid to Oswald was part of the peace settlement Theodore had managed to negotiate.[16]

By the time Bede was completing his *History*, c.731, Mercia had, in his estimation, supreme power in the south of England: all those kingdoms which 'reach right up to the Humber together with their various kings' were, Bede wrote, subject to Aethelbald.[17] This may be something of an exaggeration, but the death in 725 of King Wihtred of Kent and the subsequent division of his kingdom between Wihtred's sons may have given Aethelbald an opportunity to augment his influence in Kent. By chance, the following year saw the abdication of Ine of Wessex. Turmoil followed, most probably again to the benefit of Aethelbald. Influence in both kingdoms was, of course, essential now to the power of any Mercian king, since Mercia throughout its history would always be handicapped by its lack of ports and it was ports and trade which were now the key to the economic success of any kingdom.

Despite the remarkable stability given to eighth-century Mercia by Aethelbald and Offa, it should not be imagined that these two had found some magic formula for prosperity and peace between them. There are, in any case, very real contrasts to be found between the two reigns. For a start, each seems to have had very different dynastic strategies. Offa, Alcuin complained, spilt more blood than anyone could estimate in order to secure the succession of his son. The heirless and unmarried Aethelbald, on the other hand, led such a dissolute life that the Anglo-Saxon missionary St Boniface, now archbishop of Mainz, felt protest was necessary.

With the support of seven other missionary bishops, Boniface wrote to Aethelbald of Mercia (who, he claimed, wielded 'the glorious sceptre of imperial rule over the English'), urging him to reform his way of life: the fact that the king had not married could possibly be commendable, but rumours had reached Boniface that the king had by no means chosen chastity, but rather that he wantonly slept with nuns – as had before him, Boniface alleged, King Osred of Northumbria and King Ceolred of Mercia, both of whom were now in Hell. Eternal damnation was a looming certainty for

Aethelbald as well, unless the king could reform his ways by living chastely and by showing greater respect for the monks and priests of Mercia and for their possessions. 'He who seizes the money of his neighbour', thundered Boniface (possibly quoting St Jerome), 'commits iniquity; but he who takes away the money of the Church commits sacrilege.'[18]

Boniface's fulminations seemingly did not go unheeded. In 747, King Aethelbald summoned a council to meet at Clovesho (possibly, but not certainly, Clovesho is to be identified with Brixworth in Northamptonshire), where a significant reforming programme was put forward.[19] Laity as well as clergy attended and, for the first time at a synod in England, *Anno Domini* dating was used, together with the regnal year of the Mercian king. The proceedings were, however, opened not by the king, but by the archbishop of Canterbury and the primary concern of the council was with the conduct and duties of the clergy. The correct administration of the sacraments, following Roman rites and customs, together with the proper education of the laity, were of paramount importance. A clear division was to exist between the sacred and the secular – priests were not to sing the liturgy in such a way that could made them seem akin to secular poets; laymen must not frequent monasteries. This two-tier view of the Church was of course intended for the benefit of both. Between them, a well-disciplined clergy and a well-instructed laity could together create a holy society, pleasing to God. But it was not only by their prayers that the Church was to protect its kings. Two years after Clovesho, at Gumley, came the first record of that key decree insisting that monasteries contribute to the building of bridges and the repair of forts (though henceforth, by way of a telling recompense, they should not feel obliged to provide kings with hospitality). In the future, all ecclesiastical land, even if temporarily held by a layman and even if exempt from other forms of tribute, must yet contribute to 'the building of bridges [and] the necessary defences of fortresses against enemies'.[20] In the decades that followed, comparable clauses would be repeated again and again. Thus, a grant of 822 from the king of Mercia to the archbishop of Canterbury specifies:

I will free the aforesaid land from all servitude in secular affairs, from entertainment of king, bishop, ealdormen or reeves, tax-gatherers, keepers of dogs, or horses or hawks, from the feeding of all those who are called *faestingen* ... except military service against pagan enemies, and the construction of bridges and the fortification or destruction of fortresses against the same people[21]

Just ten years after the meeting at Clovesho, Aethelbald was dead. The circumstances are both mysterious yet clear: it was his own bodyguard who had assassinated him. The *Anglo-Saxon Chronicle* of 757 that records his death makes compelling reading. The entry begins, curiously, not with Mercian affairs, but an epic tale concerning the death of the West Saxon king Cynewulf.[22] Cynewulf had become king in 757 by deposing King Sigeberht 'because of his unjust acts'. Sigeberht had at first kept Hampshire, though this too he subsequently forfeited because he murdered a loyal ealdorman. Sigeberht was thereupon driven into the Weald by Cynewulf, where he lived 'until a swineherd stabbed him to death by the stream at Privett, and he was avenging the ealdorman'. Cynewulf, the annalist goes on to tell us, had often fought great battles against the Britons. This may have given him heroic status, but seemingly not regnal security, so that even after many years he felt the need to expel Cynheard, brother of the king (Sigeberht), whom he had deposed decades earlier. But Cynheard, who had got wind of the king's intentions, went with his own band of followers to the place where it was known the king would be with his mistress. A terrible fracas ensued: Cynewulf wounded Cynheard; retainers of Cynheard killed Cynewulf; Cynheard offered terms to Cynewulf's followers, but all to a man refused them and 'they continued to fight until they all lay dead'. Next morning, as the news of the king's death spread, further retainers of the dead king came to where the body of their lord lay. Cynheard attempted to bargain with them from behind locked gates: if they would but give him the kingdom they would have both land and money. And, said Cynheard (by way of further inducement), some of their kinsmen had already taken his side. 'No kinsmen', retorted the thegns, 'were dearer to them than their lord.' A bloody fight ensued; the gates were broken into and Cynheard killed. 'And in the same year', continued the chronicler, 'Aethelbald, king of the Mercians was slain at Seckington, and his body is buried at Repton.'[23]

A scribal error was clearly at work here so the dates are confused, but the juxtaposition of the stories is suggestive. Why was it that Aethelbald was killed? Was he, like Cynewulf and Cyneheard, also involved in some deep-rooted feud? We will never know, but a recent suggestion has a high degree of plausibility about it: it connects Aethelbald's death with an expedition against Mercia in 756, launched by Onuist, king of the Picts, in alliance with Eadberht, king of Northumbria. Aethelbald had himself invaded Northumbria in 740, at a time when Eadberht had been at war with the Picts. Now, or so it seems, Picts and Northumbrians were allies, determined to strike at Mercian power. They failed, defeated (probably) at Newborough, near Lichfield. Despite the victory of the Mercians, the battle could, conceivably, have spelt the demise of Aethelbald if (as has been conjectured) it was not he who was the hero of the day.[24]

After some years in exile and 41 more as ruler, Aethelbald is indeed hardly likely to have still been in his prime. Aethelbald still belonged to a world in which the hold of any king over his throne remained deeply precarious. His thegns might protect him; they might also turn against him. As yet, no divinity hedged any king. Every king needed protection against assassination; in eighth-century Northumbria, between 756 and 800, three kings were murdered (with another two deposed). Given Offa's own taste for murdering anyone who might have stood in the way of his son's succession, it is a testimony to his power that he himself escaped assassination.[25] It is the nature of that power that needs now to be examined.

Tenth-century charters call Offa 'the king of the English', even 'king of the whole country of the English'. In his own day, he never achieved any such accolade, nor is there any evidence that he could or would have aimed at these titles. Nonetheless, it does not seem fanciful to imagine that Offa thought well and grandly of himself. His very name, Offa, would have recalled the legendary Offa, king of Angeln, a figure who features in the genealogy of Mercian kings, as well as in the poetic record. As king, his achievements have been made difficult to assess because we have no contemporary chronicler to guide us – the lack seems all the greater, given that for Northumbria we have Bede and for Wessex the *Anglo-Saxon Chronicle*. The evidence for Offa's reign is, nonetheless, sufficiently rich and diverse to make it possible to conclude that, while Mercian England is emphatically not the prototype for a united England, it is undoubtedly a very different place from Bede's.

Fig. 16: Offa's gold coin

Offa had come to power just six years after the Carolingians had replaced the last Merovingian ruler in Frankia (on the grounds that he was 'useless'). This transition had been marked by the anointing of the new king, Pippin, at Soissons in 751, at a ceremony possibly performed by none other than Boniface of Mainz. Three years later, the pope gave this coup his final seal of approval by anointing Pippin's two sons, Charlemagne and Carloman. Around the same time, Pippin displayed his new authority by reforming the Frankish coinage. Its silver content was restored and the method of manufacture changed. And every coin was now to bear both the name of the king and the mint. Shortly after his accession, Offa instituted a similar reform, albeit with some differences – Mercian coins named the king and the moneyer, but not the mint, and a greater freedom of design was evidently permitted.

Offa, who had no Bede to chronicle his reign, had at least 37 moneyers.[26] They operated from London, Canterbury and, it is thought, Ipswich. Their designs were highly innovative and it can be argued that between them they do much to make up for our lack of a contemporary Mercian historian. For a start, the location of the mints is significant. There is scant evidence that there was ever a mint in the Mercian homelands. As a landlocked kingdom it had no ports so its trading capabilities were sorely restricted. Access to Hamwic, via Oxford, was possible, but not enough. Control of Kent was vital and by the 760s it had fallen to Offa, together with its Canterbury mint. Local leaders, chafing at the extent of Mercian dominance, attempted with some success at the Battle of Otford in 776 to regain their independence, only to lose it again within the decade. East Anglia, with its flourishing town of Ipswich, was another area vital for Offa's prosperity. Here, Offa exerted power by marrying a daughter to the East Anglian king, Aethelberht, seemingly reserving to himself the right of coinage. An attempt by Aethelberht to break free from his father-in-law's domination can be seen from the coin that Aethelberht nonetheless dared to mint in the latter part of his reign and which gave him the title 'Rex'; the design showed the wolf that nursed Romulus and Remus and thus carried the implication that Aethelberht's family name (Wuffingas) had imperial connotations. Such audacity may have cost Aethelberht his life, for Offa had him killed in 794. Meanwhile, no coinage at all has survived from the kingdom of the East Saxons and very little from Wessex.

Despite any military effort expended by Offa to maintain his conquests, it is not as a warrior that he wanted to be depicted. His coins show no helmets, no spears. Instead, we have a curly headed king, almost certainly fashioned on the prevalent image of King David; portraits were modelled on classical images and, perhaps most surprisingly, we have a gold coin inscribed with the words 'Offa Rex' written across it in imitation of an Islamic coin. The Latin and the Arabic do not match up – that is to say, one or the other is upside down – so it is clear the moneyer knew no Arabic. But the coin, together with those coins that bear the name of Offa's queen Cynethryth, are a striking testimony to Offa's pretensions to be a figure on the world stage. Roman emperors had put the names of their consorts on coins; so too would Offa. But such iconography was not mere antiquarianism. At the time of the minting of Cynethryth's coins there was in Byzantium an empress, Irene, whose coins bear her image, while in the Islamic world there was a caliph, Harun al Rashid, with whom Charlemagne was in regular touch. (Harun, famously, sent Charlemagne the present of an elephant.) Is it fanciful to imagine that Offa had such contacts as well? His imperial tastes are in any case well vouched for. In a much quoted letter, Charlemagne complains that the consignment he has been sent included cloaks that were not the right size and he was not pleased. Offa, for his part, had asked for black stones which Charlemagne was willing to supply, but since Offa has specified the length of these stones it is, Charlemagne thinks, entirely fair to be particular about the measurements of the cloaks. For many years, these 'black stones' presented something of a puzzle. What could they be? In recent years, a solution has been found: they are black marble, quite possibly Roman *spolia* taken from Ravenna, such as those Charlemagne himself was using at his palace in Aachen.[27]

Let no walkers, as they meander along Offa's dyke, underestimate how seriously Offa took himself, his place in the world and his relationship with his 'brother' Charlemagne; but nor should it be thought this was simply some form of megalomania – Charlemagne himself called Offa his 'brother' and although relationships between him and Offa had their stormy moments, Charlemagne had every reason to think well both of his fellow Christians across the sea and of Offa, their foremost king.

Relationships between Charlemagne's family and England can be traced back to the 690s, when the Northumbrian monk Willibrord had gone to Frisia in the hope of converting those peoples east of the river Rhine, fated to be swallowed up before long into the Carolingian Empire. The Northumbrian mission was soon joined by Boniface and his circle of disciples. Such men worked with papal support, but in the first instance and by necessity in alliance too with the Pippinid family and thus, when the Pippinids seized power in 751, with the royal court itself. The famous mission to the papacy *c.*750 to ask whether it could be right for someone to have the name of king when he had no power thus included the Anglo-Saxon Burchard, bishop of Wurzburg. Once the pope had given the 'right' answer Pippin and his queen then could be anointed; the ceremony, conducted at Soissons in 751, may have been conducted by Boniface himself.

Some 30 years later it was the Northumbrian Alcuin who had the ear of the Carolingians. Alcuin (of the same family as Willibrord) was one of the foremost scholars of his day. Educated at York, he was lured away in the early 780s to his court by Charlemagne, whom he had happened to meet in Italy. Alcuin remained then in Frankia until his death in 804, but he returned to England twice, the first time in connection with the visit of George, bishop of both Ostia and Amiens, leader of the papal mission to England of 786.[28]

Quite what it was that had prompted the dispatch of Bishop George remains uncertain, but the hopes and aspirations of King

Offa cannot but be part of the story. George and his party arrived at Canterbury, where they were duly received by Archbishop Jaenberht. Thereafter, the party divided: half went to Mercia, half on to Northumbria, where reforming decrees were drawn up. With these in hand and accompanied by Alcuin, Bishop George returned to Mercia, where a second council was convened and the Northumbrian decrees adopted. So content was Offa with the proceedings that it was at this point, according to a later papal letter, that Offa promised to send to Rome 'every year ... as many mancuses as the years had days, that is 365'.[29] Just one year later, despite fierce opposition from Canterbury, the see of Canterbury was divided: papal permission was given for a new see to be established at Lichfield. Its archbishop, Hygeberht, chosen by Offa is thought to have consecrated Offa's son, Ecgfrith. In this way, or such was the hope, Offa would become the founding father of a new Mercian dynasty. Offa can of course have had no premonition of Ecgfrith's premature death in 796 only months after his own.

Lichfield kept its archiepiscopal status only until 803. Its short-lived elevation is nonetheless remarkable not least for the light it throws on Offa's ambitions. Since 784/5 (following the death of its king, Ealhmund), Offa had again been able to exercise direct control over Kent and it was not impossible that he had planned to give Kent as a sub-kingdom to the anointed Ecgfrith, in the wake of his possible marriage to Bertha, a daughter of Charlemagne – a match that would have substantially augmented Offa's power in southern England. But the expectations here were all on Offa's side: content though Charlemagne was to contemplate the marriage of his son, Charles, to Aelfflaed, a daughter of Offa's, he had no intention of allowing any daughter to leave his side to go to England and so angered was he by Offa's attempt to bargain that even the proposed match between Charles and Aelfflaed was called off and a trade embargo imposed. Once more, Alcuin appears on the scene, swearing loyalty to his friends on both sides of the channel while he attempts to make peace. By 796, Alcuin could write to Offa: 'be it known to your reverend love that the lord King, Charles [Charlemagne], has often spoken to me of you in a most loving and loyal way, and in him you certainly have a most faithful friend ... He is also sending fitting gifts to you.'[30]

Alcuin's letter of the following year concerning the premature death of Ecgfrith in 797 – 'that most noble young man has not died for his own sins; but the vengeance for the blood shed by the father has reached the son' – is often taken as if it were Alcuin's considered verdict on the whole of Offa's reign, whereas even in the same letter Alcuin, after lamenting the state of his native Northumbria, 'almost destroyed by internal quarrels and false oaths', can continue to 'let the Mercians maintain the good, temperate and pure conduct, as Offa laid down for them, that they have a blessing from God, a stable kingdom and a strength against their enemies'.[31] No one, of course, could deny that Offa was much hated, certainly outside his heartlands – Kent attempted to break free from Mercian domination within months of his death – but no Dark Age king could survive who was not also ruthless. The interesting question must always be this: what could a king do to make his ruthlessness not only effective, but even perhaps palatable?

In the case of Mercia, which bred no contemporary chronicler, much of the evidence must be archaeological; the work is still ongoing, varied and controversial. For decades, Mercian power has of course been epitomized by Wat's and Offa's Dyke; debates about these great works are even now not yet settled, even if they undoubtedly stand as testimony to the manpower Mercian kings could muster.[32] But, as the forthcoming work of John Blair will show, Aethelbald and Offa had interests that went far beyond their western frontier; revolutions on many fronts were in progress. Thus Blair suggests that the power of Mercian kings in the eighth century depended not only upon the extent to which they were able to put a halt to the dangerous possibilities (adumbrated by Bede in his letter to Egbert of York), whereby 'bogus' minsters deprived kings of land and of fighting men, but, further, that it depended precisely upon the kings' successful imitation of monastic landholding and management.[33] Thus, whereas the great buildings of the seventh century had been minsters, in the eighth century the landscape would be transformed by centres held under royal control. Kings of Mercia would necessarily still travel throughout their kingdom, but they also had, in effect, the beginnings of a capital: Tamworth. This was where you might expect to find Mercian kings at Christmas, where at least some records were kept and where from the ninth century, if not before, there was a water mill.[34] The fortifications around the town, thought formerly to be post-Viking in date, are now considered to be of a much earlier date, even if they were then subsequently re-built in the post-Viking era. Similarly, the fortifications at Hereford and at Winchcombe must no longer be dated to the reigns of Aethelflaed and Edward, but rather to the eighth century.[35] In response to the Viking invasions, repairs and rebuilding were doubtless essential, but Mercia under Offa was already a well-fortified kingdom. It had to be. Its creation had depended on reducing to client status the power of subordinate kings; its well-being depended now on the successful management of its resources – salt, lead, wool and iron. This was not a society geared to war but rather to prosperity. But prosperity depended on peace, on the guarding of resources and specifically of the places where production was in process.

Even the most cursory study of place names will suggest how rapid were the developments across the kingdom of both 'towns' or 'tuns' and fortifications – 'burhs'. Quite suddenly after c.760 a crop of 'tun' names appear.[36] The possibility of archaeological investigations of such places is necessarily limited by their continued settlement. However, on the river Nene, some 30 miles from Brixworth (which boasts one of the finest Anglo-Saxon churches in the country) and 15 miles from Northampton, lies the recently excavated site of Higham Ferrers, a site of some 100 acres which provides an idea of the scale and complexity of a Mercian estate centre.[37]

Across the river from Higham Ferrers lies Irthlingborough. In 784, Offa was here, as his signing of a charter testifies. Offa can be expected to have had with him a retinue of around 100 – but they will not have gone hungry. The complex included a horseshoe-shaped enclosure which it can be assumed acted as a stock pen, together with six buildings – possibly two of these provided houses for workers, while the other four seem to have been used for storage. The most remarkable discovery on the site, however, must be the malting oven. Analysis of the grains suggests that prestige barley malt was made here, fit indeed to brew ale for a king.

Just as Irthlingborough was close to Brixworth, so, near to Tamworth, was Lichfield. Palaces and cult centres were interdependent. No king, since the days of the conversion to Christianity, could expect to rule without the help of holy men, sometimes alive (for example Guthlac), sometimes dead (as was Chad). Lichfield, where Chad was buried, was of course the seat of a bishop, even for a few years an archbishop, but it was its possession of Chad's body which made it a source of numinous power. Chad had been Mercia's fifth bishop and had died in 672. Not long afterwards, a new church of St Peter's was built at Lichfield and it was there that Chad's body had been taken and was venerated. Just recently, in 2003, during restoration work at the cathedral, a limestone angel, some 600 mm tall, was unearthed from beneath the nave.[38] The angel had been broken into three large portions before being buried. Why remains a matter of speculation but there is nothing to suggest vandalism. The angel wears bright yellow, his wings are open and he is poised in such a way as to suggest he had just alighted. The supposition that he had originally formed half of the end panel of a tomb which had once housed Chad is irresistible. The work is likely to date from the late eighth century and thus would have been made at around the same time as the St Chad Gospels. Indeed, both may plausibly have been intended to honour Ecgfrith, on the occasion of his anointing as the appointed heir and to celebrate the new status of Lichfield as a metropolitan see. Chad had been a favourite of Bede's (and Mercia is known to have had a copy of the *Ecclesiastical History*) and it must be of more than passing interest that Bede's account of Chad was translated into Old English, very possibly still within Offa's lifetime, and that Bede had graphically described how when the moment had come for Chad to die, his brother, Cedd, coming to fetch Chad's soul, had 'descended from the sky with a host of angels'.[39]

Might Offa himself have read Bede? It is not impossible. Offa, the tyrant, could nonetheless be described by Alcuin as a ruler 'intent on education' who would know how to take care of a pupil Alcuin had sent him: 'Do not let him wander in idleness or take to drink.'[40] Both faces are of course wearable: Offa's power – and his legacy – was made manifest by his patronage of the arts just as much as by the erection of new fortifications. The Lichfield scriptorium, or so it seems, continued to flourish after his death.[41] The Lichfield angel was only one of a number of Mercian angels. Breedon on the Hill, also close to Tamworth (but to the north), boasts another.[42]

Breedon was once an Iron Age fort; its revived fortunes as a minster began with a colony of monks sent from Medeshamsted (today's Peterborough) sometime in the 680s under the abbacy of Hedda, later bishop of Lichfield. Breedon's sculptures, however, belong not to the period of Hedda's office but to a time much closer to the Lichfield angel. What is particularly striking about the Breedon sculptures, however, are the Byzantine influences to which they are clearly and heavily indebted. The Breedon angel has seemingly arrived to give Mary the news of her pregnancy – like the Lichfield angel, he also gives the appearance of having only just landed – but somewhat unexpectedly he has a panel to himself. It is, nonetheless, clear that he expects an audience: his right hand is raised in the Greek form of blessing – the thumb touching the ring finger. Mary, meanwhile, is elsewhere; she has a panel of her own in which she appears carrying a book (a symbol of the incarnation), facing her audience in the manner of a Byzantine icon.[43] Indeed, throughout the church, most notably in the two friezes around its walls, are motifs – vine scrolls, birds and animals – taken from Byzantine sources – vine scrolls, birds and animals. The challenge, as ever, is to imagine the impact of the sculpture in full colour. At nearby Sandbach (still in the diocese of Lichfield), where at least two crosses were erected, their power may have been further accentuated by the use not only of paint but probably also used metalwork as part of the decorative technique.[44]

The prosperity which Mercia enjoyed under Offa's grip he will have been expected to share with his loyal followers, those who had risen thanks to his patronage. One such is the Ealdorman Aethelmund.[45]

Under 802 the *Anglo-Saxon Chronicle* records his death. Aethelmund, once a thegn in the independent kingdom of the Hwicce, had (perforce) transferred his allegiance to Offa, after Offa had absorbed the Hwicce into his kingdom. Aethelmund had then become its ealdorman. When Aethelmund died it was in battle, defending his province against the men of Wiltshire. His body was taken by his son Aethelric to be buried at the church at Deerhurst. Thereafter, Aethelric went on pilgrimage to Rome. On his return in *c*.807, Aethelric confirmed the grant of certain lands to Deerhurst 'for me and for my father Aethelmund, if it may befall me that my body would rest there ... on this condition, that the community there shall make firm their vows, just as they have promised to me'. What Aethelric then set about to do is, seemingly, to transform the church at Deerhurst, even if his death in 824 may have occurred before the commission was completed. The work testifies to the influence of Rome on Aethelric and provided a further example of the use of polychrome as used also at Lichfield; it was not only a cathedral then that could employ the finest craftsmen Mercia

Fig. 17: Sandbach Crosses, Sandbach

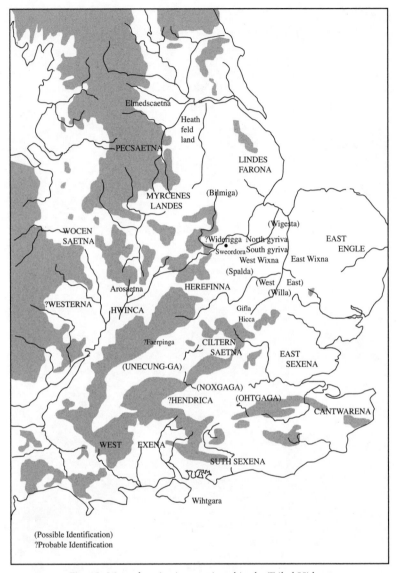

Fig. 18: Map of territories mentioned in the Tribal Hidage

Fig. 19: All Saints' Church, Brixworth

Fig. 20: The Priory Church of St Mary's, Deerhurst

could muster. The cultural prosperity of Offa's reign clearly left a rich and widespread legacy: the Deerhurst animal heads have much in common with the pointer of Alfred's Jewel (see Figure 23), a reminder of how much Alfred in his renaissance may have owed to Mercia and its craftsmen, even if everything, in his words, had been 'destroyed and burnt' by Vikings. It is to those Vikings and to Alfred that we must now turn.

5

KING ALFRED, THE VIKINGS AND THE RISE OF WESSEX

Now after Easter when the Emperor was heading back into Frankia, a king of the English sent envoys to him to ask the Emperor to grant him permission to travel through Frankia on his way to Rome on pilgrimage. He also warned the Emperor to devote even more careful attention and concern to the salvation of the souls of those subject to him. For the minds of the English had been quite terrified by a vision one of them had seen. The king took pains to send the Emperor a detailed account of this vision, which went as follows:

The vision of a certain pious priest of the land of the English, revealed to him after Christmas while he was transported out of the body.

One night when that pious priest was asleep, a certain man came to him and told him to follow him ... This guide then led him to a land he did not know at all and there he saw many wonderful buildings standing. One was a church into which he and his guide went and there he saw a lot of boys reading ... and he could see ... that their books were written not only in black letters but also in letters of blood ... He asked why the books were written out like that ... and his guide answered: 'The lines of blood you can see in those books are all the various sins of Christian people, because they are so utterly unwilling to obey the orders and fulfil the precepts in those divine books. These boys now, moving about here and looking as if they were reading, are the souls of the saints who grieve every day over the sins and crimes of Christians and intercede for them so that they may finally be turned to repentance some day ... [But] if Christian people don't quickly do penance for their various vices and crimes ... then ... for three days and nights a very dense fog will spread

over their land, and then all of a sudden pagan men will lay waste with
fire and sword most of the people and land of the Christians along with
all they possess.

(*Annals of St-Bertin*, 839)[1]

The last years of both King Offa and the Emperor Charlemagne
were overshadowed by the new fear presented by what, at
the time, seemed the sudden appearance of the Vikings. Their
sacking of Lindisfarne in 793 had sent shockwaves across Europe.
Alcuin of Northumbria, now one of Charlemagne's chief advisers,
wrote anguished letters back home to both the king of Northumbria
and to the community at Lindisfarne: 'what assurance is there for
the churches of Britain, if St Cuthbert, with so great a number of
saints, defends not his own?'[2] It is likely that it was in light of this
catastrophe that Offa now placed military obligations on the people
of Kent that specifically mentioned the possibility of pagan attacks.[3]
Yet, however shocking and terrifying these early coastal raids might
be, they were of minimal significance compared with the warfare
that was to follow.

The particular terror the Vikings inspired can be attributed in
the first instance to their seafaring skills. The unexpected speed
with which such raiders in their newly designed ships could arrive
(and leave) made both preparation and retaliation difficult in the
extreme. Before the raid on Lindisfarne no one had imagined (as
Alcuin's letter testifies) that inroads of the kind the Vikings now
perpetrated could be made from the sea. To be sure, it would not
be long before these same Vikings also sought to build settlements
and it is undoubtedly the case that their raiding had never been
an activity entirely separate from their trading. Nonetheless, the
fashion for minimizing their impact flies in the face not only of
the laments of their contemporaries, for whom they were indeed
a scourge sent by God in punishment of manifold 'crimes and
vices', but also of recent archaeological discoveries. Thus it now
seems likely that their early victims included not only the monks
of Lindisfarne but also the equally prestigious Pictish community
of Portmahomack on the Tarbat peninsula in north-east Scotland,
a rich and hugely important centre of sculpture and vellum
production, burnt beyond recovery in the late eighth century and
only recently rediscovered.[4]

The eventual success of the kingdom of Wessex under King Alfred in finally halting the Vikings is a familiar story that needs only little re-telling. Less well known is how it was that Wessex had managed to surpass Mercia as England's most powerful kingdom many years before the Viking attacks provided it with the opportunity of consolidating (and then extending) this position. Yet, as the (admittedly partisan) *Anglo-Saxon Chronicle* tells the story, certain landmarks seem clear: in 825, Ecgberht, king of Wessex, defeated the Mercians; just four years later, continues the *Chronicle*, 'King Egbert [*sic*] conquered the kingdom of the Mercians, and everything south of the Humber; and he was the eighth king who was "Bretwalda."'[5] The seventh king in this famous list had been the Northumbrian King Oswiu, following the accolade provided by Bede. How far the skipping over of any eighth-century Mercian – whether it be Aethelbald or Offa – was intended as a deliberate slight can be no more than a guess, but there can be little doubt that Ecgberht himself had deep-seated reasons to distrust Mercian power. As a young boy he had sought the safety of exile at the court of Charlemagne in 789, the very year when the king of the West Saxons Beorhtric had married a daughter of Offa's, whose offspring (Offa will have hoped) would then rule in Wessex. On the death of Beorhtric, in 802, Ecgberht had been able to return to England where, very possibly with Carolingian help, he had successfully claimed the kingship.[6]

Ecgberht's mastery of Mercia after his victory of 825 was short-lived, but there is no reason to think this had any long-lasting implications for his standing and authority. Without guaranteed access to ports, Mercian power had always been precarious; of far greater importance for Ecgberht's position within Southumbria was therefore his relationship with Kent. For the first decades of the ninth century, Mercia had been able to continue to exercise control here (while intermittently squabbling with its archbishops), but in 825, in the aftermath of Ecgberht's victory, the men of Kent both accepted his authority and took Aethelwulf, son of Ecgberht, as their sub-king; with him at their helm, a new relationship was forged between Church and ruler. In 838, at Kingston-on-Thames, a long-standing land dispute between king and archbishop was settled and a new pact spelt out: Ecgberht and Aethelwulf and their heirs were henceforth promised 'firm and unbroken friendship from ... Archbishop, Ceolnoth ... and from all his successors'.[7]

Fig. 21: Silver ring, c.775–850

This was an agreement that held; it is notable that throughout the tenth century royal West Saxon consecrations regularly took place at Kingston (where Aethelwulf himself may have been consecrated as part of the proceedings of 838). Kingston, as the last place upstream where the River Thames is tidal, had about it a numinous aura.

Ruling Kent brought with it the responsibility of fighting off Vikings from the Channel coast as well as from Wessex. A Viking band attacked Sheppey, on the north coast of Kent, for the first time in 835. The following year, Ecgberht had to contend with an attack in what is now Somerset. Two years later, Vikings struck yet further west. In the 840s, when Ecgberht had been succeeded by his son Aethelwulf, attacks are recorded on London, Rochester, Romney Marsh and Southampton. In 851, Vikings returned to England, making five separate raids; thereafter, they wintered in Sheppey. These were no longer random raids.

It is against this background that in 856 King Aethelwulf set off for Rome.[8] The ground seems to have been laid already by an entourage sent in 853 that had included Aethelwulf's youngest son Alfred (whom the pope may well have blessed in some form without, as was later claimed, actually anointing him. That Alfred

Fig. 22: The Fuller Brooch, British Museum

then went to Rome again, in his father's company, is also possible). Before leaving England, Aethelwulf had settled the inheritance of his kingdom should he not return: Wessex was to be divided between his two elder sons. The sons may well have expected their father to stay in Rome; after all, Aethelwulf would not have been the first king of Wessex to abdicate and end his days there. But Aethelwulf had other plans. On his way home, to the consternation of his two sons, the king took as a new wife none other than the 12-year-old Carolingian princess Judith. The match was perhaps prompted by a need to co-operate with his father-in-law, Emperor Charles the Bald, against the mounting Viking threat; even without this, the opportunity of adding Carolingian blood to his dynasty may have seemed irresistible to Aethelwulf, despite the family tensions it would necessarily create.

In the event, by chance rather than design, the match between Aethelwulf and Judith led eventually to the succession of Alfred. Aethelwulf died only two years after the marriage. Judith, as yet childless, was immediately taken by the eldest prince, Aethelbald, to be his wife. Five years later, Aethelbald himself died, and still there were no heirs. During the next 11 years two more of Alfred's brothers also died. And thus, in 871, it was the turn of Alfred to become king.

With the accession of Alfred, we are presented with a Dark Age king for whom the evidence suddenly seems plentiful. But plentiful, in this case, also means controversial and in need of particularly careful scrutiny. A number of the achievements long attributed to Alfred turn out on closer inspection to be either exaggerated or fabricated. The much loved story of how the king in hiding from the Vikings was so pre-occupied by his plight that he burnt the cakes he had been set to watch is derived only from a tenth-century legend. The notion that Alfred founded the English navy will not bear scrutiny. Many of the so-called Alfredian burhs must be attributed instead to his son Edward. The number of books the king is thought to have translated from Latin to English is now questioned.[9] His *Life*, written by his priest Asser, though generally accepted as genuine, is nonetheless regarded as a work tending towards the hagiographical.[10] Yet, however many qualifications are made, the conclusion remains: Alfred was indeed remarkable.

When Alfred became king in 871, it was far from clear that the West Saxons would be able to stem the Viking advance. The year 865 had seen the arrival of 'the great army' when (according to the *Anglo-Saxon Chronicle*) Vikings 'ravaged all eastern Kent', despite having been promised money if only they would leave.[11] The winter of 866 they then spent in East Anglia, where they were given horses. In 867, they reached York where 'an immense slaughter was made of the Northumbrians'. In 868, Alfred, together with his brother Aethelred, the then king of Wessex, joined forces with the Mercians against a Viking force which had reached Nottingham but the encounter was inconclusive. The year 869 saw Vikings back in York. In 870, a Viking army killed King Edmund of East Anglia and took possession of the kingdom. The *Chronicle*'s entries noting these events verge on the laconic, but in 871 the pace changes: a party of Vikings who now have named leaders reach Wessex. Aethelred and Alfred fight them at Reading where they lose. Four days later, they fight them again at Ashdown; the Vikings are put to flight, but not before night-time and in any case, at a battle just a fortnight later, it is the Vikings who win. It is, as the *Chronicle* tells it, a tempestuous year. Aethelred and

Alfred lose 'many important men'. Aethelred himself dies. Alfred becomes king and continues the fight, but he loses his first battle and at the end of the year there is no alternative but to make peace.

For the next seven years, the Viking advance must have seemed inexorable and its menace ever greater. No longer content with tribute and treasure, the Vikings now aimed to control kingdoms. In Mercia, they drove King Burgred overseas and set up a puppet king, Ceolwulf, who promised that the kingdom would be 'ready for them on whatever day they wished to have it'. In the North of England, the Viking leader Healfdene 'shared out the land of the Northumbrians and they proceeded to plough and to support themselves'. Then, in 878, a Viking army advanced into Wessex, 'and settled there ... and the people submitted to them, except Alfred'.

The Anglo-Saxon chronicler describing the winter and spring of 878 (and likewise Asser, who relies heavily for his account on the *Chronicle*) depicts a scene of such courage and heroism that the cautious historian will feel tempted to mistrust it, all the more since the *Chronicle* seems to have been put together only in the 890s, at a time when the Vikings were again threatening Wessex and encouragement was badly needed. Yet what is striking about the passage in question is not so much its general tenor but rather its precision, the degree of local knowledge it shows and the caution Alfred took before engaging the Vikings in what turned out to be the decisive Battle of Edington of 878.[12] The story is not so much the tale of a miraculous victory but rather of a slow, careful and uncertain campaign. Thus it was in January, after Twelfth Night of that year, that a Viking force advancing from Exeter had captured the royal vill at Chippenham. Alfred, forced to take flight, 'journeyed in difficulties through the woods and fen-fastnesses with a small force'.[13] By Easter, the king was ensconced at a fort in Athelney. From there he was able to rally some of the men of Somerset and to begin to harry his enemy, but it was only seven weeks later (thus around Pentecost) that he felt ready to take decisive action. He rallied not only followers from Somerset, but now also from Wiltshire and from Hampshire – and they received him, so Asser tells us, 'with immense joy ... as if one restored to life'.[14] Together, this newly constituted army advanced across Alfred's estates before finally engaging with the Vikings at Edington in Wiltshire. Despite the victory on the battlefield, it took a fortnight before the Vikings submitted and only then (according to Asser) because, after they had fled from Edington, Alfred had been able to pursue them and to besiege them in their stronghold, where 'hunger, cold and fear' finally wore them down.

For Alfred, no lasting peace could be made with the Vikings before, or unless, they converted to Christianity. His was not a war of 'Englishmen' against 'foreigners' so much as it was a war of Christians against heathens. The dating of religious festivals the *Chronicle* gave is deeply significant. Quite apart from any missionary zeal Alfred may have felt towards converting the Vikings, there was also the simple fact that for any lasting peace to be made, a shared religious language was essential. Only two years before Edington, Alfred had already tried to make peace with the Vikings and had made a treaty with them, whereby they had promised to leave his kingdom. For the first time on record, both Asser and the *Chronicle* tell us, they had sworn on Christian relics to keep their word – but 'practising their usual treachery', they had nonetheless broken their word, killed their hostages and made off.[15] Now, after Edington, came the opportunity for a new dispensation. Once more, the Vikings promised to leave Alfred's kingdom, but this time the peace would be sworn between Christians: Guthrum, the Viking leader, promised to accept baptism, taking Alfred as his godfather. The ceremony took place with all due solemnity at Aller, an island close to where Alfred had earlier prepared for his assault on the Vikings. 'And [Guthrum] was twelve days with the king, and he honoured him and his companions greatly with gifts.'[16]

Political expediency may appear to lie behind Guthrum's conversion and adoption of his new identity; maybe it did, maybe not. But of the depth of Alfred's own faith and of his sense of purpose there can be no doubt. For him, the fight against the Vikings was indeed a battle for the Christian faith. From an early age Alfred may well have imagined that he had been chosen by God for some special mission: the reasons behind his visits to Rome as a young child remain something of a mystery, but they are likely to have made a strong enough impression on Alfred to suggest to him that already as a 4-year-old, and the Benjamin of the family, he had been singled out for greatness.[17] Similarly, his bookish precocity, illustrated by Asser's famous story of how he beat his elder brothers in memorizing a book of poetry, can be seen as marking him out

Fig. 23: The Alfred Jewel

not only as a scholar in the making but also as a child of destiny, foreordained to protect the Christian faith.[18]

Scholarship for Alfred was never a pursuit to be undertaken for its own sake; scholarship rather led to the acquisition of wisdom and thus to the knowledge and love of God. In an ideal world, everyone seeking wisdom would be able to read the necessary Latin texts in the original. But this was not an ideal world: on top of the shortage of teachers was the fact that too many libraries had been 'ransacked and burnt'.[19] But, for Alfred, a solution was at hand: reading works in translation had always been a respectable alternative and infinitely preferable to remaining in a state of ignorance. Alfred therefore would 'turn into the language that we can all understand certain books which are the most necessary for all men to know'.[20]

How much the king himself wrote of the so-called 'Alfredian texts' which followed on from this decision remains a subject of constant debate. Most scholars would now attribute to him at least the Old English rendering of Gregory the Great's *Pastoral Care*, a much freer translation of both Boethius' *Consolation of Philosophy* and of Augustine's *Soliloquies*, as well as the first 50 psalms of the Psalter. But the other works that were likely translated under his patronage, such as the Old English Bede, or assembled (as was the *Anglo-Saxon Chronicle*), are also crucially important for understanding the cultural revolution that Alfred was determined to spearhead.[21]

Alfred's mission, as set out in the preface to his translation of the *Pastoral Care*, is unequivocal. The pursuit of learning is not esoteric; it will bring benefits, here and now. Thus success in warfare and prosperity is intimately linked with the acquisition of wisdom:

> Remember what punishments befell us in this world when we ourselves did not cherish learning nor transmit it to other men. We were Christians in name alone … Therefore we have now lost the wealth as well as the wisdom [of our ancestors], because we did not wish to set our minds to the[ir] track.[22]

In remedy, Alfred is sending to every bishop in his kingdom a copy of Pope Gregory's *Pastoral Care*, together with a book-marker (*aestel*) of quite some value (the equivalent of the price of 50 oxen). Book and book-marker are not in general to be removed – times are still uncertain: 'it is not known how long there will be such learned bishops as, thanks be to God, there are now nearly everywhere'.[23] But it was not only bishops who were expected to be learned. So, too, if they wanted to keep their jobs, were lay officials. This was all very well, Asser opines, for the younger generation who had grown up expecting an education, but for their elders it could be very taxing. Nonetheless, even those who found it especially difficult to learn to read had to attempt to make progress by getting their sons or relatives, or even their slaves, to read out books in English 'day and night' so that they might make at least some progress in literacy.[24]

Alfred's pursuit of wisdom coupled with the illnesses from which Asser tells us he suffered from youth have sometimes been seen as difficult to reconcile with the image of the young warrior (also given to us by Asser) rushing at his Viking enemies like a wild boar, or with the military strategist who after his victory at Edington set about implementing a hugely ambitious plan whereby Wessex would in future be defended by what amounted to a standing army and a network of heavily fortified towns or 'burhs'. The contradiction is more apparent than real. 'Wisdom', for Alfred, had wide-ranging implications, practical as well as ideological. In his translation of Boethius' *Consolation of Philosophy*, the king, personified as 'Mind', explains in his dialogue with 'Wisdom' precisely how, in order to rule virtuously a king needed resources: he needed praying men, fighting men and working men. Each of these three groups required material support, whether it be land, weapons or food and ale. But each must be guided by wisdom: 'no man may bring to bear any skill without wisdom'.[25] But for Alfred this was a wisdom tempered always by humility; his physical afflictions endowed him with something of the quality of the saviour Christ and thus, by analogy, the body of the king could represent the body of his suffering land.

For there can be no doubt that the land of Wessex did suffer: despite Alfred's victory at Edington and despite his new relationship with Guthrum, sealed in time by the treaty which granted him East Anglia, there were further Viking forces to combat. The protection of Kent and of London from Viking power was vital for the king's prosperity and security. Quite when and how the now diminished kingdom of Mercia itself submitted to Alfred is far from clear, but possession of the once Mercian city of London sealed the achievement. 'That same year' [886], reports the *Anglo-Saxon Chronicle*, 'King Alfred occupied London, and all the English people that were under subjection to the Danes submitted to him. And he then entrusted the borough to the control of Ealdorman Aethelred.' What the *Chronicle* does not make clear is that Aethelred, having succeeded Ceolwulf as ruler of Mercia, had been forced into a position of dependence on Alfred after his defeat, in *c*.881, at the Battle of Conwy, a battle fought to avenge the Mercian slaying of a former ruler of Gwynedd. Aethelred, finding it impossible to recover from this humiliation, submitted to Alfred. The terms were generous. Alfred not only gave London to him, he also married him thereafter to his daughter, Aethelflaed. In return, Alfred both expected and received Aethelred's steadfast loyalty and the recognition of a kingship that extended now over all of southern England.[26]

Once he had London in his hands, Alfred proceeded to rebuild it, restoring it splendidly and thus, according to Asser, 'making it habitable again'.[27] Pre-Viking London had been centred on present-day Aldwych, but after the Viking attack of 842 most of this old city had been abandoned. Across his kingdom Alfred had set to work to create fortified towns (or burhs) protected by manned walls in response to the threat posed by the Vikings. London was no exception. Here, as in a number of other cities, this necessitated the rebuilding of Roman walls, as well as the laying out of streets on a grid pattern. The Burghal Hidage, a document usually dated to the ninth century, gives detailed information as to how 33 such towns were to be garrisoned. The figures provide an extraordinary testimony to the perceived threat the Vikings posed, of the resources needed to counter this level of danger and of the determination of the kings of Wessex to muster these. Within Wessex itself, nowhere was to be further than 20 miles away from a burh; everyone could therefore expect, if necessary, to be able to take refuge behind walls – but the cost of this provision was high: 27,000 men were needed to maintain the network. In addition, Alfred expected his nobility to serve in what amounted to a standing army; at any one point in the year, or so Asser tells us, half of those whom the king could conscript would be on active service with the other half at home taking care of their estates.[28] The effectiveness of the system was put to the test when a new army of Vikings returned to Wessex in the early 890s and was rebuffed. 'By the grace of God', reported the *Anglo-Saxon Chronicle* under the year 896, looking back over the past three years, 'the [Viking] army had not on the whole afflicted the English people very greatly.'[29] Nonetheless, the burden imposed by Alfred's military reforms should not be underestimated. Not everyone in Wessex shared the king's sense of urgency; maintaining morale was never going to be easy while there were, on the one hand, Jeremiahs who intimated that Christianity was doomed, and, on the other hand, men who left building projects unfinished or who hurried home regardless of circumstances when their days of duty were up.[30] Alfred, on the other hand, Asser assures, was indefatigable:

> even though all his sailors were exhausted, once [the king] had taken over the helm of his kingdom ... he did not allow it to waver or wander from course ... for by gently instructing, cajoling, urging, commanding and (in the end when his patience was exhausted) by sharply chastising those who were disobedient, and by despising popular stupidity and stubbornness in every way, he carefully and cleverly exploited and converted his bishops and ealdormen and nobles, and his thegns most dear to him, and his reeves as well ... to his own will and to the general advantage of the whole realm.[31]

Asser's own work seems to have been written in the early 890s, in an attempt to endear the Welsh to Alfred, their new lord. Difficult though it is to establish an exact chronology, it now seems likely that it was the fall-out from the Battle of Conwy which enabled Alfred to emerge as the only credible protector of South Wales, but that it was only some ten years later that he was further able to extend his power in North Wales, receiving then the submission of Anarawd of Gwynedd, a ruler who had become disillusioned with his previous alliance with the Vikings of Northumbria and who seems to have now become anxious about possible Viking attacks from across the Irish Sea. Be that as it may, there is no evidence that Asser's work was ever very widely read. There is a sharp contrast to be made here with the *Anglo-Saxon Chronicle*, a work compiled at about the same time as Asser's *Life* and widely used by him, equally driven by a strong political purpose and which would over time come to be seen as a foundational text of English national identity.[32]

Asser, as well as those who worked on the *Chronicle* and on the other so-called 'Alfredian' texts, was part of the glittering circle Alfred gathered together at his court in his determination to make it a centre of 'wisdom'. Central to it, Asser tells us, were four Mercian and two Frankish scholars. A letter from Fulco, archbishop of Rheims, giving Alfred permission to 'poach' the priest Grimbald, likens Grimbald to a 'watch-dog' who will know how to 'keep far from hence the savage wolves of the impure spirits which threaten and devour ... souls'. (Alfred, it transpires, had sent the archbishop actual dogs in exchange, to help in the hunting of those 'visible wolves' of Rheims which God had sent in punishment for sin.)[33] The metaphors implicit here need to be taken seriously for there can be little doubt that Alfred saw the Vikings as dangerous as any wolves. Modern distaste for holy wars should not be allowed to disguise the fact that Asser never describes the Vikings as anything other than *pagani* and never does he suggest that Alfred is fighting for 'England'. The king's struggle with the Vikings was a war of Christians against heathens, as a ninth-century sword from Abingdon, whose hilt is decorated with evangelist' symbols, so graphically illustrates.[34] As such, it had the character of many an Old Testament struggle; Alfred correspondingly could be portrayed sometimes as David, sometimes as Solomon, who in return for his righteous living and constant vigilance could indeed expect to be rewarded with wealth and wisdom and with the power and peace to dispense both.

In 891/2, the *Anglo-Saxon Chronicle* noted the portent after Easter of a star 'which is called in Latin *cometa*. Some men say that it is in English the long-haired star, for there shines a long ray from it, sometimes on one side, sometimes on every side.'[35] Just the next year saw the return of Vikings who had been forced to cross over from Boulogne in consequence of the famine caused by a disastrous harvest. Despite the verdict of the chronicler for 896 'that the army had not on the whole afflicted the English people very greatly', these were not easy years, nor, even on the dispersal of the Viking army in the summer of 896, was there peace.[36] The Vikings now took to raiding along the South Coast, thus putting to the test Alfred's new ships which proved to be far from perfect. 'That same summer', continued the *Chronicle*, 'no fewer than 20 ships, men and all, perished along the south coast.'[37] To say that Alfred's final years ended in despair would be to overstate the case but there seems to have been little to celebrate. The *Chronicle* has no entry for 897 beyond the record of two deaths and nothing for 898/9. Then, in 900, comes the notice of Alfred's death, followed immediately by an account of the rebellion of Alfred's nephew, Aethelwold, against the new king, Edward, and of Aethelwold's flight to Viking Northumbria, where he is said to have gained support for his bid to be accepted as Alfred's heir. Aethelwold's rebellion, short-lived though it was, illustrates how misleading it can be to allow simple distinctions of Christian/pagan or Viking/Anglo-Saxon to dominate the history of ninth-century England.[38]

Aethelwold was the son of one of Alfred's elder brothers. He was himself considerably older than Edward (perhaps by as much as ten years) and had every reason to consider himself throne-worthy. The convention whereby the crown could be expected as a matter of course to pass to his eldest son of the previous king was not yet established. There is, then, nothing surprising about Aethelwold's bid for power. More surprising, perhaps, is the support he was able to muster. Having, with some panache, staked his claim – he had occupied the royal residence at Wimborne, where his father had been buried, and had helped himself to a nun, presumably of royal blood to further bolster his claim – he was then forced to flee to Northumbria (and to relinquish the nun) and here, seemingly, he found allies with whom to plan his campaign. In 902, he went by sea to Essex, together with a fleet 'which was subject to him'; the next year he is said to have 'induced the army in East Anglia to break the peace so that they harried all over Mercia'.[39] Such a challenge finally provoked Edward to counter-attack; in the Battle of the Holne that followed 'a great slaughter was made on both sides'. Aethelwold himself was killed, but it was hardly a glorious battle for Edward. It is not even clear (from the *Chronicle*'s report) that Edward was in full control of his own army – the men of Kent are reported as 'lingering behind … against the king's command' as the king was attempting to muster his forces (in consequence, they bore the brunt of the attack).[40] One of the casualties was the ealdorman Sigehlm. Some 15 years later, Edward took as his third wife Sigehlm's daugher, Eadgifu.

With Aethelwold safely dead, Edward could proceed to proclaim his inheritance, and to bolster it with symbolic statements of his power as well as with military might. Thus, New Minster at Winchester, dedicated in 901, became the burial place both of his mother and of Alfred, moved by Edward from the Old Minster to this new foundation. In Mercia, meanwhile, Edward's sister, Aethelflaed ('the Lady of the Mercians'), together with her husband, ealdorman Aethelred, were building themselves a new cult centre in Gloucester (to where, following the Battle of Tettenhall, they moved the bones of the Northumbrian king St Oswald). But the following year Aethelred was dead and despite the continued loyalty of Aethelflaed to her brother any prospect of an independent Mercia would prove illusory. The ultimate victor at Tettenhall would prove to be Edward.

The Battle of Tettenhall took place while a Danish army, who had 'ravaged with great ravagings' across Mercia, were making their way home. According to the chronicler Aethelweard, the Danes had broken a truce made with Edward and Aethelred, but now as they struggled to cross the river Severn together with their booty, suddenly 'squadrons of both Mercians and West Saxons' moved against them. In the ensuing battle the Vikings suffered severe losses: thus no fewer than three Vikings kings together with many of their chief men 'hastened to the hall of the infernal one'.[41]

For Edward, the Battle of Tettenhall of 910 proved a turning point. Whereas King Alfred's efforts had been dedicated to the protection of the heartlands of his house and to the recovery of Kent, what was at stake after 910 was the capture from the Scandinavians of lands beyond Wessex, notably the kingdoms of Northumbria, East Anglia and Viking Mercia. In the absence of written records by any Viking (theirs was still a runic literature) it remains difficult to reconstruct the history of their settlements, which were in any case subject to fluctuation, but in the years that followed Tettenhall, Edward, together with the help of his sister, implemented a policy both of consolidation but also now of conquest: in 912 Edward was in Essex building burhs at Witham and at Hertford and 'a good number of the people', reported the *Chronicle*, 'who had been under the rule of the Danes submitted to him'; in 913, Aethelflaed built burhs at Tamworth and at Stafford. In 914, Edward accepted the submission of 'the principal men who belonged to Bedford, and also many of those who belonged to Northampton'. In 916, it was the turn of Maldon. The following year saw both Derby and Colchester fall to Edward and his sister. The fighting that year, as described in the *Chronicle*, seems to have been particularly intense, bitter and bloody but, for Edward and his army, it was also effective: by the autumn, 'many people who had been under the rule of the Danes, both in East Anglia and in Essex submitted to him ...'.[42] But in 918 Edward was faced with an entirely new political scenario.

The expulsion in 902 of Norse settlers from Dublin had created an explosive situation. Their leader Ragnall had responded by moving across the water, setting up camp on the Isle of Man whence he attacked western Northumbria. Ironically, Edward's victory at Tettenhall had left York prey to the militantly pagan Ragnall (or Ragnald). Before the arrival of Ragnall, Vikings and Northumbrians had seemingly been able to reach various forms of accommodation. Ragnall now upset all such compromises. The Northumbrian ruler (Eadwulf) accordingly fled to Scotland to seek help from King Constantine. To no avail – Ragnall defeated their army at the Battle of Corbridge in 918. The year 918 also saw the death of the Lady of the Mercians, Aethelflaed. Edward now moved swiftly to establish direct control himself.[43]

The Battle of Corbridge created a new sense of emergency. At Tamworth, also in 918, Edward received the submission not only of Aethelflaed's Mercia but also of the kings of Wales. Edward next moved to Nottingham, which he captured and fortified; thence to Thelwall, Manchester and Nottingham and, by 920, to Bakewell. At Bakewell, according to the *Anglo-Saxon Chronicle*, Edward achieved something of a triumph, receiving the submission not only of the king of the Scots but also of Ragnall 'and of all who live in Northumbria, both English and Danish, Norsemen and others, and also of the king of the Strathclyde Welsh and all of the Strathclyde Welsh ...'.[44] The entry provides a grand finale to Edward's reign – and but for the mention of the building of one more burh, it is the last we are to hear of the king before the record of his death in 924. But the question must be: does it stand up to scrutiny? Is such a scenario at all plausible? The recent suggestion that some sort of truce was brokered makes more sense than to imagine that Ragnall would have so willingly and easily accepted Edward's lordship. The triumph over the North of a southern king was yet to come.[45]

Edward's death in 924 brought in its tide a reminder of the continued fragility of the unity of any kingdom of the 'Anglo-Saxons'. Wessex had expected Edward's son, Aelfweard, to be their king, but the Mercians choose Athelstan. Athelstan was Edward's son by his first wife and seemingly had been brought up not at the

Wessex court but rather in Mercia in the care of Aethelflaed.[46] It is quite possible that the Mercians were still smarting at the removal from their midst of Aethelflaed's daughter, Aelfwynn, who, on her mother's death, had been abruptly spirited away and, in the words of the *Mercian Register*, 'deprived of all authority'.[47] In the event, conflict between the brothers was avoided by the sudden death, in 924, of Aelfweard. A year later Athelstan was crowned on the boundary between Wessex and Mercia, at Kingston, explicitly as the ruler of two peoples. An actual crown, rather than the customary helmet, was used for the ceremony.[48]

Relying, as it were, on crown rather than on helmet, Athelstan took the bold step in 925 of opening negotiations with Sihtric, brother and successor in Northumbria of Ragnall. Sihtric was a formidable warrior, renowned for his savage reconquest of Dublin in 917. Nonetheless, it seems from his coinage that as ruler of Northumbria he was ready to find some form of accommodation with Christians. Such a supposition is confirmed by Sihtric's willingness to come to Tamworth, in the heart of the Mercian kingdom, to meet Athelstan and even to seal their friendship by taking one of Athelstan's sisters as his bride. Given that at about the same time one of Athelstan's half-sisters was being sought at by Hugh, duke of the Franks (and that another would later marry Otto I of Germany), the marriage would indeed have provided Sihtric with an entrée into the courts of Europe – Paris, for the first but not the last time, may well have seemed worth a mass. But it is impossible to do more than guess what Sihtric's ambitions may have been, for in 927 he died and with him, or so it must have seemed, the hope of any peaceful union between Northumbria and Athelstan.

On Sihtric's death, his kinsman Guthfrith immediately left Dublin to claim York. Athelstan, somehow, was able to outwit him, though whether by battle or by diplomacy is far from clear. The *Anglo-Saxon Chronicle* does not even mention Guthfrith.[49] It simply (and grandly) claims that Athelstan both:

> succeeded to the kingdom of the Northumbrians; and ... brought under his rule all the kings who were in this island: first Hywel, king of the West Welsh, and Constantine, king of the Scots, and Owain, king of the people of Gwent, and Ealdred, son of Eadwulf from Bamburgh. And

they established peace with pledge and oaths in the place which is called Eamont, on 12 July, and renounced all idolatry [in other words any alliance with Guthfrith] and afterwards departed in peace.[50]

Although it is likely that the chronicler is claiming too much for Athelstan's power over Northumbria and that its actual ruler was indeed Ealdred of Bamburgh, 927 can, nonetheless, be taken as a date fit to rank alongside 878, when Alfred had defeated Guthrum, or 886, when he had taken London. In 927, as in 878, this was a peace made between Christians; in 927 as in 886 new political identities were being forged, however precariously. Henceforth, in his charters, Athelstan would be named not 'king of the Anglo-Saxons' but rather 'king of the English', even 'king of all Britain'.[51]

If the sources for 927 are tantalizingly scarce, the same cannot be said of the great battle won by Athelstan at Brunanburh ten years later, but, by way of prelude to Brunanburh, mention should first be made of the visit in 934 of Athelstan to the body of St Cuthbert. St Cuthbert, having survived the attack on Lindisfarne in 793, had finally been found a new home in the late ninth century at Chester-le-Street and it was to here that Athelstan made his pilgrimage bringing with him lavish gifts that included a picture of himself in a pose of deep reverence, holding an open book before St Cuthbert. This is the first known picture of an early medieval ruler and its meaning is as controversial as is the occasion: what was it that had prompted Athelstan's visit? Might it have been a response to the power vacuum caused both by the death in 934 of Guthfrith of Dublin and of his rival, Ealdred, the de facto king of Northumbria? Was Athelstan seeking the blessing of Cuthbert on the expedition north which he would make after his visit to the shrine? For on leaving Chester-le-Street, Athelstan, according to the *Anglo-Saxon Chronicle*, proceeded north and 'ravaged Scotland'.[52] And then, when he went home, he took back with him King Constantine, named as a 'subregulus'. The following year, 935, Constantine was still (or was it again?) to be found in the king's company, this time in attendance at a great court held in Cirencester, along with the Welsh kings Hywel Dda, Idwal and Morgan. But two years later, in 937, came the backlash. Olaf, son of Guthfrith, mounted a renewed Viking attack from Dublin, joining forces both with the Strathclyde Welsh and with the Scots. Constantine, in other words, had had enough of being Athelstan's lackey. Although it is not clear exactly when Constantine switched sides, his marriage – even if the date is uncertain – to a daughter of Olaf's is a strong indication of the grievances he nursed at his status within Athelstan's 'empire'. For Constantine and his allies, the time had come to curb the seemingly limitless ambitions of the kings of Wessex.

Olaf and his combined forces met Athelstan at Brunanburh. The site of the battle has never been identified with any certainty, though it probably took place at Bromborough on the Wirral. Athelstan's victory became the subject of one of the most stirring of the poems contained in the *Anglo-Saxon Chronicle*. Here, Constantine is presented as 'a hoary-haired warrior', a survivor doomed to suffer the death of his son and kinsman. 'Never yet in this island before this', the poet assures us, '... was a greater slaughter of a host made by the edge of the sword, since the Angles and Saxons came hither from the east.'[53] Yet for all the triumphalism of the poem, the rejoicing was premature. Within two years Athelstan was dead and his empire in tatters. Olaf Guthrithson lost no time in claiming the kingship of Northumbria; within months he had captured Tamworth and retaken those towns soon to be known as the Five Boroughs of the Danelaw. Yet Olaf's triumph, too, was to be short-lived; by 941, he also had died; by 942, King Edmund, Athelstan's half-brother and successor (and himself a Brunanburh veteran), had recovered the lost territories; he, too, merited another, albeit briefer, poem in the *Chronicle*. In 946, he was dead as well, killed, or so it was recorded, in a brawl at Pucklechurch, near Bath. His brother, Eadred, succeeded him.

King Athelstan, unusually for a medieval king, had never married, perhaps because he had so rich a supply of half-brothers eager to succeed him (one of whom he is suspected of murdering) and ready to continue what must often have seemed the thankless task of conquering and holding the kingdom of York. The ability of the Vikings to find allies among those who resented the power of the kings of Wessex and who were therefore ready to acquiesce in Viking rule helps explain the rapid oscillations of power. A glance at the career of Wulfstan, archbishop of York, is instructive here. Seemingly appointed to the post by Athelstan in 931, Wulfstan nonetheless disappears from view between 936 and 941. He re-emerges in 939, not in the company of King Edmund, but rather as a supporter of

Olaf Guthfrithson; yet, in 942 and 944, he is once more to be found at the English court and he was present at the coronation of King Eadred in 946. But then, in 947, when Eric Bloodaxe (from Norway) had become king of York, Wulfstan no longer appears at Eadred's court, even though he returns between 948 and 950, at the point when the Northumbrians themselves have, at least temporarily, gone over to Eadred. It is no wonder then, that in 952, when the Northumbrians had again returned to their allegiance to Eric Bloodaxe, it seems that Eadred decided the time had come to place Wulfstan under some sort of house arrest and, furthermore, to make sure that, even when set free, he never again returned to the North.

The kingdom of York finally fell to the English in 954 with the expulsion of Eric by the citizens of York. But it would not be long before the advent of the 'second Viking age' and the conquest of the whole country by the Danish Swein Forkbeard in 1013. But the England of 1013 was of course very different from the England of Alfred, or even of his grandchildren.

6

GODES RICE: GOD'S KINGDOM

And I say in truth that the time was blessed and delightful in England when King Edgar advanced Christianity and established many monasteries; and his kingdom was flourishing in peace, so that one never heard of any Viking army, except for those of the people themselves who live permanently in this land; and all the kings of the Welsh and the Scots who were in this island came to Edgar – once, on one and the same day, eight kings together – and they all submitted to Edgar's rule.

(Aelfric, *Life of St Swithun*)[1]

Aelfric, abbot of Eynsham in the early eleventh century, combined his sense of the Christian duties a king should exercise with a strong streak of realism. He understood how much England had suffered in consequence of its particular vulnerability as an island and how from the moment of the attack on Lindisfarne in 793 the 'natives' of the British Isles had had to fear unpredictable sea-borne raids led by fleets of 'foreigners', many of whom had subsequently settled. Although Athelstan's victory at Brunanburh in 937 had marked a turning point in the advance northwards of the authority of Wessex, its kings, Aelfric knew, could never be complacent. Vigilance had always to be their watchword. Nonetheless, as Aelfric saw it, under King Edgar there had indeed been a golden age.

Between 954, when the Viking kingdom of York had fallen, and the renewal of Viking attacks stand barely three decades. For 17 of these years, Edgar was king. A glance at the *Anglo-Saxon Chronicle*

Fig. 24: Saint Aethelthryth of Ely from the Benedictional of St Aethelwold

Fig. 25: King Edgar seated between St Aethelwold and St Dunstan, from the
Regularis Concordia

makes it look as if these were years when nothing much happened. The verdict of Frank Stenton in his magisterial work on the Anglo-Saxons still has resonance: 'it is a sign of Edgar's competence as a ruler that his reign is singularly devoid of recorded incident'.[2] Nonetheless the Anglo-Saxon chronicler recorded that 'in [Edgar's] day things improved greatly'.[3] It might be appropriate then to consider, as far as we can, how 'things' stood when Edgar became king, taking stock first of the nature of the new kingdom which Athelstan had created, and to which after a rapid succession of kings – Edmund (939–46); Eadred (946–55) and Eadwig (955–59) – it had fallen to Edgar to strengthen and embellish.[4]

Kings had long exercised control over their lands, and displayed their power, by holding assemblies at favoured locations throughout the year. Anxiety lest such meetings should be interpreted as proto-parliaments led historians over many decades to eschew the use of the word 'witan' for such assemblies. Recent historiography, however, has reintroduced the term since it is clear that it was generally accepted that certain kinds of business could indeed only be transacted with the consent of a substantial number of the king's wise men, in other words, in the company of his 'witan'.[5] A 'normal' gathering of the court was not considered to be a sufficiently august arena in which either to make new laws or grant land; for such weighty matters a more representative assembly of 'the wise' was needed. In addition, there were occasions when even if there was no pressing business in need of attention, a grandiose display of authority nonetheless seemed appropriate.

Athelstan has a well-established reputation as a king for whom his witan was of particular importance. This need cause no surprise: the unprecedented size of Athelstan's kingdom meant that new ways had to be found whereby the king could keep in regular touch with ealdormen from the more distant parts of his realm. It has, however, also to be recognized that some of the particular characteristics of Athelstan's assemblies are due to one scribe (known to historians as 'Athelstan A') who during his period of office (928–34/5) seems to have taken a special delight in the drawing up of a lengthy witness lists.[6] But even the very employment of this scribe points to Athelstan's own sense of his dignity. Thus Athelstan was the first English king to appear crowned on his coins – and very probably the practice of crown-wearing, when the king would ceremonially

Fig. 26: Saint Swithun of Winchester from the Benedictional of St Aethelwold

don his crown, dates from his reign.[7] Athelstan regularly held
assemblies at Christmas, Easter and sometimes, too, at Whitsun,
and it seems highly likely that such occasions seemed appropriate
both for crown-wearings and feastings and for the conduct of royal
business.

Athelstan's assemblies were large-scale events, sometimes
attended by around a hundred of his nobles, many of whom would
have travelled quite some distance to be with the king – Athelstan
did not on the whole go to meet 'his people'; they were expected
to come to him. And come they did: an archbishop or two could
always be expected together with a goodly number of bishops and
abbots, ealdormen and local nobility. Welsh princes might be in
attendance; striking, too, is the number of Scandinavian names. Such
assemblies were doubtless intended to create a sense of confidence
in the new political community that was emerging after the traumas
and conflicts of the previous century, but the strategy had its risk: the
triumphalism of Athelstan's court fuelled grievances which could at
any moment erupt, as Brunanburh amply demonstrated.

The legislation emanating from the meetings of Athelstan's witan
in the years before Brunanburh is, however, in the main remarkable
for the evidence it reveals of Athelstan's concern with law and order.[8]
The sheer number of codes – six at the least, a record for any tenth-
century king – and the evidence the codes reveal about the process
of law-making suggest something of the problems Athelstan had
to face in governing his newly enlarged kingdom – even allowing
for the fact that there is no evidence (until the reign of Edgar) that
the king was attempting to legislate for the Danelaw. A constant
problem was evidently theft. Punishments were harsh. If the value
of the stolen goods was over eight pence, the death sentence was
invariably imposed, though the method varied, depending on the
status and age of the accused: stoning, drowning or hanging were all
possibilities. However brutal such penalties may seem, they were not
thoughtlessly imposed – thus, on consideration, Athelstan raised the
age for the death penalty from 12 years to 15, since he 'and those
with whom he had discussed the matter' had come to the conclusion
that to kill anyone at the younger age was 'too cruel … furthermore
for so little as he had discovered was being done elsewhere'.[9]
Athelstan's legislation was thus part of an ongoing conversation
with 'his bishops, his ealdormen and all his reeves'; the statutes for

a London peace-guild, for example, indicate how local participation worked hand in hand with royal admonitions.[10]

Athelstan's legislation was also a reflection of his belief in his role as Christian king and therefore as the representative of God on earth:

> Now you [the reeves] are to hear, says the king, what I grant to God and what you should perform of pain of disobedience to me ... And you are to guard both yourselves and those whom you should admonish against the anger of God and against disobedience to me.[11]

Offences against God were offences against king Athelstan's legislation and now stretched even beyond death. Thus, his Grately law code of *c.*930 contains the first reference to burial in consecrated ground, or rather to those to whom it will be denied:

> And he who swears a false oath, and it becomes known against him, is never afterwards to be entitled to an oath, nor is he to be buried in consecrated ground when he dies, unless he has the witness of the bishop in whose diocese he is that he has done the penance for it as his confessor prescribed for him.[12]

The newly intense partnership between bishop and king would come to fruition in the tenth-century reform movement. But sacrality has never been an infallible bulwark against the fragility of power. Upon the death of Athelstan in 939, any idea that England was now a united country once again proved to be a fiction. York re-established itself as a separate kingdom, to be fully regained only in 954. And, further South, it is far from clear that the notion of England united under just one king had as yet been accepted. Such a concept had been foreign both to the Carolingians (of France) and would be hard won by the Ottonians (of Germany); provision for each royal son (sometimes sequentially) seemed the natural order of things even if it was not the most politically savvy. In England, Athelstan's childlessness had temporarily eased, but by no means solved, the situation: two (short-lived) half-brothers Edmund and Eadred succeeded him, both of whom were pre-occupied with recovering the kingdom of York, but when Eadred died in 955 (a year after the final capitulation of York) old divisions re-appeared: the circumstances are hard to unravel but it is clear from the *Anglo-Saxon Chronicle*

Fig. 27: Preface to the blessing for Palm Sunday, from the Benedictional
of St Aethelwold

that some form of power sharing was planned between the brothers Eadwig and Edgar: Eadwig's power base was to be in Wessex and Edgar's in Mercia. It was only Eadwig's death in 959 that provided Edgar with the chance to become sole ruler – and thus, as the *Anglo-Saxon Chronicle* put it, 'king over all Britain'.[13]

It has long been assumed that Edgar when he became king inherited a kingdom whose organization had been already rolled out in the reign of Edward the Elder and of his sister, Aethelflaed, the Lady of the Mercians. It was their achievement (it has long been supposed) that once lost lands had been recovered from the Vikings, that the administrative practices already known in Wessex could be (and were) imported into the newly conquered territory. Thus, the 'Five Boroughs' had been quickly divided up into shires over which were placed ealdormen. These shires had courts which (as later legislation indeed makes clear) were expected to meet twice a year; meanwhile every month were held meetings of a hundred courts; hundreds (each made up of a hundred hides, a hide being by tradition enough to support one family) were made responsible for day-to-day peace-keeping within their area. The chief men of the hundred were expected to chase malefactors, to bring them to justice and to impose fines; persistent offenders might well be outlawed.

Of the administrative efficiency of the late Old English state there can be no doubt. Tried and tested, its structures survived not only the Danish conquest by Cnut, but even the Norman Conquest of 1066 and well beyond – only in 1974 were the shires of Anglo-Saxon England subject to any radical revisions.[14] But the origins of its institutions may not, or so it has been argued recently, be quite as ancient as has long been assumed. Fresh arguments suggest that the reign of Edgar, far from being a time when 'nothing happened', may be precisely when those systems long in place in Wessex could finally and systematically be extended across the country.[15] It was the particular circumstances of Edgar's reign which made this possible: no new Viking incursions were troubling England; as for long-settled Danes, these were singled out by Edgar for their loyalty: '... I am to be a true lord to you while my life endures, and am very pleased with you because you are so eager for peace'.[16] It was precisely this unwonted peace which provided the opportunity for the extension across the kingdom of those measures long tried and tested in the heartlands of Wessex.

Such peace demanded careful safeguarding. It was of course something of a commonplace that the Vikings had been God's punishment for the sins his people had committed; in consequence, the prayers of the faithful supported by alms were the first line of defence. But despite this belief in the efficacy of prayer, neither under Alfred, Edward, nor indeed under Athelstan were any strenuous efforts made to make good the damage Vikings had inflicted upon those chief centres of prayer, the minsters. Numerous communities simply disappeared and, although it is impossible to be precise as to the extent, it is, nonetheless, clear that much ecclesiastical property passed into the hands of laymen. In some cases, strategic considerations caused church lands to be swapped, but more often, particularly in Northumbria and in the Midlands, much ecclesiastical land was lost, never to be recovered. But in the reign of Edgar, a number of monks, supported by the king, decided the time had come to call a halt to any further such alienation and to attempt to restore the monastic life to the (perceived) golden days of Bede. No longer was the piety of the king, his example or his exhortations, to be relied on as a sufficient safeguard for the kingdom. The peace of Edgar's reign now presented an opportunity to establish not only administrative reforms but also – as the other side of the same coin – full time practitioners of prayer who would in future work, ceaselessly, to protect the kingdom, to ensure its unity and stability and to safeguard it from attack.

Tenth-century monastic reform, as the consequent movement is frequently called, is in fact something of a misnomer: it was not so much a reform movement as a radical re-interpretation of the shape and purpose of monastic life and of the role of king and queen, both as patrons and as mediators with God. But, like many revolutionary movements, it claimed to be nothing of the sort: the professed intention was a return to the past, seen through the lens of the *Rule of St Benedict*. 'Monasteries' now came to replace the 'minsters' of an earlier era, with a new emphasis being placed on uniformity of customs, and on the superiority of the prayers of the chaste monk over the married clergy who had of late come to occupy a number of sees.

Much of the inspiration for the tenth-century monastic movement came from the Continent, where a comparable zeal for 'reform' was manifest, famously, but by no means exclusively, exercised through the monastery of Cluny, in Burgundy, and at Fleury, in the Loire. Throughout the tenth century, English contacts with the Continent were, of course, extremely close and the numerous marriage links, which were never narrowly 'political', brought in their wake cultural connections with endless ramifications.[17] Louis IV of France, for example, fostered at the court of Athelstan, later married Gerberga, sister of Otto I (and therefore sister-in-law of Athelstan's half-sister Edith). When Dunstan, one of the three main leaders of the monastic movement in England (both in his role as abbot of Glastonbury and later as archbishop of Canterbury), was for a time banished (seemingly because he had expressed his displeasure at King Eadwig's sex life) he had found refuge in Ghent, thanks to the support of Count Arnulf I; Arnulf's mother had been a daughter of King Alfred's. Arnulf placed Dunstan in the care of Abbot Womar at the reformed monastery of St Peter's. On the death of Arnulf, it was Otto's sister Gerberga who became regent for his son, seemingly smoothing her path by making grants to Womar for Arnulf's soul. Subsequently, Womar became sufficiently well-enough known in England for his death to be mentioned in the *Anglo-Saxon Chronicle* (he seems to have been a visitor to Winchester). Not all monastic connections were, however, quite so complex; nor must they overshadow the very particular context of the movement in England.

Our starting point must be East Anglia, home once to some of the most prestigious monastic houses of the conversion period (Ely, for example, and Iken) and endowed with two bishoprics – one at Elmham and the other (probably) at Dunwich. By the ninth century, both sees had vanished and there is no evidence of any trace of monastic life having survived the arrival of the Great Army and subsequent Viking settlement. But by 917/18, East Anglia had been recovered by Edward the Elder and in 932 he appointed his kinsman Athelstan as its ealdorman. Athelstan's influence was immeasurable – hence his nickname of 'half-king'. Both Athelstan Half-King and his wife were deeply committed to the restoration of diocesan and monastic life in East Anglia and it is therefore highly significant that the future King Edgar was fostered in his household and that Edgar may later have been given as his tutor none other than the monastic reformer, Aethelwold, monk of Glastonbury, abbot of Abingdon and later bishop of Winchester. When Dunstan was banished, Athelstan resigned (or was forced out of office), whereupon he retired to the monastery at Glastonbury, of which he was a benefactor (as he was also of Abingdon). He was succeeded as ealdorman of East Anglia by his son, Aethelwine, whose commitment to the cause of monastic reform seems to have equalled his father's. The third reformer to join Aethelwold and Dunstan was Oswald, bishop of Worcester and later archbishop of York. On Oswald's return to England – he had spent six impressionable years at the monastery of Fleury (a community whose claim to possess the body of St Benedict gave it immeasurable clout) – his foundation at Ramsey, in 965, was made possible by the gift of estates that had belonged formerly to Aethelwine's mother.[18]

Edgar, then, when he came to the throne, had already received a formidable education in 'the right order of things'. Aethelwold had perhaps been his tutor; Dunstan, the friend of his foster-father. King Eadwig (whom he succeeded) may (or may not) have been the profligate painted by later sources but the salacious story of how he had behaved on his coronation day (cavorting with two women) presented a nice contrast to high-minded Edgar. Not that Edgar himself would prove to be above marital scandal but he had (it would seem) a sense of occasion which Eadwig seemingly lacked. A king's private morality should never be confused with his perception of his office and Edgar, without a doubt, had an exalted sense of who, as king, he was and of how the prayers of reformed monks could support, glorify and safeguard his reign and his kingdom.

Tenth-century prayer was not (or not simply) a matter of pious supplication. It had a power, for good or ill, that is difficult now to fully comprehend. The prayers of the righteous formed an essential defence system for the security and safety of king and kingdom, but such prayers had to come from the mouths of those considered to be already close in spirit to the angels: in other words, from those who were sexually pure. To the reformers it seemed appropriate that the storm troops of the country be based in monasteries, in particular in monastic cathedrals. In consequence, the prayers of cathedral priests who had no particular respect for celibacy were no longer considered efficacious: as King Edgar himself put it 'they availed [him] nothing'.[19] In the future, cathedral priests were to be sexually pure, to possess no private property and to live in strict adherence to the *Rule of St Benedict*. Only then would their prayers be of a quality to ensure the salvation of king and kingdom. It was in this spirit, and driven by this conviction, that it became acceptable for Aethelwold, in conjunction with King Edgar (and with the backing of Dunstan as archbishop of Canterbury), to organize, in the February of 964, a swoop on 'the evil-living clerics' of the Old Minster at Winchester, replacing them with reformed monks from Aethelwold's foundation of Abingdon, a group of whom were standing in readiness by the door of the Winchester minster, poised to enter and evict 'the impious blasphemers'.[20]

As well as the reform of the Old Minster, Aethelwold took in hand both the New Minster at Winchester and the women's community of Nunnaminster. Thereafter, he turned his attention to Milton Abbey, in Dorset; to Chertsey, in Surrey; in East Anglia to Peterborough, Ely and Thorney. Meanwhile, albeit less frenetically, Aethelwold's partners in reform were also hard at work; Dunstan endowed and reformed Malmesbury and (probably) Westminster; Oswald had Ramsey (as already mentioned) built to house monks. At Worcester itself, while Oswald was bishop, change came slowly but nearby Winchcombe, Pershore and Evesham were all fully monasticized on his watch. In the reformers' ideal world, Benedictine houses might well have been established throughout the length and breadth of the land; if the pace of reform seems to have slowed somewhat after 971, this can be attributed to lack of opportunities rather than to a lack of fervour: the new establishments were not cheap to run and the gathering together of enough property to finance each enterprise is likely to have depended both on the ruthless exploitation of random opportunities and on chance circumstances which were beyond orchestration (such as the deaths of bishops and the release of their individual holdings). Moreover, even if the number of reformed houses before the Conquest never exceeded 50, their influence was out of all proportion to their number since it was from just such houses that the pre-Conquest episcopate came to be drawn.[21]

The reformers' manifesto was given shape in the *Regularis Concordia* (The Monastic Agreement), a document that established the set of customs which Edgar and the reformers wanted observed in monastic houses the length and breadth of the land. It is not clear when the text was first drawn up, but it was approved at a synod held at Winchester, sometime around 970, where bishops, abbots and abbesses all 'raised their hands' in support 'lest differing ways of observing the customs of one rule and one country should bring their holy conversation into disrepute'.[22] No matter that in the days of Bede, which the reformers were happy to extol as a golden age, a range of customs had been accepted as normative. Now what was seemingly required was uniformity, under the direction of the king. The initiative and patronage behind the movement were manifestly royal. Influential though the customs of both Fleury and Ghent were (and acknowledged as such in the preface to the *Concordia*), as far as the extent of prayers for royalty were concerned, the English customs were unique: at every office (except Prime) two psalms and three collects were to be said for the king and the queen and after each mass a further psalm for each was to be said, together with a further prayer.

The drawing up of *Concordia* is usually attributed now to Aethelwold himself (rather than, as hitherto, to Dunstan).[23] The much quoted story of how Aethelwold tested the obedience of one of his monks at Abingdon by asking him to plunge his hand into boiling water all too easily gives the impression that the reform movement was oppressive, authoritarian and dour. And doubtless, in certain respects, so it was.[24] But at the same time, and however paradoxical it may appear, the reformers' vision had about it a breath-taking splendour and magnificence that was undoubtedly designed to be both celebratory and inclusive. All Christians, and not only monks and nuns, had parts they could play. In this respect, Aethelwold's sense that his mission was to restore the lost glory of the days of Bede was not entirely misplaced. Tenth-century Winchester now functioned, as had eighth-century Wearmouth Jarrow, as a mission centre and monastic showcase.[25] The scale of the building works at Winchester associated with Aethelwold is staggering: the bishop acquired a new residence; the Old Minster, a magnificent west work; the New Minster, an imposing western tower. Whether the citizens themselves welcomed all this building (it necessitated much land clearance) may be doubted, but there need be no reason to be over-sceptical about the welcome they were asked to give to the translation of St Swithun, the ninth-century bishop of Winchester, to the new west end of the Old Minster. This was a celebration in which the whole community was to participate:

each person from Winchester, of whatever age and sex – whether slave or nobly born, whosoever dwelled in that town – was to proceed barefoot over the three miles, and was to meet the holy patron with reverence, so

that every tongue might magnify God in unison and the ethereal radiance
would shine everywhere through the chanting, and St Swithun would be
translated to the city with glorious acclaim.[26]

The very discovery of Swithun's body was presented as an exercise
in reconciliation, given that one of the priests whom Aethelwold
had expelled from the Old Minster was chosen to play a key role in
the saint's exhumation. When the number of miracles subsequently
worked by Swithun proved wearisome to the monks, Aethelwold
roundly chastised them for their sloth; by day or by night, just as
soon as a sick person had been cured the monks were to hurry,
without delay, to the church to sing the *Te Deum*.[27]

Aethelwold's commitment to the cause of reform finds its manifesto
not only in the *Regularis Concordia*, but also in the iconography of
his Benedictional (a book of blessings a bishop might use during
mass); Aethelwold's volume was not only exceptionally sumptuous,
it was also notably 'political' in that the images it contained
reinforced time and again the very particular role Aethelwold
envisaged both king and queen should play in the establishment of
God's kingdom on earth. No opportunity was missed to exalt the
nature of kingship – the three magi who bring gifts to Christ each
wear crowns, unusually for the time, and their first gift to Christ is of
a crown; in the next illustration, of Christ's baptism, the Holy Spirit
anoints him as both king and priest, while angels invest him with
crown and sceptre. At the same time, it is important to note those
images in the Benedictional that suggest the participation in services
of the laity, for example, as part of the processions of Palm Sunday
and seemingly as spectators during the dedication of a church by the
bishop.[28]

Impossible though it is to be certain of the date of the
Benedictional, the suggestion that it must be understood in relation
to Edgar and Aelfthryth's coronation at Bath in 973 is compelling.
This coronation is itself something of a mystery: by 973, Edgar
had already been king for 14 years and it is hard to imagine that
he had eschewed any crowning when he had first become king.
The year 973, however, was for Edgar a significant date. That year,
Edgar entered his thirtieth year. He was thus the same age as Christ
when he had begun his ministry. How far this was a compelling
motive for a second coronation is conjectural, but there is every

reason to imagine that a number of reasons will have pointed in the same direction: keeping up with the Ottonian rulers of Germany (given Otto I's imperial coronation in Rome in 962); the need to strengthen the claims of Queen Aelfthryth's sons (as opposed to that of Prince Edward, an elder son but born from an earlier union); a wish for a display of glory to accompany the vigorous assertion of Edgar's authority as king of all England, such was also proclaimed by Edgar's reform in 973 of his coinage, whereby a uniform currency was ensured throughout the kingdom.[29]

Whatever the precise mix of motives for Edgar's coronation, there can be no doubting the splendour of the occasion. The choice of the Roman city of Bath added a touch of imperial glamour to the ceremony. It may well be, too, that the meeting reputed to have taken place immediately afterwards at Chester when British kings (whether it be Aelfric's 'eight' or the mere six noted in the *Anglo-Saxon Chronicle*) pledged their allegiance to Edgar was designed to suggest that he had indeed achieved some sort of *pax Romana*.[30] It would be a mistake, however, to interpret this occasion as purely ceremonial: the possibility of attacks from the Norse Irish had never gone away. The peace of Edgar's reign had been won neither by luck, nor by prayer alone. Edgar's was a Church militant and the militancy took many forms. Thus the 'naval force' which is said to have accompanied Edgar to Chester could well represent the invention of 'shipsoke', a system of taxation designed to provide the king with the fleet long acknowledged to be necessary for defence. But meanwhile there was much to celebrate. Edgar was king now of a country united by its currency, by its system of local government and hopeful that its supplications to God were sufficiently powerful to both please and appease him.

Yet within two years of his coronation at Bath, Edgar was dead. The succession dispute that followed, between Edgar's two sons, Edward and Aethelred, landed the country in civil war. The conflict provided an ideal opportunity for anyone who felt that the monastic reformers had arbitrarily and unjustly appropriated their lands (as doubtless they had) to rebel and pillage, but there is little evidence for any widespread rejection of the reformers' ideals as such: this was less an ideological protest than a 'not in my back garden' reaction. As for the succession, the reformers' themselves took up positions in opposing camps – Aethelwold seemingly backing

Aethelred, son of Queen Aelfthryth, while Dunstan favoured, and subsequently crowned, Aethelred's older half-brother, Edward. The shocking murder just three years later of Edward, while out hunting in Wiltshire, seems particularly grotesque, given the exalted spectacle of kingship Edgar had so recently displayed. To contemporaries it may have seemed no more and no less than a reminder that the devil never sleeps. At the time, everyone of course knew this. The devil and his minions were never far away: one of the very first miracles performed by St Swithun after his translation in 971 was to rescue a seemingly blameless citizen of Winchester from the clutches of the three furies (to wit: two naked women with swarthy hair, together with a taller woman, dressed in shining white).[31]

The devil could not be combated in monasteries alone, nor indeed had the reformers ever imagined this to be so. A striking difference between the English monastic reform movement and its continental exemplar lies precisely in the pastoral role which the reformed communities in England chose to exercise. It was monks, from the moment of St Augustine's arrival in Canterbury in 597 and of Aidan's at Lindisfarne in 635, who had been foremost in providing pastoral care and instruction to the laity and the tenth-century reform movement continued this tradition. No one better demonstrates this than Aelfric (with whom this chapter opened).[32]

Aelfric had been a pupil of Aethelwold's at Winchester but around 987 he was dispatched to Cerne, in Dorset, to a monastery newly founded (or perhaps re-founded) by Aethelmaer, son of the ealdorman Aethelweard; as well as being a figure of political importance, Aethelweard was responsible for a Latin translation of the *Anglo-Saxon Chronicle* for his cousin Matilda, abbess of Essen, and both he and Aethelmaer were the indispensable patrons of Aelfric's work. After Aethelweard's death, when Aethelmaer had perhaps fallen from political grace, Aethelmaer moved to Oxfordshire, where he founded a community at Eynsham (as with Cerne, this was perhaps a re-foundation), taking with him Aelfric to become its abbot. At both Cerne and Eynsham, Aelfric was prolific; while at Cerne, he wrote 80 homilies in the vernacular (divided into two volumes) on a range of subjects suitable for use either as preaching texts or as devotional reading. A third collection of *Lives of the Saints*, written specifically for Aethelweard, was followed by further translations from the Old Testament designed to be read by educated laymen (notably Aethelmaer and Aethelweard themselves). Such was Aelfric's reputation that he was soon in demand as a writer of 'official' prose, composing the pastoral letters to his clergy sent both by Wulfstan, archbishop of York (with whose millenarian views Aelfric was much in sympathy), and by Wulfsige, bishop of Sherborne. As a devoted schoolteacher, Aelfric also wrote a Latin grammar for his pupils and a colloquy designed to give them practice in speaking Latin. But it is the lasting influence of Aelfric's first books that is particularly impressive: around 30 manuscripts (dating from the tenth to the thirteenth centuries) of the early homilies are still extant. An examination of such manuscripts suggests that copies were made into little booklets so as to provide ready access to priests in search of sermons, a remarkable testimony indeed of the success of Aelfric's ambition to 'tell written learning to all God's people together'.[33]

Aelfric's sermons were, then, heard not only in his own churches but also across the country. He had a concept of a national Church, imbued in him most probably by Aethelwold; for both, there were therefore three saints who deserved particular honour: St Benedict, the 'father' of monasticism; Pope Gregory, whose project it had been to send monks to England in order to convert the country; and, lastly, St Cuthbert, a saint who had come to stand for a united England.[34] Quite how Cuthbert had been so co-opted is not entirely clear, but, undoubtedly, it mattered to the reformers of the tenth century – and to their kings – to have his support. Had not Athelstan, on his journey North, made a point of honouring Cuthbert? For was it not Cuthbert, or so the story went, who had appeared to King Alfred on the eve of his battle against Guthrum, promising him immediate victory together with the prospect that his heirs would one day rule all England?[35] Impossible though it is to date the origins of this story with any confidence, what is clear is that, throughout the tenth century, 'southerners' felt little compunction in appropriating the support of northern saints for their cause. There could, of course, be no prospect of bringing Cuthbert himself southwards, but it was a different matter with other northern saints: by the mid-tenth century, Oswald had long been settled in Gloucester; Wilfrid was in Canterbury; Benedict Biscop in Thorney. But it would be with the support of such saints, duly honoured in their new surroundings, that reform could hope to percolate across the country.

The bitter blow dealt to such hopes by the death of King Edgar in 975 and the turmoil that followed should not, however, obscure the rich evidence there is for the vitality and diversity of religious practice that nonetheless developed across England in the late tenth and eleventh centuries. Alongside the reformed monasteries, 'unreformed' minsters continued to flourish and alongside these can be detected the earliest parish churches. Tracing the history of these new places of worship is not easy; often it is only through disputes about dues owed that distinctions become visible – thus in Aethelred's law code of 1014 the fines due for violation of a 'chief minster' as opposed to 'a smaller minster' or to a 'still smaller' [church] and finally to a 'field church' are to be distinguished from each other. Since the tenth century (but probably not before) it had become obligatory to be buried in consecrated ground, with the exception of certain criminals, but the question could still arise as to who should receive the funeral dues (the soul-scot), supposing the deceased was not buried where he would normally be counted as a parishioner. Aethelred legislates accordingly: 'it is best that soul-scot be always paid at the open grave. And if any body is buried elsewhere, outside the proper parish, soul-scot is nevertheless to be paid at the minster to which it belonged.'[36]

The 'proper parish' in this context is a 'rihtscriftscir', that is to say the place where the deceased would normally have gone to confession and then to mass. How far such recommendations were observed is of course impossible to know, but the evidence that Christian belief and practice were neither perfunctory nor merely ritualistic is plentiful. From the moment of baptism, each Christian had been entrusted to a guardian angel whose role it was to provide protection against the ever present dangers presented by devils. At no point was such an angel needed more acutely than at the hour of death when Satan and his minions would do their best to claim the soul of the dying man or woman. This was a time for a final confession, absolution and communion, but necessarily there must have been countless occasions when men died without these rites and when the help of the soul's guardian was particularly vital: such an angel, it was hoped, could then present God with a record of all the good deeds the deceased had done in his life. For the truly wicked there could of course be no remedy – to imagine that at the Last Day some such men might be rescued by the Virgin from the eternal flames of Hell was, argued Aelfric, an exceedingly dangerous heresy. The most the 'average' Christian could hope for was a time of preparation and cleansing in a proto-purgatorial realm; never was there room for even a glimmer of complacency.[37]

The 'average' Christian could be expected to have made his confession and taken communion, if not every week, at least with some regularity throughout the year.[38] He would have known both the Lord's Prayer and the Creed, but rote learning was not expected. Various translations were available to help understanding; what mattered was that laymen should have a grasp of both texts so that 'they may know what to pray for to God and how they shall believe in God'.[39] There was also a considerable body of vernacular verse, telling in dramatic detail of the adventures of saints and the perils of Hell.

At some point in the tenth and eleventh centuries, such texts were collected into three codices: the *Vercelli Book*, consisting of assorted homilies and verse; the lavishly illustrated Junius manuscript, full of Old Testament narratives, starting with the creation of the world; and the Exeter book, not illustrated but which contains both religious and secular poetry. (The manuscript of *Beowulf*, together with a poetic version of the Old Testament story of the slaying of Holofernes by Judith, is the last of the four great manuscripts that have preserved all that we have of Anglo-Saxon verse.) The merest acquaintance with any of these texts highlights the dramatic intensity with which Christian truths and doctrines were conveyed. There was no shirking the brevity of life, nor the realities of death – 'A house was built for you before you were born. Earth was your appointed end before you emerged from your mother' – nor the fate of the body in the grave: 'ferocious worms [then]ravage the ribs; in swarms they gulp down carrion thirsting for gore ...'.[40] But it was the horrors of the Last Judgment before which all else must pall:

> the earth will tremble and the hills will crumble and collapse; the slopes of mountains will buckle and subside, and the horrible roar of the rough sea will greatly distress the mind of every human being. All above the sky will ... become black and dusky ... the stars will ... plummet ... [and] then the celestial troops will come.[41]

But despite these terrors, there was always hope for the penitent, provided, that is, that he had confessed truthfully. The responsibility must always lie with the sinner:

The confessor cannot see through the flesh into the soul, whether someone is telling him the truth or a lie ... Nevertheless, every vice and impure evil can be healed, if it is told to just one person but no one can hide a stainful sin for which he has not atoned on that harsh day when the multitude will see it.[42]

But it was of course not by texts alone that the men and women of Anglo-Saxon England knew about their God and his saints. Every year in the ecclesiastical calendar was a ritual year and every ritual had its own particular story to tell. Every church year was, also, costly and always had been. By the time of Edgar's reign new taxes had been added to those Bede would have recognized: to churchscot (a render of grain, paid already in the reign of King Ine) were added further impositions: 'a tithe of all young stock is to be rendered by Pentecost and of the fruits of the earth by the Equinox and all churchscot is to be rendered by Martinmas'. Woe betide the backslider:

if anyone will not render the tithe as we have decreed, the king's reeve is to go there, and the bishop's reeve and the mass-priest of the minster to which it belongs, and to assign him the next tenth; and the remaining eight parts are to be divided into two, and the lord of the land is to succeed to half, and the bishop to half, whether it be a king's man or a thegn.[43]

But feast days nonetheless remained a time of celebration, most notably those that took place just before and during spring. The processions envisaged on such days were necessarily easier to 'stage' in places where there was more than one church but groups of churches were by no means unusual in Anglo-Saxon England; Canterbury from its earliest days had three.[44]

Let us start the ritual year on 2 February with Candlemas, a feast that marked Mary's churching after the birth of Jesus, known therefore as the Purification. Ever since at least the seventh century, this was a feast which had been celebrated in Rome. Whether it had been introduced into England before 900 is uncertain; by the time of the *Regularis Concordia* an elaborate liturgy had been composed. To Aelfric, what particularly mattered was the involvement of the laity: 'you must on the mass day that is called The Purification of St Mary bless candles and bear them with praise singing, both monks and laity, in procession and offer them, so burning, after the gospel to the mass priest with the offering song'. Participation by all mattered: 'although some men cannot sing they can nevertheless bear those lights in their hands because on this day that true light, Christ, was carried to the temple who freed us from darkness and will bring us to eternal light'.[45] On this occasion, every man and woman was Simeon, the New Testament figure, who, when the infant Christ was taken into the temple, had recognized who he was: 'just as this one [Simeon] did not see death before meriting to see Christ the Lord, so also may we obtain eternal life'.[46] On Ash Wednesday, the laity again had its role: after the priest had marked his own forehead with the ashes he had blessed, it was the turn of the whole congregation to be similarly marked. Thereafter, a procession preceded the celebration of mass. Everyone now was Adam: '[men must] have in mind that they came from earth, and afterward will return to dust, just as the Almighty God said to Adam after he had transgressed against God's command ... you are dust and to dust you will return'.[47]

The climax of the liturgical year was Holy Week, starting with Palm Sunday, a day marked by palm (or rather branch)-bearing processions in imitation of Christ's arrival in Jerusalem, together with the apostles, when, as described in the Gospels, Christ was feted by the crowds. Remarkably, as Robert Deshman has pointed out, in the illustration for Palm Sunday in Bishop Aethelwold's sumptuous Benedictional the apostles have no place. It is the 'ordinary' crowd – including a woman – which is depicted.[48] Once such a crowd has processed, then follows mass. Later in the week, the laity again have prominent roles: on Maundy Thursday a selected group of poor have their feet washed and they are fed; ritualized charity, but nonetheless meaningful. On Good Friday, the *Regularis Concordia* has this suggestion to make in a passage that, even abbreviated, deserved to be quoted at some length:

> if anyone should care or think fit to follow in a becoming manner certain religious men in a practice worthy to be imitated for the strengthening of the faith of unlearned common persons and neophytes, we have decreed this only: on that part of the altar where there is space for it there shall be a representation as it were of a sepulchre, hung about with a curtain, in which the holy Cross, when it has been venerated shall be placed in the following manner: the deacons who carried the Cross before shall come forward and having wrapped the Cross in a napkin there where it

was venerated, they shall bear it thence ... to the place of the 'sepulchre' ... On the holy day of Easter ... four of the brethren shall vest, one of whom, wearing an alb ... shall enter and go stealthily to the place of the 'sepulchre' and sit there quietly, holding a palm in his hand ... the other three brethren, vested in copes ... shall enter in their turn and go to the place of the 'sepulchre' step by step, as if searching for something. Now these things are done in imitation of the angel seated on the tomb and of the women coming with perfumes to anoint the body of Jesus. When, therefore, he that is seated shall see these three drawing nigh ... he shall begin to sing softly and sweetly, *Quem quaeritis* [whom are you looking for] ... the three shall answer together, *Ihesum Nazarenum* (Jesus of Nazareth).[49]

Much has been made of this passage in any history of the development of the religious drama of the Middle Ages; but, not the least interesting part of the ritual, the way in which monks, representing the women, are also the messengers of the resurrection (whereas in the Gospels, it is the apostles Peter and John who find the grave cloth).[50] Thus after the singing of the *Quem quaeritis*, the monks, as 'women', are given the news that Jesus has risen and asked by the 'angel' to spread the news by showing the cloth in which the Cross had been wrapped (the Cross having meanwhile been taken away) to the congregation, singing as they do so *Surrexit Dominus de sepulchro* (The Lord has risen from the tomb). Strikingly, this is the version of events further developed by Aelfric in his homily for the day urging his audience, as he does, to be like the women of that first Easter Sunday.

On many levels, no other occasion in the Christian year can surpass Easter; but there could yet in Anglo-Saxon England be many reasons for processions at other times: rogations, just before Ascension Day, when crops were blessed; patronal saints' days; burial processions. Necessarily, participation on such occasions is no evidence of the kind of orthodoxy which Aelfric was seeking; nor can any other measure be found for this – nor, it can be argued, should the attempt even be made. Orthodox beliefs seldom (if ever) exist divorced from more heterodox opinions; clearly this was so in Anglo-Saxon England. Nonetheless without having at least some sense of Aelfric and the thought-world of his contemporaries the dramas that were to unfold in the eleventh century will make no sense.

7

THE VIKING RETURN

Things have not gone well a long time now at home or abroad, but there has been devastation and persecution in every district again and again, and the English have been for a long time now completely defeated and too greatly disheartened, through God's anger; and the pirates so strong with God's consent that often in battle one puts to flight ten, and sometimes less, sometimes more, all because of our sins ... But all the insult that we often suffer we repay with honouring those who insult us; we pay them continually and they humiliate us daily; they ravage and they burn, plunder and rob and carry on board; and, lo, what else is there in all these events, except God's anger, clear and visible over this people?

(Wulfstan, *Sermon of the Wolf to the English*)[1]

King Edgar's premature death in 975 – he is thought to have been no more than 32 – resulted in one of those succession disputes which were so regular a feature of English kingship (both in this period and beyond). On this occasion the two claimants were half-brothers, both of whom were still children. Gossip and counter-gossip have made it difficult to fully unravel who supported which brother and why but the dispute necessarily provided a platform for magnates, lay and ecclesiastical, to air their grievances, to display their rivalries and to parade their local loyalties. The backers of the elder brother, Edward, included Dunstan, archbishop of Canterbury; the ealdorman of Essex, Brythnoth (hero-to-be of the Battle of Maldon of 991); and Aethelwine of East Anglia. His rival, Aethelred, who was as yet only around seven years old, had his own powerful allies, notably Aethelwold, bishop of Winchester, and Aelfhere of Mercia, and he had the inestimable advantage of having as his mother Aelfthryth, a crowned queen, whereas it is quite uncertain (despite various rumours) who Edward's mother really was. The division of the kingdom, which once would have seemed the simplest choice, does not seem this time to have been considered. Given the outcome of events, this can, however, hardly have been because kingship had become a more exalted office: by the end of 975 Edward had been accepted and consecrated as king; by the spring of 978 he was dead, seemingly murdered while on a hunting expedition in Dorset (close to the spot where Corfe Castle now stands). Who did it will never be known; nor whether it was manslaughter or a carefully planned assassination. Queen Aelfthryth before long became identified as the chief suspect and though there is no evidence of her complicity the circumstances surrounding the death and even more the subsequent delay in giving the king a proper burial necessarily provided grounds for suspicion, speculation and rumour. For months the king's body lay hidden before it was finally recovered and transported with honour to Shaftesbury, to the house founded by King Alfred. By the turn of the millennium, a cult had developed round the king's tomb and, in 1001, Edward was recognized as a martyr and a saint; by then, it was not hard to attribute the return of the Vikings to the murder of this anointed king and to seek his help in their defeat.[2]

May 979, meanwhile, had seen the consecration of Aethelred as king. Whatever the precise year of his birth, he can as yet have been little more than a boy. For the first five years of his reign, he perforce accepted the guidance both of his mother, Aelfthryth, and of Bishop Aethelwold, but there were tensions. In 980, the completion of Aethelwold's Old Minster in Winchester seemingly provided an opportunity for reconciliation and celebration, an occasion when 'all who had previously seemed his enemies ... were suddenly made, as it were, sheep instead of wolves'.[3] But the equilibrium did not hold. On the death of Aethelwold in 984, Queen Aelfthryth appears to have been banished from her son's inner circle and Aethelred now entered upon a period that came to be known as a time of 'youthful indiscretion', years when licence was seemingly given to favoured magnates to plunder ecclesiastical property; then, in 993, came an

Fig. 28: Nineteenth-century representation of the treacherous moment before the murder of Edward the Martyr

abrupt change of direction. That year, according to the *Anglo-Saxon Chronicle*, 'the king had Aelfgar, son of Ealdorman Aelfric, blinded'.[4] Uncertain though the circumstances are, it seems that Aelfgar, having initially been one of those to profit from the king's generosity with Church lands, then found himself exposed to public disgrace while Aethelred, in a notably public statement of repentance, apologized for misfortunes that had happened 'partly because of the ignorance of my youth – which is accustomed to practise different behaviour – partly also because of the detestable covetousness of those men who ought to counsel me for my benefit'.[5]

The year 993 was of course an ominous year. By then it had become clear that the Vikings were again presenting a serious and sustained menace to the peace and prosperity of the kingdom. The sporadic raiding of the 980s could be ignored but the Viking fleet that had arrived in 991 and that had inflicted a defeat on Ealdorman Byrhtnoth and his men, so terrible that it became the subject of the heroic verse, *The Battle of Maldon*, was of a different order.[6] After this battle, the practice was resumed (and now with regularity rather than, as hitherto, as an occasional measure) of buying off the Vikings in order to get some respite from their renewed attacks, but the relief gained by paying out these sums proved to be short-lived. One disaster now followed another in quick succession; in 994, for example, the Vikings committed 'the greatest damage that ever any army could do, by burning, ravaging and slaying, both along the coast, and in Essex, Kent, Sussex and Hampshire; and finally they seized horses and rode as widely as they wished, and continued to do indescribable damage'.[7]

It has long been recognized that the highly coloured account of these years given by the *Anglo-Saxon Chronicle* needs to be read with care. Whoever the chronicler was, he is writing with the benefit of hindsight: Aethelred, by then, was dead, the Danish King Cnut was on the English throne and it was time to apportion blame. Recent assessments of Aethelred attempting to rehabilitate the king have done their best to correct the impression of royal incompetence and poor leadership which the *Chronicle* so vividly presents. Emphasis is placed now on Aethelred's attempts at diplomacy – his alliance, for example, already in 991 (so before the Battle of Maldon) with Richard of Normandy whereby each ruler promised not to harbour the enemies of the other (an alliance Aethelred further consolidated by marrying Emma, daughter of Richard, in 1002). Then, in 994, the king acted as sponsor at his baptism to the Viking leader Olaf Tryggvasson (just as King Alfred had done for the Viking Guthrum) in the reasonable hope that Olaf would concentrate now on the conquest of Norway and that the strengthening of his hand against Swein of Denmark (another thorn in England's side) would help to keep both Swein and Olaf safely engrossed with projects beyond English soil and shores. It must also be recognized that the Vikings of Aethelred's later years were a more formidable force than the Vikings of earlier invasions and that their ambitions (as the subsequent conquest of England would show) were of a different order.[8]

Yet even when all allowances have been made for Aethelred, there can be no escaping the fact that the record of his reign still makes dispiriting reading. The large sums of money paid out to the Vikings, both by way of peace settlements and as a way of giving support to one group of Vikings to fight another, became over the years increasingly steep – after the Battle of Maldon a mere 10,000 pounds was paid out; in 1018 the figure was 72,000 (these at least are the figures in the *Anglo-Saxon Chronicle*).[9]

One reaction is to admire the administrative skills that made the collection of such sums possible; another, equally important, is to consider the corrupting effects that so much cash could have on a society as yet unused to the dynamics of a moneyed economy; it can be no accident that the Anglo-Saxon word 'rice' which had once meant 'powerful' underwent, in the eleventh century, a shift in meaning, and began now to mean simply 'rich'. The circulation of large numbers of coins necessarily created a very different sense of wealth than had existed in the world of ring givers and gift exchange. Ready supplies of money tended to encourage both corruption and greed.[10]

Time to return to 993: it is a year that repays close attention. Since the Battle of Maldon of 991, the sense of crisis generated by further setbacks and defeats had been aggravated by the death in 992 of those two 'elder statesmen', Oswald, archbishop of York, and his friend and ally the ealdorman of East Anglia, Aethelwine, from either of whom Aethelred might reasonably have been expected to seek advice. In their stead, Aethelred recalled to court his mother (she re-appears now as a witness to royal charters) and turned to the men who were in effect the heirs of the monastic movement of Edgar's day, to men such as the archbishop of Canterbury, Sigeric; Aethelweard, patron of Aelfric of Cerne; Wulfgar, abbot of Abingdon. At Pentecost of 993, the king summoned a great synodal council (held at Winchester) in which he questioned how it was that in the past few years (since in fact the death of Bishop Aethelwold) things had not gone well for his country, how he had concluded that he had been badly advised and how he now regretted in particular the fact that he had sold the abbacy of Abingdon. This sale, the king accepted, had necessarily placed him under a curse which, both for the safety of his soul and for the well-being of his people, must now be lifted. Accordingly, some weeks after the synod, the king solemnly restored to Abingdon its rights; the monks in return said 1,500 masses, and sang 1,200 psalters for the redemption of Aethelred's soul.[11]

However dramatic a moment Aethelred's breast-beating of 993 may seem, it should not necessarily be regarded as extraordinary; what is rather more extraordinary is that it is only recently that it has been placed in its appropriate context. In its concentration on the growing powers of the state and in the origins, already in the Anglo-Saxon period, of an embryonic 'parliament', English medieval scholarship has often failed to allow for the extent to which the sacrality of later Anglo-Saxon kingship was a quotidian reality. If King Edgar had been the Good Shepherd, Aethelred by the same token could be the prodigal son. No one should imagine that Christocentric kingship provided only one role – what mattered always was the grace of humility, and the willingness of the king to atone for sin and to share in the sufferings as well as the triumphs of his people.[12]

Aethelred's confession of 993 was to be followed by further acts of reparation to churches (for example to Rochester and to Winchester) which had suffered during the king's 'youth', and by renewed veneration of Bishop Aethelwold whose death was seen now as marking the moment when the king had begun to stray from the path of righteousness.[13] Aethelwold's Old Minster at Winchester had been magnificently enlarged and embellished (it had a new tower topped by a golden weathercock); now it was re-dedicated, bringing with it reminders of the reconciliations of the earlier dedication of 980. Then, in 996, Aethelwold was declared a saint. His body was duly and solemnly translated into the choir of the church from where he could reasonably be expected to watch over the king and to guide his steps.[14]

By 996, then, Aethelred might well have imagined that with his misspent youth behind him and with Olaf Tryggvasson, the foremost Viking of those same years, now busily fighting for the crown of Norway (and the conversion of its people to Christianity) he had at last successfully enlisted God and his saints on his side. The *Anglo-Saxon Chronicle* for that year (a source known for its hostility to Aethelred) has nothing to report beyond the consecration of Aelfric as archbishop of Canterbury (in succession to Sigeric who had died the year before). But the peace was illusory: already in 997 Vikings were back, this time raiding both Cornwall and Devon 'and they took with them to their ships indescribable booty'; in 998, they were in Somerset, Dorset and the Isle of Wight. In 998, according to the *Chronicle*, 'they went inland everywhere into Dorset as widely as they pleased and the English army was often assembled against them ... but always the enemy had the victory in the end'.[15] From then on, as the *Chronicle* reports it, the news became steadily grimmer: in 999, English efforts to stem the raiding did nothing but add to the oppression of the native people, waste money and encourage further attacks; 1000 saw a fiasco at sea; 1001 was 'in every way grievous'. The sense of desperation evinced by the *Chronicle* is corroborated by the order it reports the king as having issued in 1002 to the effect that 'all the Danish men who were in England' were to be killed 'because the king had been informed that they would treacherously deprive him, and then all his councillors, of life, and possess the kingdom afterwards'.[16]

The order for the massacre of 1002 was without a doubt carried out, though only for Oxford is the evidence clear. Aethelred's charter to the Oxford monastery of St Frideswide's renewing its privileges told the story in unabashed detail: following the king's order, the Danes of Oxford had fled to the monastic church, presumably expecting to take sanctuary there. It was to no avail: the natives of Oxford and the surrounding area pursued their victims and when they found they could not drive them out, they set the church on fire.[17]

But who precisely were these Danes?[18]

The men and women of the Danelaw, long integrated into English society and subject to English law, cannot conceivably have been the intended victims; but the 'cockles' may well have included those Danes whom Aethelred had originally employed as mercenaries to help fight off other marauding bands. The *Anglo-Saxon Chronicle* for 1001 reports how one Pallig had joined the Viking force that had been ravaging Hampshire, thereby deserting Aethelred 'in spite of all the pledges which he had given him. And the King had also made great gifts to him in estates and gold and silver.'[19] Alliances between kings and Vikings were nothing new but desertion of this kind was not to be tolerated and may well explain the order for the massacre of 1002. And there is a further intriguing (if unverifiable) twist to the story: according to the twelfth-century historian William of Malmesbury, the victims of 1002 included not only Pallig himself but also his son and his wife Gunnhildr, and Gunnhildr (or so William reports) was a sister of Swein of Denmark. Swein's subsequent attacks on England may thus have been no more and no less than a form of blood feud.

Whatever the truth behind William's story, there can be no doubt that from 1002 onwards Viking attacks intensified and at the same time so too, according to the *Anglo-Saxon Chronicle*, did the scale of treachery within Aethelred's ranks. Thus, in 1003, when Swein moved into Wiltshire, Ealdorman Aelfric, rather than resisting this advance, 'up to his old tricks ... he feigned him sick, and began retching to vomit ... and thus betrayed the people whom he should have led'.[20] The following year saw Swein in Norwich where the East Anglian Ulfcetel put up a heroic defence, but, at a crucial moment, a number of his own men failed him and in a final battle 'the flower of the East Anglian people was killed'.[21] The year 1005 brought peace, but only because a terrible famine in England drove the Vikings home. By 1006 they were back, causing such terror (according to the *Chronicle*) that men feared the whole country would be destroyed.

Aethelred's response to the events of 1006 was to lash out at his court circle, just as he had done when faced with the crisis of 993.[22] Wulfgeat, a member of the king's household, was deprived of all his property. Aelfhelm, the ealdorman of Northumbria, was murdered and his two sons blinded, but, whereas in 993 Aethelred had turned to men of unquestioned loyalty, for example to the archbishop of Canterbury, Sigeric, and to the West Country ealdorman Aethelweard, and later to his son Aethelmaer, in 1006 it would be Eadric Streona and his brothers who were among those who now came to the fore. Given Eadric's later conduct, it is not hard to see how it was that he would later earn the sobriquet 'The Acquisitor', while Aethelred for his turn would come to be called *unraed* 'the ill-advised' (later mistranslated to 'unready').

The unfolding of the 'palace revolution' of 1006 is nonetheless hard to track with any precision.[23] It is, for example, difficult to know whether Aethelmaer's retreat at this juncture from court life to the monastery of Eynsham, which he re-founded (placing over it as abbot Aethelwold's former pupil, Aelfric), was a decision taken by Aethelmaer because he was pushed, because he was disillusioned with Aethelred's judgement as king or because both he and Aethelred felt prayer was the best response to the dire situation in which the English now found themselves. The deep despair of these years is certainly palpable and, as in 993, Aethelred knew God was an ally he must appease. The foundation charter for Eynsham was on this point unusually explicit, echoing closely the sense of crisis portrayed by the *Chronicle*:

> because in our own days we endure the fires of war and the pillaging of our wealth, and also from the most savage assault of the rampaging barbarous enemies, and from the manifold oppression of heathen peoples and of those afflicting us almost to the point of extinction, we perceive that we live in perilous times; so it is very fitting that we, on whom the ends of the world are to come, should look with diligent care to the needs of our souls.[24]

Throughout these years of crisis (and indeed beyond, for he died only in 1023) the most persistent and the most influential voice belongs to Wulfstan Lupus. Little is known of Wulfstan's background before he became bishop of London in 996 (a post he held until his promotion in 1002 to the sees of York and of Worcester) but he was already recognized then for 'the very sweet eloquence of [his] wisdom' and known by then for his preoccupation with the approaching end of the world.[25] Five of his sermons, one in Latin and four in the vernacular on the subject of the last days, date from his time as London's bishop. While it had long been held that no one could, or indeed should, know the exact time when the world would end, it was really not possible, and perhaps even irresponsible, not to take stock of the approaching millennium and not to allow for the possibility that the Vikings were its harbingers. 'Foreigners and strangers severely oppress us', wrote Wulfstan:

> just as Christ clearly said would happen in his gospel ... [and] it is also written that the sun will grow dark before the world ends and the stars will fall because of people's sins ... liars and false Christians will quickly fall from correct belief and eagerly bow down to the Antichrist and honour his helpers with all their might.[26]

The passing of the year 1000 seemingly did nothing to dampen Wulfstan's apocalyptic fears; his sense of imminent danger chimed in all too well with the ever greater threats the Vikings posed. Their return in 1006 had led to further payments of geld – and 'gifts' of provisions – 'they were supplied with food throughout England'.[27] In response, a meeting was called at the behest of both archbishops, Aelfheah of Canterbury and Wulfstan of York, to be held in 1008, at Enham, in Hampshire, at Pentecost (a time of the year when it would be particularly appropriate to invoke the help of the Holy Spirit). The legislation that followed has long been attributed to Wulfstan's pen. It is strikingly comprehensive:

> horrible perjuries and devilish deeds of murder and manslaughter, of stealing and spoliation, of avarice and greed, of over-eating and over-drinking, of deceits and various breaches of the law ... and evil deeds of many kinds are condemned so that God will at once become gracious to this nation.[28]

But moral behaviour will not in itself be enough: practical steps must be taken too – ships were to be built 'unremittingly over all England'.[29] And ships were indeed built, so many, according to the *Chronicle* for 1009, that:

> there were more of them than ever before, from what books tell us ... and they were all brought together at Sandwich and were to stay there and protect this country from every invading army. But yet we had not the good fortune or honour that the naval force was of use to this country, any more than it had been on many previous occasions.[30]

And why? Not, in the first instance, because of new Viking attacks, but precisely because of a breach of those bonds of 'peace and friendship' which Wulfstan at Enham had been so anxious to promote.[31] A quarrel broke out between a brother of Eadric Streona's and a certain Wulfnoth, in the course of which 80 of the ships got smashed to bits in a storm. The rest were taken back to London. Sandwich was thus left unprotected – and, in August, in sailed an 'immense raiding party' led by the formidable Viking leader, Thorkell.[32] The king called for an emergency meeting to be held at Bath. It is once more Wulfstan who kept the record of the proceedings.

The meeting at Bath was held already late in the year. There was no time now for further military measures to be taken against the Vikings. What was imperative was for the English to recognize their sins and to throw themselves on God's mercy: only then would they be able to withstand their enemies. A mandatory programme of prayer and fasting was therefore drawn up. The whole nation was to fast on bread, herbs and water on the Monday, Tuesday and Wednesday before Michaelmas and everyone was to go barefoot to church to make his confession; slaves were to be freed from work so that they too could be included. The food that would otherwise have been eaten was to be distributed to the bed-ridden and those too weak to fast. Monastic communities at each of the Hours were to sing Psalm 3 'O Lord, how they are multiplied that trouble us'. In addition, the whole country was to be taxed with the money so collected being distributed in alms. These were age-old remedies, long known, for example, in Carolingian Frankia and not altogether unknown in England, but the scale of the programme envisaged in 1009 was nonetheless unprecedented. Nor was it restricted to just three days. 'Until things become better', a mass was to be said every day in each minster 'with special reference to the need which is now urgent for us'.[33] Moreover, it is highly likely that it is to just this time that a special issue of silver pennies belongs, showing on the obverse an image of the Lamb of God and on the reverse a dove, symbol of the Holy Spirit. Both Lamb and Dove would have been known from the liturgy of the mass as symbols of peace and of community and it is possible that just at this juncture concerned magnates took to wearing brooches depicting the dove – to date, three such brooches have been discovered, probably all emanating from the same workshop. The sense of crisis was palpable.[34]

The extraordinary measures of 1008 and of 1009 proved, however, to be of no avail. As described in the *Chronicle*, 1010 saw worse Viking devastation than ever before, lamentable English leadership and a total breakdown of morale: 'Finally there was no leader who would collect an army, but each fled as best he could, and in the end no shire would even help the next.'[35] The year 1011 was no better. Attempts to make peace with the Vikings or to buy them off failed miserably: 'for all this truce and tribute they journeyed none the less in bands everywhere, and harried our wretched people, and plundered and killed them'.[36] The year 1012 saw a spectacular tragedy. In the autumn of the previous year the Vikings had 'through treachery' managed to enter Canterbury and to take prisoners, many of them clergy. In return for the city's liberation, they asked for 48,000 pounds. The sum was duly collected and handed over, as agreed, by the following Easter (13 April). But then a further sum, as ransom for the release of Archbishop Aelfheah, was demanded; this Aelfheah himself refused to sanction. On 19 April, during a drunken feast, anger against the archbishop erupted. Aelfheah was seized and:

> shamefully ... put to death. [The Vikings] pelted him with bones and with ox-heads, and one of them struck him on the head with the back of an axe, [so] that he sank down with the blow, and his holy blood fell on the ground and so he sent his holy soul to God's kingdom.[37]

The consequences of Aelfheah's murder were startling. Thorkell, the Viking leader who since 1009 had been terrorizing the country, now switched sides. In return for the substantial sum needed for the upkeep of his fleet of 45 ships, Thorkell promised allegiance to Aethelred.[38] But if Aethelred had imagined there would now be peace, he could not have been more mistaken. Within a matter of months, he had a new, yet more powerful invader to face – King Swein of Denmark. Last seen in England in 1005, Swein now returned – with a vengeance – this time accompanied by his son Cnut. Within a matter of months, Swein had received the submission of everywhere north of Watling Street; Aethelmaer, last seen in retirement in the monastery of Eynsham, responded to the crisis by leaving his monastery seemingly so as to provide leadership in the west, but on seeing that resistance was futile, he too submitted. 'All the nation', declared the *Chronicle*, 'regarded him [Swein] as full king.'[39] Aethelred and Thorkell, who for a time had held out in London, now bowed to the inevitable. Thorkell remained in London, but Queen Emma and the royal children, Edward and Alfred, retreated to Emma's natal Normandy where, after Christmas, they were joined by Aethelred.

Swein had been accepted by a people weary of war; but he was not, or not yet, a crowned king of England and when he unexpectedly died in February 1014 it was not, in the event, to his son, Cnut, that the English turned, but rather to Aethelred, as being their rightful lord and king. Certainty (as ever in this period) is not possible but the likelihood is that the impresario here was Archbishop Wulfstan and that this was the occasion when he delivered his celebrated

Sermon of the Wolf to the English. In this sermon, Wulfstan bitterly chastised the English for their lack of fidelity to God, and to their kings: 'Edward[the Martyr] was betrayed and afterwards killed ... and afterwards Aethelred was driven from the country.'[40] The Vikings are thus presented as God's way of punishing a people who have utterly lost their moral compass, just as previously the English had themselves been let loose on the profligate Britons. But, for Wulfstan, the situation now was yet more desperate – time was short: 'the world is in haste and it nears the end'. The call for repentance was urgent:

> let us do what is necessary for us, turn to the right ... let us order our
> words and deeds rightly ... and keep carefully oath and pledge, and have
> some loyalty between us without deceit ... let us save ourselves from the
> surging fire of hell torment.[41]

But King Aethelred's return, however welcome, was to be conditional. The English throne could again be his 'if', so the *Anglo-Saxon Chronicle* reports, 'he would govern [his people] more justly than he did before'. For his part (again, according to the *Chronicle*), Aethelred promised that 'he would be a gracious lord to them, and reform all the things which they all hated; and all the things that had been said and done against him should be forgiven, on condition that they all unanimously turned to him without treachery'.[42]

How far Aethelred could realistically have been expected to keep Cnut at bay and to restore peace is a moot point, but the first months of his return at least will have given cause for cautious optimism. Wulfstan remained the man behind the throne, drafting legislation designed to emphasize the sacrality of the royal office and the godliness to which all should aspire – the king was described now as 'Christ's deputy in a Christian people' while the people for their part were to 'zealously honour the true Christian religion ... and loyally support one royal lord'.[43] Meanwhile, Aethelred's first campaign against Cnut succeeded in dislodging him from his base in Lindsey, even if Cnut's subsequent savagery (he mutilated his hostages) will have dampened any rejoicing. Aethelred, moreover, was by now around 50 years of age – a considerable age for any Anglo-Saxon king – and the death in June 1014 of his eldest son, Athelstan, had added to an already volatile situation.

Fig. 29: Lenborough Hoard

The sequence of events following Athelstan's death is difficult to unravel but it would seem that Aethelred's second son, Edmund, now attempted to bolster his position as the new heir, a move which Eadric Streona, still Aethelred's favourite, was determined to resist. Treachery and murder became again the order of the day. In the summer of 1015, Cnut returned to England determined to pursue conquest. Aethelred fell ill; at a crucial moment Eadric, surmising which way the wind was blowing, deserted Aethelred. His one miscalculation would be that Cnut would reward him for this; once he had become firmly established, though not before, King Cnut did not hesitate to have him executed.

In April 1016 Aethelred died. Cnut's conquest of England, well under way, was not yet complete. Edmund had his supporters. At a Battle at Ashingdon, in October 1016, he claimed the ancient heartland of his house, Wessex, leaving Cnut with both Mercia and Northumbria. The plan exposes the fragility of English unity; it failed only because Edmund died just a month after the battle, thus presenting Cnut with an easy opportunity to take over Edmund's share. Rivals were now eliminated or isolated – Edmund's younger brother was murdered; his half-brothers, Edward and Alfred, took refuge in Normandy. To their story (and to the story of their mother, Emma, whom Cnut married) we will need to return, but we should consider first how Cnut governed his newly acquired kingdom and how he fashioned his rule.

Thanks to Henry of Huntingdon, writing in the twelfth century, Cnut has become remembered as the king who learnt the limits of his power by allowing the tide to sweep over him as he sat by the sea-shore:

> jumping back, the king cried, 'Let all the world know that the power of kings is empty and worthless, and there is no king worthy of the name save Him by whose will heaven, earth and sea obey eternal laws.' Thereafter King Cnut never wore the golden crown, but placed it on the image of the crucified Lord in eternal praise of God the great king.[44]

What makes this anecdote of particular interest is that it seems as if Cnut was indeed obsessed with crowns as a display of both his regality and his piety.[45] His earliest coins, minted not long after his accession, portray him wearing a crown, even though this was far from the norm. In the portrait of Cnut and Emma that forms the frontispiece of the *Book of Life* given by the royal couple to Winchester in 1030/1, Cnut is depicted with a crown of a design similar to that shown on his coins except that it now has an extra arched bar spanning its centre. This bar transforms the crown into a symbol of imperial power since it was precisely a crown of this design that German emperors wore. Henry II, after his coronation as emperor in 1014, had hung his crown above the altar at St Peter's, where it is highly probable that Cnut himself saw it when he visited Rome in 1027 in order to attend the imperial coronation of Conrad II.

There was, of course, nothing hyperbolic or exaggerated about Cnut's imperial claims. The attraction of becoming king of England for Cnut must always have been that it could furnish an easy supply of money and men to enable him to pursue his ambitions elsewhere. Cnut was no younger son in search of new lands and although he had a brother, Harald, who laid some claims to Denmark, by 1019 Harald had disappeared from the scene, leaving Cnut's claims to the Danish throne unchallenged. Cnut was also determined to regain control of Norway, which (with the help of the Swedes) had slipped from his father's hands. The chronology here is uncertain, but in a letter to the English sent soon after his Rome visit of 1027, Cnut already calls himself 'king of all England, and of Denmark and of the Norwegians and of part of the Swedes'.[46]

The consequences for England of Cnut's imperial dreams were dramatic and far-reaching. By 1017, he had divided the country into four. Wessex he kept for himself; East Anglia he gave to Thorkell; Mercia to Eadric Streona; Northumbria to a Norwegian, Erik of Lade. These divisions may always have been envisaged as temporary, intended to facilitate the collection of the huge sums (10,500 marks from London and 72,000 from the rest of the country) that Cnut was demanding so as to be able to pay off and send back to Denmark many of those who had helped his conquest. Given Eadric's track record, it is indeed hard to imagine that Cnut could have singled him out for any permanent post of responsibility and, indeed, by Christmas he had been executed. Nor was his the only head to roll. The *Anglo-Saxon Chronicle* gives the names of Cnut's other victims: Northman, the son of Ealdorman Leofwine of Mercia; Aethelweard of Wessex; and Brihtric of Devonshire; all were killed in 1017. To this list of native 'casualties' should be added the names of those who had died during the intense period of fighting that had culminated in the Battle of Ashingdon, where, in the words of the *Anglo-Saxon Chronicle*, 'all the nobility of England was there destroyed'.[47] Hyperbole, perhaps, but the sense of desolation, treachery and savagery the *Chronicle* gives is hard to discount. Nor was it only those in the South of England who had suffered. In Northumbria, in 1016, Edmund's ally Uhtred, despite having surrendered, had been executed on the orders of Eadric, along (or so it came to be remembered) with 40 of his followers.[48]

Although it is generally assumed that Cnut was crowned, there is in fact no record of such a ceremony; nor is it even certain at what point he accepted Christianity, though it does seem he was not baptized as an infant.[49] But during his early years as an English king, while he was still learning how to present himself as a Christian leader, Cnut had the fortune to be able to rely on the help and guidance of Wulfstan of York. Whether Wulfstan regarded Cnut as having been sent by God to punish the sins of the English or as a harbinger of the last days (or both) must remain an open question, but there can be no doubt that Wuflstan was a pragmatist: the work he had begun under Aethelred he would continue now under Cnut. His message of repentance would be the same. In 1018, at a meeting in Oxford that was minuted by Wulfstan, the English and Danes (according to the *Anglo-Saxon Chronicle*) 'reached an agreement'. Quite what was discussed on this occasion is uncertain, but it would seem to have taken place soon after Cnut, now furnished with the requested tribute, had sent back to Denmark his troops (with their well-lined pockets) keeping back only 40 ships to act as a permanent fleet. After the meeting, Wulfstan could accordingly report that there was now 'peace and friendship' between Danes and English; that all had promised to obey the laws of King Edgar and that 'they would with God's help investigate further at leisure what was necessary for the nation'.[50] And so indeed they did. The results, as found in the lawcodes known as I and II Cnut, have sometimes been seen as perplexing documents, more akin to homilies than to law codes; such a distinction would have meant very little to Wulfstan himself.

Law, for Wulfstan, was God's law.[51] In his codes he was not attempting a new legislative framework; rather what interested him was the re-iteration of old laws, occasionally elaborated or modified, and only sometimes supplemented. He was content to repeat as necessary laws that went back as far as the seventh century. Wulfstan could preach with a shattering sense of urgency. At the same time, he knew how to bring some perspective to England's woes. Its history provided Wulfstan with lessons as well as consolations – his were not the only times when God had been angry with the inhabitants of the island. Gildas had told of the sins of the British and their punishment; Alcuin had lamented the destruction of Lindisfarne, but had taught that the chastisement of God could yet be a sign of his love; King Alfred had faced the Vikings confident that the cultivation of wisdom could bring him military success; King Alfred's translation of Pope Gregory's *Pastoral Care* was a book which we know Wulfstan read with particular care; the copy he annotated survives to this day.

With Wulfstan's help, Cnut could be seen as a Christian ruler and there is no doubt that Cnut was proud of this image and cultivated it assiduously. It mattered to him that he could take his place among the Christian elite of Europe, that he could journey to the papal court at Rome, arrange a marriage alliance with Emperor Henry II and present rich gifts to potentates across Europe. He was well aware that this new representation of himself as a Christian ruler might in some circles raise eyebrows: the bishop of Chartres, thanking him for a gift, indeed expressed delighted surprise at finding not a 'prince of pagans' but rather 'a most generous benefactor to churches and to the servants of God'.[52] But despite ostentatious displays of his Christianity, Cnut never attempted to repudiate his past. At the Old Minster, in Winchester, it is possible that the stone fragment depicting a scene from a Scandinavian saga was commissioned by Cnut.[53] Certainly at his court, Cnut continued to expect and to encourage the traditional Skaldic verse of his homeland: this, for example, is how it seemed appropriate for his victories against the English to be celebrated:

> Strong Scylding, you performed/a feat of battle under the shield;/the blood-crane[raven] received dark morsel at Ashingdon./Prince, you won by fighting a great/enough name/with a mighty sword nearby/to the north of the Forest of Dean, and it seemed a slaughter to his retinue.[54]

Given the complexity of Skaldic verse as well as the linguistic differences between Old Norse and Anglo-Saxons, it is impossible to be sure that the English among Cnut's court circle would have necessarily understood all that was being sung in a praise-poem such as this.[55] By contrast, it would have taken no particular skill to understand that Cnut, *more Danico*, had two wives: sometime between 1013 and 1016, during the attempt by Cnut's father Swein to strengthen his position in the midland, he had been married to Aelfgifu of Northampton, by whom he had two sons, Swein and Harold Harefoot (to Harold we must return later). However, no sooner had Cnut become king of England than he married again – this time taking as his wife Emma of Normandy, the widow of Aethelred. During the succession disputes that followed Cnut's death, attempts were made to denigrate Aelfgifu by calling her a concubine, but, during Cnut's lifetime, there is no evidence that anyone criticized Cnut's polygyny, despite the strict views of Wulfstan on the proper enforcement of Christian marriage.

After Cnut's death, the competing claims of his children by both marriages, together with the claims of the sons of Emma and Aethelred, would see the return of mayhem and murder, but it must be said that once Cnut had established himself as king, England under his rule seems to have enjoyed a period of relative peace. The question to be asked is at what cost? Constructing any narrative for the reign is made difficult by the laconic entries given in the *Anglo-Saxon Chronicle*. But does this silence represent surly acquiescence in Cnut's rule or relief at the peace he had been able to impose – or both? The limited evidence that we have would seem to suggest that Cnut himself remained ever vigilant: in 1021, for example, Thorkell was banished, just in case he had been plotting against Cnut during the king's absence in Denmark in 1020. And London, ever suspect since it had been loyal to Edmund until his dying day, was always kept under close supervision.

London was crucial to Cnut, since it was there that he kept his fleet of (initially) 40 ships, manned by *lithsmen*, who were paid for out of the heregeld (the tax instituted by Aethelred in 1012 to pay for his Scandinavian mercenaries and not abolished until 1051). Cnut gradually reduced the number of ships he had on 'stand-by', but, nevertheless, there will have been times during his reign when London was housing as many as 3,000 of his mercenaries. It would have been hard not to feel that here was a city under occupation, all the more since the city's assembly was, in the time of Cnut, known not by an Anglo-Saxon name, but by the Danish name 'husting' and it met under a 'staller'; 'stallers', also a name of Scandinavian origin, were members of the king's household who among their other duties might be expected to lead men into battle. Something of the tensions within the city can be sensed through the accounts of the translation of St Aelfheah's relics from London to Canterbury. This was a sensitive moment given that Aelfheah had been murdered only some 12 years earlier by drunken Vikings. His body was thus a natural focus for any resistance to the new regime. Cnut therefore felt it expedient that he pay Aelfheah special honour by moving him to Canterbury and that the move would make it easier for him to control his cult there than it would be in London. The late eleventh-century account of the translation recounts an elaborate plot, involving housecarls, who both incite strife and then control it, as Cnut attempts to smuggle the body out of the city, in a graphic reminder of how in London no love was lost on Cnut.[56]

'Housecarls' were once assumed to form Cnut's standing army; it is now thought rather that they should be seen as the equivalent of household knights. But the likelihood is that Cnut did have a number of armed garrisons. In the nineteenth century, evidence of the burial of a Viking warrior and his horse was discovered in the River Thames, on the edge of Oxford, close by a church dedicated (now) to St Clement's. Although there is no evidence for this church before 1120 and although it is generally assumed that the burial must be no later than 1000, it is hard not to connect this find with the large number of dedications to St Clement that spring up in the first decades of the eleventh century and to postulate that there may have been a number of garrison churches strategically positioned by river bridges. St Clement's churches, are found, for example, in just such positions at Norwich, Cambridge, Worcester and Rochester.[57]

Cnut died at Shaftesbury in 1035. He was buried at Winchester, close it seems to the tomb of St Swithun, a final expression of the claim already made in the Winchester *Book of Life*, that he was heir to the traditions of the house of Wessex. There is, of course, a profound irony here in that it was precisely Cnut's advancement of Godwine, as Earl of Wessex, that would so fatally harm the chances of the last scion of the Wessex dynasty, Edward the Confessor, of governing with the authority Cnut had been able to impose. However, during Cnut's reign, there is no sign of Godwine acting as 'the over-mighty

Fig. 30: The Gokstad ship, Vikingskipmuseet, Oslo

subject'; rather he was one, albeit the most powerful, of a number of English men from hitherto insignificant families on whom Cnut increasingly came to rely in his latter years. To be sure, Cnut did not ignore his Danish followers – men such as Tovi the Proud, whose grandson emerges in the Domesday book as a prosperous landowner with possessions spread across many shires – but what is striking is the emergence of a new class of Englishmen who now appear as witnesses on royal charters and who in the main had displaced the old aristocracy of the tenth century. Such men had no appetite for a repetition of the strife of their grandfathers' day. Contrary to expectation, the world had not ended in 1000 (as Wulfstan had feared), nor even in 1033, the millennium of the Crucifixion – another suggested date. There was even good weather.[58] Given peace, these men could thus enjoy the fruits of their estates, display their status and enjoy all manner of new luxuries.[59] Nevertheless, circumstances would sometimes conspire against them.

On Cnut's death the fragility of his empire (and indeed once more of the unity of England) was again exposed. The complexities caused by Cnut's two marriages proved to be considerable. Queen Emma claimed that when she had married Cnut he had given his word that it would be her children alone who would have any claim to the English throne; in other words, Cnut's sons by Aelfgifu of Northampton would be passed over (as indeed would Emma's sons by Aethelred). When Cnut died in 1035, Aelgifu's sons, Swein and Harold Harefoot, had, in fact, already acted as regents for their father in Norway and Denmark, respectively, so that the road might have seemed clear for Emma's son Harthacnut to have England.[60] But when Cnut died, Harthacnut was in Denmark, rather than in England, which made it difficult for him to press his claim, whereas Harold Harefoot, who had no intention of relinquishing what he considered to be his right to reign (as had his father) over a united kingdom, was in England. Old enmities now re-appeared, with Leofric of Mercia and the fleet at London supporting Harold while Godwine and the men of Wessex backed Harthacnut. The result was that once again England was divided, as it had been when Cnut himself had first been accepted as a king of the English (and as had happened too in 955). This time the reality of the division was marked by the appearance, albeit briefly, both of coins bearing the name of Harold and of those bearing the name of Harthacnut.

How long the division would have held, it is impossible now to know. For Emma, Harthacnut's failure to arrive in England seriously undermined his position. At this juncture, the sons Emma had borne Aethelred, having spent Cnut's reign in the safety of Emma's natal country Normandy, made a dramatic appearance in England, seemingly summoned by their mother in her determination to prevent Harold from asserting his claim to be sole ruler. The elder of the two, Edward, went straight to Winchester in order to join his mother there, but Alfred made his way to London so as to meet Harold. But instead of the expected parley, Alfred and his entourage were arrested. His men were treated with various forms of brutality; Alfred himself was put on a ship bound for the monastery of Ely. While on board, Alfred was blinded, and soon afterwards he died from his injuries. This much is not in dispute; what will never be known for sure is whether the letter asking Edward and Alfred to join her was indeed written by Emma or whether (as she herself later claimed) the letter was a forgery penned by Harold Harefoot so as to give him the chance of eliminating his rivals. Nor can it ever be certain whether it was Harold or Godwine who was responsible for the orders to blind Alfred; but what is clear is that Godwine had undoubtedly (and seemingly suddenly) abandoned Harthacnut and, with him, Emma. Harold was now proclaimed king of all England; Emma was put on a ship and sent to Flanders (in a memorable phrase from the *Chronicle* she was 'driven out without any mercy to face the raging winter').[61]

At this juncture, fate introduced a further twist: Harthacnut, having resolved his Danish problems, was now determined to make good his claim to the English throne. How much support he would have been able to muster was never put to the test because Harold died unexpectedly, thus removing the need for any fight. 'The nobles of almost the whole of England sent to Bruges for Harthacnut', reported the *Chronicle*, '... thinking they were acting wisely.'[62] It did not take long for the nobility to regret their choice. 'During the time of his reign', the *Chronicle* continues, '[Harthacnut] did nothing worthy of a king as long as he lived.'[63] It is a telling phrase. Magnanimity had long been expected from kings. Harold's record may not have been promising, but Harthacnut's actions were unprecedented. In 1040, he gave orders that Harold be dug up from his grave at Westminster and that his body be thrown into the River Thames; the following year, the men of Worcester killed two of the king's tax-collectors – he had imposed a particularly severe tax so as to pay off the large fleet he assembled in preparation for his anticipated fight for the throne of England before the death of Harold obviated the need. In fury, Harthacnut 'had all Worcestershire ravaged'. The *Chronicle* then goes on to report how Harthacnut's surviving half-brother, Edward, arrived in England to join the royal court.[64] Whether Harthacnut felt Edward-at-court was safer than Edward-in-exile is impossible to say, but in the event it proved, as we shall see, a propitious move.

8

ENGLAND *TEMPORE REGIS EDWARDI*

> 1041: And soon in that year there came from beyond the sea Edward, his brother [of Harthacnut] on the mother's side, the son of King Ethelred, who had been driven from his country many years before – and yet he was sworn in as king; and he thus stayed at his brother's court as long as he [Harthacnut] lived.
>
> (*Anglo-Saxon Chronicle*)[1]

The return to England in 1041 of Aethelred's son Edward is a puzzling episode: was it that King Harthacnut, already a sick man (he was to die the following year), was in search of a successor? Or had Harthacnut already made so many enemies (not least by the high levels of taxation that he levied) that he needed a new ally? How far might the invitation have been engineered by Queen Emma, mother of both Harthacnut and Edward, in an attempt to make good the family rifts she had herself, through the pursuit of her own political ambitions, done so much to create? All such suggestions are possible, even probable, but none is as straightforward as the evidence provided by an early twelfth-century preface to a compilation of Anglo-Saxon legal documents. Here we are presented with a clear narrative: Edward, it appears, is recalled at the bidding of the bishop of Winchester and of Earl Godwine. Acting with them are 'the thegns of all England' who have gathered together at a place called *Hursteshevet* where it was allegedly settled that 'he would be received as king only if he would guarantee to them upon oath that the laws of Cnut and his sons should continue in his time with unshaken firmness'.[2]

A recent analysis of the proceedings at *Hursteshevet* has put forward substantial reasons for accepting that the meeting did indeed take place (however late the evidence may be) and convincing arguments for the importance of the occasion as well as its location.[3] The place has been identified as Hurst Beach, a spit of land on the Hampshire coast, easily accessible from the Isle of Wight. Given that the Isle of Wight was sometimes used as a staging post on the way to and from Normandy, and given too that islands (which Hurst Beach approximates) were often deliberately chosen for delicate negotiations, this seemingly obscure location becomes readily intelligible. For both ideological and practical reasons, it was a highly suitable spot. What, then, of the oath and what of the company?

Cnut's laws – not unsurprisingly, given their monumental character – had become the yardstick by which good government and justice could be measured. The idea that a king needed to govern 'justly' had, of course, long been understood – it was, for example, only on such terms that Aethelred had been allowed to return in 1014 – but the great codifications of English law made for Cnut by Wulfstan, archbishop of York, further enshrined notions of what was right and proper for the well-being of a kingdom. At the time of the Hurst Beach meeting, those present had plenty of reason to feel justice was again in jeopardy. Quite apart from the possible motives of Godwine and of the Bishop of Winchester in the negotiations with Edward (and any guess as to what these might be is indeed likely to implicate Queen Emma, now ensconced in Winchester), equally intriguing is the presence of the thegns and their sense of what could be expected of kingly behaviour. Who, indeed, were these thegns? And within the highly theocratic kingdom for which Wulfstan (and therefore Cnut) had legislated, what roles might they be expected to play?

The thegns of Hurst Beach cannot, in reality, have been the 'thegns of all England', but we can suppose a company of 'king's thegns', led by a posse of earls.[4] The increase in the eleventh century of 'ordinary' thegns had been worrying to a moralist such as Archbishop Wulfstan – in the mid-eleventh century, there may have been as many as four thousand such – but 'king's thegns' remained a select company numbering perhaps only a hundred. The status of any thegn depended not only on the possession of land (an average village was the minimum expected holding), but also on the duties he was expected to exercise at local courts and in military attendance on the lord to whom he had commended himself. King's thegns did not necessarily have vast estates but their responsibilities were commensurate with their status; should they themselves flout the law, it was the king himself who would hear their case. If found guilty they were likely to be charged larger fines than would have been demanded of an 'ordinary' thegn. Their experience of court life and of manifold duties they might be asked to undertake for their king would then have stood them in good stead for any putative expedition to Hurst Beach.[5]

This supposed Hurst Beach contingent did not have long to wait to enjoy the fruits of their 1041 enterprise, nor (it may be imagined) to congratulate themselves on their prescience. Edward was already at court early in 1042; then, on 8 June came the unexpected death of Harthacnut while at a wedding feast for the daughter of Osgod *clapa* to Tovi the Proud. Both Osgod *clapa* and Tovi had belonged to Cnut's court circle and as such it seems that after Harthacnut's death their days were numbered: Osgod *clapa* was outlawed in 1046; the fate of Tovi the Proud is more difficult to trace, but it would look as if he, too, fell out of favour, as did his son Athelstan, much of whose property passed to Harold Godwineson. For Edward, there would always be scores to settle. For decades to come, the threat of further Scandinavian incursions remained potent; Osgod himself attempted a revenge attack in 1049, successfully plundering the shores of Essex, even if much of his booty was subsequently lost at sea.

Edward's insecurities can hardly cause surprise. Edward had returned on conditions not unlike those imposed on his father Aethelred in 1014 and which Edward will have had good reason to remember. Edward will have been about 7 when he had first gone into exile the year before; what is noticeable is that it was this young boy who was then chosen just the following year to act as guarantor of his father's good faith and to relay his promise to his people that he would 'be a gracious lord to them, and reform all the things which they all hated'. In return, 'every Danish king [was declared] an outlaw forever'.[6] The triumph of Aethelred's return was, of course, to prove remarkably short-lived: within two years the king lay dead,

England again had a Danish King and Edward was starting a new period of exile that this time was to last some 25 years, bitterly interrupted only by the traumatic events of 1036 when the visit he made together with his brother Alfred culminated in Alfred's murder and the accession the following year of his half-brother Harold. It need then cause no surprise that Edward can appear a wary king, no more so than when his relationship with the Godwine family is considered.

The politics of Edward's reign were indeed dominated in one way or another by the family of the Godwinesons. Given the likely complicity of Earl Godwine in the murder of Alfred, any reconciliation must have required considerable forbearance and there can be no doubt that Edward harboured bitter memories concerning those many years-in-waiting and in particular the ways in which his mother had abandoned him and his ancestral rights. In 1043 (according to the D-text of the *Anglo-Saxon Chronicle*), Edward rode to Winchester, where he confiscated all his mother's treasures 'which were beyond counting, because she had formerly been very hard to the king, her son, in that she did less for him than he wished both before he became king and afterwards as well'. At the same time according to the *Chronicle*, her faithful ally Stigand, bishop of Winchester, was deprived (in the event, temporarily) of his office 'because he was closest in his mother's counsel'.[7]

On his ride to Winchester, Edward had been accompanied by the earls Siward of Northumbria, Leofric of Mercia and Godwine of Wessex. This was not a band of friends; both Siward and Leofric were deeply dismayed by the power of the Godwinesons and between them they and their families encapsulate the history of Edward's reign. A brief summary of their careers and of their families' fortunes therefore repays attention. Let us start with Siward.[8]

Siward was apparently Danish; in the *Life of Edward the Confessor*, he is described as 'earl of the Northumbrians, called in the Danish tongue "Digara", that is "The Strong"', and, as earl, he evidently acquired a somewhat fearsome reputation even if Edward's *Life* praises not only the severity but also the effectiveness of his justice: robbers were mutilated or killed, whatever their class, and for once the North knew 'the quietness of peace'.[9] Siward has a particular place in historical memory, through his championing of the cause of his uncle Malcolm in his fight against Macbeth, as immortalized by Shakespeare, but stories of his prowess abounded much nearer his own time. In Henry of Huntingdon's *History*, for example, he appears to fit every stereotype required of the heroic, Christianized Viking. He thus remains faithful to Scandinavian traditions, founding a monastery dedicated to St Olave, where he insists he will be buried as befits a warrior. But his fatal illness was dysentery and the thought that he might share 'the ignominious death of a cow' is so appalling to him that he calls out 'At least clothe me in my impenetrable breastplate, gird me with my sword, place my helmet on my head, my gilded battle-axe in my right, that I, the bravest of soldiers, may die like a soldier.'[10]

Siward's heir was Waltheof. When Siward died, in 1055, Waltheof was only a boy, but there can be little doubt that the choice of Tostig, son of Earl Godwine, to succeed to the earldom in his stead would have caused Siward deep distress, as indeed it did perhaps too to Earl Leofric who is likely to have hoped for the earldom for his own son, Aelfgar. Neither Siward nor Leofric had any bonds tying them to the Godwines; together, they had in fact attempted to resist the creeping influence of the family over Edward (even if during the crisis of 1051/2, as we shall see, they accepted that civil war should be avoided and that the presence of the Godwines had somehow to be tolerated). The appointment of Tostig to the northern earldom was, however, to prove a disaster.

In the *Life of Edward the Confessor*, Tostig, nonetheless, appears in a glowing light: pious, well-connected (he was married to Countess Judith of Flanders) and wise. There can be no doubt of his ambition: he and Judith appear to have been lavish patrons of Durham Cathedral and much is made in the *Life* of Tostig's journey to Rome in 1061 and his encounters with Pope Nicholas II. But among the local nobility he was far from popular. The exact causes of their discontent are hard to unravel, but it seems as if Tostig may have tried to abolish some of the customs enshrined in the 'Danelaw' provisions which Edgar and Aethelred had made. In any case, so far as the rebels were concerned, Tostig had to go. In his stead, they asked for Morcar, a younger son of Aelfgar who had been passed over in 1055. The rebels' ferocious attack on Tostig's hall in York in 1065 seems to have taken both Tostig and King Edward by surprise (both at the time were hunting together in Wiltshire).

Henrietta Leyser

Tostig's brother, Harold, was sent North to attempt to bring peace, but to no avail. Within a matter of weeks, Edward capitulated: Tostig sailed to Flanders and Morcar took his place. What could not, of course, have been foreseen is that Tostig's attempt to return in 1066 would not only lead to his own death at the Battle of Fulford the same year, but would also so seriously weaken Harold's fighting power that he, too, would that year fall in battle – before William the Conqueror at Hastings.

Morcar himself survived 1066; he came, it must be said, from a family of survivors.[11] His grandfather Leofwine had kept his position, even though his eldest son was among those murdered in Cnut's purge of the native aristocracy of 1017. Leofwine seems to have died sometime after 1023; at some point thereafter, difficult to determine with any certainty, his son Leofric rose from the shrievalty of Worcester to an earldom. He soon became embroiled in national politics, supporting Harold against Harthacnut; in this way, he placed himself in the opposing camp to Earl Godwine and during Edward the Confessor's reign he often appears as a thorn in Godwine's side, at the same time as trying to keep the peace. Thus, in the crisis of 1051 (during Edward's attempt to emancipate himself from the grip of the Godwines), Leofric did all he could to support Edward, while still counselling against any action that could precipitate civil war. In 1057, his son Aelfgar succeeded to the Mercian earldom on his father's death, whereupon he was forced to relinquish his position as the East Anglia earl. This earldom was then passed to Gyrth, brother of Harold Godwineson. It was not therefore surprising that Aelfgar pursued his father's dismay at the ever-rising power of the Godwine family, but with more force and less diplomacy than his father, and twice incurring exile as a result.

We come finally to the last of the trio who rode to Winchester in 1043: Godwine of Wessex. The origins of Godwine's family are far from certain; all that can be safely said is that it was under Cnut that Godwine rose to power.[12] According to the highly partisan *Life of King Edward,* at an early stage in his career as king of England, Cnut invited Godwine to accompany him to Denmark on a trip which seemingly sealed their friendship. Godwine now took the place previously occupied by Thorkell the Tall, the earl of East Anglia, with whom Cnut had recently quarrelled. Godwine was appointed Earl of Wessex and as such, judging by the witness lists to charters, became the premier earl, but little is otherwise known of his career during Cnut's reign and it is only during the succession crises following Cnut's death that Godwine appears centre stage – and in very questionable light: there can be little doubt that he had a significant part to play in the murder of Edward's brother Alfred, despite the oath he subsequently swore that all he had done was to obey the orders of the then king Harold Harthacnut. Nevertheless, once Edward became king, Godwine seems to have found royal favour; by then he was evidently so powerful that Edward dared not antagonize him; instead he significantly advanced the family's wealth and influence. Godwine's eldest son Swein became earl of Hereford, a position he only temporarily lost, despite periods of exile, for various sins (once for the abduction of the abbess of Leominster in the hope of obtaining her lands and once for the murder of a cousin). Godwine's second son, Harold, became earl of East Anglia; Wessex went to a younger son, Gyrth, and a nephew, Beorn, was given an earldom in the South-East Midlands. To cap it all, in 1045 Edward married Godwine's daughter, Edith.

Edward, after his death, would be cast as a Virgin King, notable for his piety and monastic qualities. It is doubtful whether in his lifetime anyone would have recognized this image. There is no reason whatsoever to believe that Edward and Edith had sworn a pact of conjugal abstinence and every reason to think otherwise. The marriage makes sense primarily as a means of securing a dynasty of Godwine-related kings and there is indeed evidence of prayers being said for royal fertility.[13] But, as the years passed and as no children appeared, Edward, now securely on his throne, had good reason to think it might be possible to rid himself of the influence of the Godwine family. In 1051, the opportunity presented itself. The details of that year vary from one account to another, but that it was a year of high drama is abundantly clear. What follows is primarily the story as the *Life of Edward* recounts it – partisan though it often is, it has narrative coherence – supplemented by the various versions of the *Anglo-Saxon Chronicle*.

First, the particular circumstances: in October 1050, the archbishop of Canterbury died. The Godwine family were anxious to secure the election of their kinsman Aelric to succeed him, but Edward overruled the nomination and, in March 1051, gave the see to the bishop of London, Robert of Jumièges. That this was part of a wider plan to limit the power of the Godwines seems clear from the evidence of castle-building by Edward's Norman followers in precisely the parts of the country where the Godwinesons held the most estates. A further castle may have been planned for Dover, intended possibly for Eustace of Boulogne, Edward's brother-in-law, newly arrived in England. In 1051, on an expedition to Dover, Eustace and his entourage became embroiled in a fight; on both sides there were casualties. Edward demanded that Godwine mete out punishment, since Kent was under his authority. Godwine refused. Edward summoned a council at Gloucester to meet on 7 September. Here, tempers flew: Robert of Jumièges accused Godwine of the murder of Alfred and now the plotting of Edward's death. Armed conflict seemed imminent; Godwine and his sons Swein and Harold summoned their armies to Beverstone, 15 miles south of Gloucester; Earls Leofric and Siward meanwhile sent for reinforcements of their troops. Nonetheless, there was no appetite for war. The *Chronicle* expressed the anxiety of the earls that such a course of action would encourage invasions from overseas and they urged peace:

> some of them [the earls] thought it would be a great piece of folly if they joined battle, for in the two hosts there was most of what was noblest in England, and they considered that they would be opening a way for our enemies to enter the country and cause great ruin among ourselves.[14]

Godwine instead was put on trial and summoned to appear before Edward in London, on 21 September, the time of the autumn equinox. But when Edward refused to give him hostages so that he could journey with security across the Thames, from Southwark where his manor was, to meet the king in his palace at Westminster, Godwine decided his safest course of action was to set sail. His sons went to Ireland, Godwine and his wife to Flanders. Queen Edith, meanwhile, was dispatched to the nunnery of Wilton: 'Sing, sister Muse, on this a piteous song', declared the *Life of Edward*,[15] while the *Anglo-Saxon Chronicle* simply expressed astonishment at Godwine's fate:

> It would have seemed remarkable to everyone in England if anybody had told them it could happen, because he had been exalted so high, even to the point of ruling the King and all England and his sons were earls and the king's favourites and his daughter was married to the king.[16]

Had Edward long anticipated a show-down with Godwine? It is impossible to say, just as it is equally impossible to know whether there is any truth in the story that Edward was planning to make William of Normandy his heir and that to this end he invited William to England in the winter of 1051. But whatever ambitions and hopes Edward may have entertained, they were soon to be dashed: within the year, Godwine and his family were back. The Thames at London, again, saw the dénouement of the scene, but this time it would be Godwines who would triumph. Seemingly, Earl Godwine had both more men at his command than had Edward and more men with a stomach for a fight; the king's men, meanwhile, as at Gloucester, were hesitant to engage in combat with other Englishmen:

> it was hateful to almost all of them to fight against men of their own race, for there was little else that was worth anything apart from Englishmen on either side; and also they did not wish the country to be more laid open to foreigners through their destroying each other.[17]

Godwine, allegedly, again protested his innocence of the original charge and was restored to favour. His family likewise recovered all their possessions and Queen Edith was returned to court. A number of 'Frenchmen' were outlawed, the king being allowed to keep only a select company of those of proven loyalty both to him 'and to all the people'.[18] Robert of Jumièges, whose election had arguably triggered the whole fracas, set off for Rome to launch an appeal, but died at Jumièges, soon after to be replaced at Canterbury by Stigand of Winchester, the very bishop whom Edward had deprived of his see when he first became king. In celebration of the end of the affair, the *Life of Edward* once more addressed the Muse: 'You too make singing tunes with leaping verse/With me rejoicing at this settlement.'[19]

Once returned, the Godwines were given more power than ever before, though Earl Godwine himself died not long after the family triumph, in April 1052. His son Harold succeeded to his earldom of Wessex; East Anglia temporarily left the family's hands, but before long it, too, had become again Godwine property. Edward's extraordinary passivity, even acquiescence and collusion in the growing power of the Godwines, has long raised the question: Edward: man or mouse? And who, given the return of his wife (with whom, for whatever reasons, he had been unable to have children), did he imagine would be his heir? These are difficult questions which not surprisingly have long been the subject of controversy, but which even in the asking raise important questions about the nature of royal power in late Anglo-Saxon England.

Earldoms, it is clear, were in the royal gift. Earls, the eleventh-century successors of ealdormen, could be made and unmade by the king and the office was not hereditary. Nor was the earldom of any fixed shape. Thus, while it is clear that earls were entitled to a share of the royal dues which each shire was expected to render to the king, it is not at all clear at any one moment which shires belonged to which earldom; earldoms could grow but they could also shrink. While such a system gave enormous powers of patronage to the king, the great families from whom earls came also had lands in their own right, together with men who were commended to them. No king then, as Edward was to find, could afford to pick a fight with an earl, unless he was sure he had adequate support from other *earlisc* families and this is precisely what Edward lacked. His years in exile, his marriage into the family of a new aristocrat (it was Cnut, as we have seen, who had 'created' the Godwines), had deprived him of the opportunity of building up a group of nobles whose loyalty was beyond question and who would stand by him with unwavering tenacity; 1052 bears witness to just this lack.[20]

The year 1052 reveals, then, a king who knew the limitations of his power. But Edward, quite as much as Earl Leofwine of Mercia, was a survivor and it would be a mistake to think that he was as yet a broken man. He still had cards to play. The fact that a Godwine could, in 1066, become a king of England does not mean that after the Godwines' triumph of 1052 this would have seemed inevitable or even likely. The Godwines lacked even a trickle of royal blood. As such, they could not possibly be considered 'aethelings', a status that could, however, most certainly be claimed by Edward's nephew, Edward 'the exile', the son of King Edmund Ironside, whom Cnut had banished in 1017. In 1054, so just two years after King Edward's capitulation to the house of Godwine, an embassy was sent to Germany (where Edward 'the exile' had married into the imperial house) and in 1057 Edward duly returned home, but he died before he could even reach court. Lack of evidence makes it impossible to cry murder, but that there was great grief at his death is recorded by the

Anglo-Saxon Chronicle (D-text): 'Alas, that was a miserable fate and grievous to all this people that he so speedily ended his life after he came to England, to the misfortune of this poor people.'[21] Even then, Edward need not have given up all hope that an 'aetheling' could yet succeed him. Edward 'the exile' had a son, Edgar, who seems to have come to England with his father, and whose claim even after the Battle of Hastings could still rally enemies of the new regime. But whether such a claim would have had more chance of success had Edward in his last years backed him with more vigour than seems to have been the case must remain an open question. Edward may have been (as many historians have suggested) pusillanimous; but equally he may have been shrewd enough to foresee the possibility that the Godwines would destroy each other or maybe he was simply sufficiently experienced to know that in any case the vagaries of fate made futile too much planning.

The years after the return of the Godwines in 1052 are often presented as the years when nothing much happened. This is of course precisely the picture which the *Life of Edward* wanted to present: with the return of the Godwines 'the whole country [could] settle[d] down in peaceful tranquillity'.[22] To be sure, the senior Godwine had died soon after his re-instatement, but once Harold had succeeded to his father's earldom, 'the whole English host breathed again and was consoled for its loss'.[23] With the appointment of Harold's brother, Tostig, to the northern earldom, Edward could now relax: 'with Harold [and Tostig] thus stationed in his kingdom, he lived all his life free from care on either flank, for the one drove back the foe from the south and the other scared them off from the north'.[24] The artifice of the picture is such that it deserves quoting at length:

> And so, with the kingdom made safe on all sides by these princes, the most kindly King Edward passed his life in security and peace, and spent much of his time in the glades and woods in the pleasures of hunting. After divine service, which he gladly and devoutly attended every day, he took much pleasure in hawks and birds of that kind which were brought before him, and was really delighted by the baying and scrambling of the hounds.[25]

Was Edward ever so carefree? It would seem highly unlikely. It also needs to be remembered that hunting for any medieval king was never merely pleasurable. Leaving aside its dangers (and who can fail to wonder whether King William Rufus, who met his death hunting in the New Forest in 1100, was assassinated or merely unlucky?), hunting provided an opportunity for conspicuous displays of power, and the ostentatious bonding of aristocrats through their feasting together on their quarry.[26] Venison now appeared regularly on the menus of the great along with an astonishing variety of game birds – pheasants and partridges; blackbirds and plovers were also consumed in large quantities. Hunting parties cemented loyalties and celebrated triumphs, though there were times when even the best laid plans could go awry. The sacking of Portskewet, in the south-east of Wales, was one such, an event sufficiently rich in significance to justify closer examination.

Throughout his reign, Edward was, with reason, wary of the unprecedented power in Wales of Gruffydd ap Llywelyn, ruler in the first instance of Gwynedd and Powys but from 1055 master also of the southern cantrefs. The frequency with which Edward held court at Gloucester and his grant of Herefordshire to Ralph of Nantes, seemingly with instructions to fortify it with castles, bear testimony to his anxieties. Particularly dangerous to Edward was the alliance that formed between Gruffydd and Aelfgar of Mercia. Aelfgar, like his father Earl Leofric, was indeed no friend of the Godwinesons, but Aelfgar was more aggressive in his resistance than Leofric had been. Aelfgar's exile in 1055 was almost certainly prompted by his resentment at the appointment of Tostig Godwineson as earl of Northumbria. In response Aelfgar allied himself with King Gruffydd (and married his daughter). Together, they sacked Hereford, putting to ignominious flight the forces of Earl Ralph. Peace was patched up and Aelfgar's exile rescinded, only to be re-imposed in 1058; once again, Aelfgar returned, this time with the help not only of Gruffydd but also of Magnus of Norway.[27] Earl Ralph had meanwhile died. Harold had taken over his earldom, while East Anglia, held by Aelfgar before he succeeded Leofric in Mercia, had gone to Harold's brother Gyrth. Was the growing power of the Godwinesons quite unstoppable?

Early in 1064, so it must have seemed: that year Harold and Tostig were set on destroying King Gruffydd. When their plot to assassinate him failed, they launched a two-pronged attack by land and sea. Gruffydd was forced to sue for peace. Encouraged by this vulnerability, a rival of long-standing, based in Dublin, seized the chance to murder him, but it was Harold who appropriated the glory for his destruction.[28] Harold now was at the height of his power as an earl; he duly planned a celebration. He would build a hunting lodge at Portskewet in the south-east of Wales ready for the start of the new hunting season. There, he would entertain the king. A lavish party was to be arranged. But then, in the words of the *Anglo-Saxon Chronicle*:

> when it was all ready, Caradoc, son of Griffith, went there with all the following he could get and killed nearly all the people who were building there, and they took the goods that were got ready there. We do not know who first suggested this conspiracy. This was done on St Bartholomew's day.[29]

St Bartholomew's day is on 24 August. Some five or so weeks later, rebellion in the North broke out against the rule of Harold's brother. Here again is the *Anglo-Saxon Chronicle*:[30]

> And soon after this [the attack on Portskewet] all the thegns in Yorkshire and in Northumberland came together and outlawed their Earl Tosti and killed his bodyguard, and all they could get at, both English and Danish, and took all his weapons in York, and gold and silver and all his treasure that they could hear about anywhere. And they sent for Morcar, son of Earl Aelfgar, and chose him as their earl, and he went south with all the people of the shire, and of Nottinghamshire, Derbyshire and Lincolnshire until he came to Northampton. And his brother Edwin came to meet him with men that were in his earldom, and also many Welsh came with him. Thereupon Earl Harold came to meet them and they entrusted him with a message to King Edward, and also sent messengers with him, and asked that they might be allowed to have Morcar as their earl. And the king granted this and sent Harold back to them at Northampton on the eve of St Simon and Jude. And he proclaimed this to them and gave them surety for it and renewed there the law of King Cnut.

The feast of St Simon and Jude falls on 28 October. Between the humiliation of Harold at Portskewet and the fall of Tostig in the North, there had then been just two months. Both events show how little love there was for either of these Godwine brothers; even more surprisingly, perhaps, how little love there was between them. When the news broke of the rebellion against him, Tostig was not, in fact, 'at home'; rather, he was with the king, keeping him company

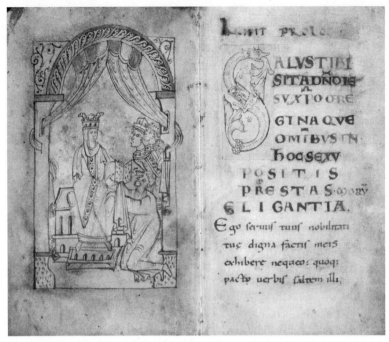

Fig. 31: Encomium of Queen Emma

in one of his many hunting grounds. According to the *Life of Edward* the king did what he could to save Tostig and to secure his restoration in Northumbria, but all to no avail and, as in 1051–52, there was no appetite for war, even though the king considered it. But we need to remember that this is the version of events which Queen Edith wanted recorded, as was the charge that it was Harold himself who had encouraged the rebellion against Tostig. There is no way of verifying this testimony. All we can know is that, by the end of the year, Tostig had taken ship for Flanders, that, in his stead, Northumbria had as its earl Morcar of the house of Leofwine and that Tostig's holdings had been divided up between Harold, Morcar and Morcar's brother Eadwine.

Whatever Edward may himself have thought about the crises of 1065 and of how they would affect any competition for his crown, he must at least have felt assured of the grandeur and success of his cherished project: Westminster Abbey. Though he was not well enough to attend its consecration in the December of 1065, just

Fig. 32: Eadwine Psalter

Fig. 33: Bayeux Tapestry: coronation of Harold

weeks before his death in January 1066 (he seems to have had a series of strokes), he will have known that the abbey would now be ready and able to receive his body. Its building had occupied the better part of his reign, starting already in the 1040s, coinciding most probably with the appointment of Robert of Jumièges as bishop of London (given that there are close parallels between the designs of the new abbey church of Notre Dame at Jumièges, begun *c*.1040, and Westminster). Westminster had, of course, long had an abbey (or rather, originally, a minster), dating from the seventh century, which Dunstan, as archbishop of Canterbury, had re-founded as a Benedictine community *c*.959, but Edward's rebuilding of it was a startling assertion both of a new architectural style and of the increased prominence of London as a major international port.[31] Winchester, long the home of Alfred's dynasty, was now relegated to second place. Emma and Cnut might rest there – and Edith rebuild the nearby nunnery of Wilton – but this perhaps was all the more reason for Edward to choose to build a mausoleum for himself elsewhere. He had, too, a palace built at Westminster and the three occasions when it is known that he ceremonially wore his crown all took place in London.[32]

Crown-wearing was a piece of medieval pageantry long associated with continental kings but somehow regarded until recently as 'un-English' (on the assumption that the English knew how to govern without the need for theatrical displays of power). But it now seems certain that, at least since the tenth century, English kings had found occasions to formally 'wear crowns'.[33] It is also becoming increasingly clear that Edward was a ruler who knew about style. During his years of exile in France, he was recognized as a king-in-exile, even perhaps a king who by virtue of his rank could heal the sick. His failure to produce an heir would in time lead to his portrayal as a monastic ascetic but as suggested there is no evidence to support this picture and plenty that would suggest otherwise. Sometime around 1050, he ordered for himself a new crown made of 'plenty of gold and chosen gems' and it is hard not to believe, despite any protestations to the contrary, that he relished, quite as much as did Queen Edith who was allegedly responsible for his attire, 'the pomp of royal finery'.[34] And there can be no doubt that English fabrics were admired and coveted both at home and abroad.[35] So well-dressed, indeed, was the young aristocrat Gospatric, so luxurious his clothes, that robbers on his route to Rome mistook him for an earl.[36] And after 1066, William and Matilda were careful to keep on their payroll a certain Leofgyth, who was known for the gold embroidery she had made for Edward and Edith.[37]

England in the eleventh century was spectacularly rich and much indeed could be, and was, said with gold. Earl Godwine, on the accession of Edward, had given the king a ship decorated with a golden lion at the stern and at the prow a golden dragon; the description is given in verse but it need not be assumed that much poetic licence was involved.[38] After the murder of King Gruffydd of Wales his head was sent to Edward – but so too were the golden prow and stern of Gruffydd's ship. Display and generosity were a mark of nobility: huge effigies of Christ and of the Virgin were given to their favoured churches by, for example, both Earls Harold and Leofric. Such offerings would later become booty for the Norman Conquerors – 'extremely large gold crucifixes, remarkably adorned with jewels' were taken across the channel and distributed as plunder.[39] But it was not just earls and the king who were enjoying England's wealth; what is striking is how widespread the prosperity was. Across the country, even the small fry among the aristocracy could be found building themselves those homes and churches which would become the staple features of the English village. At the same time, one should beware of imagining that such men were 'only' village squires. Even the most modest country 'gentleman' could be expected to hold property in the town nearest his estates while grander thegns spread their affluence and their influence across

Fig. 34: Bayeux Tapestry: Harold's death

a number of towns, even in places outside their own particular jurisdiction.[40]

It was of course the wealth of England which made its conquest so irresistible to William, duke of Normandy. How or when William first considered that its kingship was a prize within his reach is far less certain – the Norman claim that, during the crisis with the Godwine family in 1051, William had visited England and been designated Edward's heir is only one story among a number in circulation. It was also rumoured (and indeed recorded in the Bayeux Tapestry) that Harold, in 1064, had sworn an oath of fealty to William; furthermore, or so it was argued, Harold's coronation was not only a perfidious act but also invalid as a ceremony because it had been performed by that notorious pluralist Stigand, archbishop of Canterbury and bishop of Winchester. And should anyone still doubt William's claim, was not William's victory at the Battle of Hastings in 1066 a sure sign that God was on William's side?

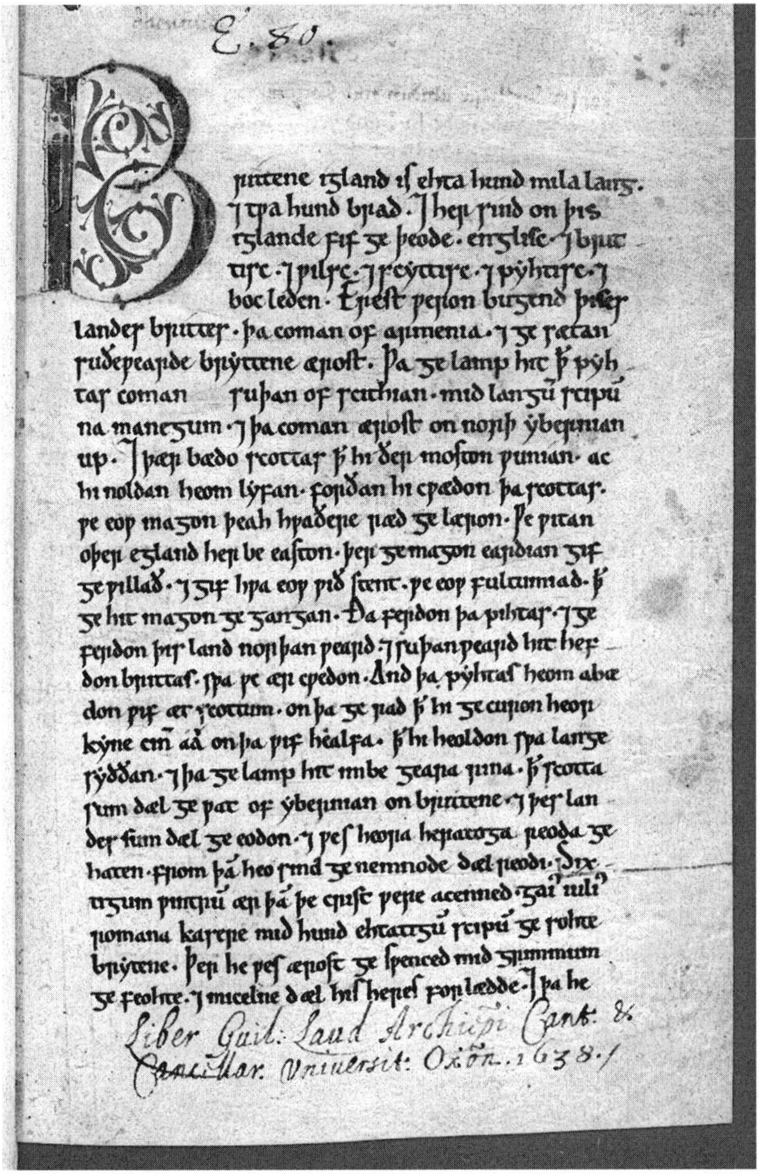

rittene igland is ehta hund mila lang.
7 twa hund brad. 7 her sind on þis
iglande fif ge þeode. englisc. 7 brit
tisc. 7 wilsc. 7 scyttisc. 7 pyhtisc. 7
boc leden. Erest weron bugend þises
landes brittes. þa coman of armenia. 7 ge setan
suðewearde bryttene erost. þa ge lamp hit þ pyh
tas coman suþan of scithian. mid langum scipu
na manegum. 7 þa coman erost on norþ ybernian
up. 7 þer bædo scottas þ hi ðer moston wunian. ac
hi noldan heom lyfan. forðan hi cwædon þa scottas.
we eow magon þeah hwaðere ræd ge læron. we witan
oþer igland her be easton. þer ge magon eardian gif
ge willað. 7 gif hwa eow wið stent. we eow fultumiað. þ
ge hit magon ge gangan. ða ferdon þa pihtas. 7 ge
ferdon þis land norþan weard. 7 suþan weard hit hef
don bryttas. swa we ær cwedon. And þa pyhtas heom abæ
don wif æt scottum. on þa ge rad þ hi ge curon heora
kyne cin aa on þa wif healfa. þ hi heoldon swa lange
syððan. 7 þa ge lamp hit ymbe geara yrna. þ scotta
sum dæl ge wat of ybernian on bryttene. 7 þes lan
des sum dæl ge eodon. 7 wes heora heretoga reoda ge
haten. fram þam heo ynd ge nemnode dæl reodi. Six
tigum wintrum ær þe crist wære acenned. gaiulius
romana kasere mid hund ehtatigu scipu ge sohte
bryttene. þer he wes erost ge swenced mid grimmum
ge feohte. 7 micelne dæl his heres for lædde. 7 þa he

Fig. 35: The initial page of the *Peterborough Chronicle*

Harold, the traitor, would not even be accorded a proper burial, and never, in Norman sources, the title of king.[41]

The Battle of Hastings was no bolt from the blue. Harold had lost no time in claiming the throne – he had been elected and crowned within days of Edward's death, with a haste which suggests he expected his title to be challenged – and by midsummer he had a fleet assembled by the Isle of Wight in readiness lest William should invade. The tragedy for Harold was that he miscalculated: on 8 September, he disbanded his troops thinking (probably) that by then the season for campaigning was over; this was perhaps bad judgement, but what followed could scarcely have been foreseen. Harald Hardrada of Norway, spurred on by Harold's exiled brother Tostig, now invaded England from the North. Landing early in September at the mouth of the River Tyne, Hardrada and Tostig together sailed inland via the rivers Humber and Ouse. On 20 September, just outside York, they met and defeated the forces of the Northumbrian earls Eadwine and Morcar. Harold's response was both swift and devastating: just five days later, he had reached York; and in the Battle of Stamford Bridge, both Hardrada and Tostig were slain.

So far, for Harold, so good, even very good, but now came the news that William had seized the opportunity the northern invasion had offered to chance his crossing. On 28 September, Norman ships, bearing not only William's men but also their horses, landed at Pevensey. Whether his elation at his victory at Stamford Bridge made Harold reckless has been much debated, since what he did not do was pause or replenish his troops, or reward them for their bravery at Stamford Bridge before making another march, this time southwards, towards the Norman encampment. The subsequent Battle of Hastings was, nonetheless, no easy victory for William, yet by the close of day, on 14 October, it was securely his; the English for their part had lost not only their king, but also the better part of their aristocracy: 'Far and wide the earth was covered with the flower of the English nobility and youth, drenched in blood.'[42]

The Battle of Hastings has long taken its place among the list of decisive battles of the world, not least because of the chance survival of the Bayeux Tapestry, with its graphic battle scenes of great Norman stallions bearing their men to victory against Anglo-Saxon foot soldiers.[43] It is as well to remember, therefore, that although the victory paved the way for William's coronation on Christmas

Day 1066, his place on the throne was never particularly secure. His claim to be Edward's heir was at best disingenuous; there were others who could – and with good reason did – challenge these alleged rights.[44] William's response was to build castles and to rule ever more oppressively; if the greatest Anglo-Saxon landowners suffered, so too did the poorest peasants. There was nothing hyberbolic about William's obituary in verse in the *Anglo-Saxon Chronicle* text: 'Into avarice did he fall/and loved greediness above all.'[45]

Norman rule was beyond doubt humiliating and harsh. Its greatest historians – William of Malmesbury and Ordericus Vitalis, themselves of mixed parentage – were conscious that the English had a cherished past, chronicled both in Latin by Bede and in the vernacular by the *Anglo-Saxon Chronicle* that took their history back to the fifth century and beyond. Against such written traditions, the Normans and pagan 'Northmen', converted to Christianity only in 912, could not hope to compete: 'O fools and sinners!' asked Ordericus Vitalis:

> Why did they [the Normans] not ponder contritely in their hearts that they had conquered not by their own strength but by the will of almighty God, and had subdued a people that was greater, and wealthier than they were, with a longer history.[46]

How, why and when English and Norman cultures, nonetheless, finally coalesced is a complex story, glimpsed from time to time in any number of surprising vignettes.[47]

Thus it was at St Albans, home of England's proto-martyr, that a holy woman of Anglo-Scandinavian descent was given the first known text of the Old French legend of St Alexis, a story hitherto known only orally.[48] This text, it seems, was a present from Abbot Geoffrey, originally a schoolteacher from Le Mans who perhaps intended to use the story as an Anglo-Norman primer for a woman for whom he had the highest regard. The woman, Christina, had first visited St Albans as a child together with her rather worldly parents, keen to view the new building the Norman abbot was erecting (after the Conquest, every Anglo-Saxon cathedral would be given a 'bigger and better' look). The trip made a deep impression on Christina, but it was the lecherous advances and devious sexual plots of a Norman bishop (right-hand man to William I and William

II) that later propelled her to flee the world, putting herself under the protection of a Norman hermit, Roger. Christina became for Roger his 'Sunday daughter', 'myn sunendaege dohter'.[49] And it was to her that he left his hermitage at Markyate. On Roger's death, Christina turned to the patronage of Abbot Geoffrey; when he too died, Christina was not forgotten. Henry II, himself the son of an English mother, ensured she was supplied with firewood.

Epilogue

Christina of Markyate was only one of a number of Anglo-Saxon holy men and women to whom the new ruling class turned for spiritual support and advice. They had, they knew, blood on their hands. Despite all arguments to the contrary, and despite the papal banner so proudly displayed by William at Hastings to add legitimacy to his cause, the battle was widely recognized as ungodly, given the death on the battlefield of a consecrated king. Penance was indeed mandated but not everyone was persuaded that the sins of the Normans could be so easily absolved – all the more so given the brutality that followed in the subsequent years. Retribution for rebellion, such as the infamous 'harrying of the north' (following a rebellion against William I in 1071), was perhaps to be expected; but there could be no excuse for the arbitrary and petty displays of power which both the Conqueror and his sons were believed to enjoy – William II, for example, according to the Anglo-Saxon monk Eadmer, arrested 50 of his fellow countrymen on a trumped up charge of having killed and eaten some of the king's deer. Writing some 75 years after the Battle of Hastings, Ordericus Vitalis put into the mouth of the Norman monk Guitmund, to whom the Conqueror had offered a job, this stark refusal:

> After carefully examining the matter I cannot see what right I have to govern a body of men whose strange customs and uncouth speech are unknown to me, whose beloved ancestors and friends you have either put to the sword, driven into bitter exile, or unjustly imprisoned and enslaved ... considering [all these things] I deem all England the spoils of robbery and shrink from it and its treasures as from consuming fire.

England under the Normans then, had a new ruling class; by 1086, thanks to the Domesday Book, the extent of regime change is all too clear. Only two men of Anglo-Saxon origin held significant amounts of land, yet in many other ways it was business as usual: no attempt was ever made to dismantle the Anglo-Saxon system of coinage, nor the institutions – the shires and the hundreds – of local government. It could hardly have been otherwise. The number of Normans who settled in England was comparatively small and there is nothing to suggest the incomers had either the will or the expertise to introduce radical change in the day-to-day management of their newly conquered country. Power was displayed in the rebuilding of cathedrals and in the construction of castles; but having married, in many cases, women of Anglo-Saxon birth, the newcomers were content to take over rather than transform the management of their newly acquired lands.

Until the reign of King John (1199–1216) kings of England saw themselves as being 'kings of the English and the French'.[1] John's recognition, following his loss of Normandy in 1204, that he was king only of the English – a formal acknowledgement that all who lived in England could by now be seen as English, whatever their ethnicity[2] – perhaps goes some way to explain John's reverence for Bishop Wulfstan of Worcester: the only Anglo-Saxon prelate to have kept his office throughout the Conqueror's reign. Worcester is where John chose to be buried; Worcester too is where, at the turn of the twelfth century, the poet Layamon was to be found writing – in English – a new history of his country. Layamon took as his sources books in English, French and Latin. Of these three cultures was England made.

Appendix: Notes on the Illustrations

CHAPTER 1

(1) Spong Hill man: pottery lid

A clay pot lid probably made to fit a cremation urn, found at the early Anglo-Saxon cemetery of Spong Hill, North Elmham, Norfolk.

The Spong Hill cemetery, much in use during the fifth century, was exceptionally large – it contained around 2,500 cremation burials of men, women and children. A number of the pots were decorated; some of the undecorated pots contained animal bones. Many of the pots held a wide range of grave goods: antler combs; tweezers; ivory rings; beads and brooches – depending on the age and sex of the deceased. The similarities with sites across the North Sea suggest that the migrants may have still been in touch with their original homelands. But three-dimensional figures such as this Spong Hill man are for this period extremely rare. S/he is the only known example of this period found in England.

Catherine Hills, Kenneth Penn and Robert Rickett, 'The Anglo-Saxon Cemetery at Spong Hill, North Elmham, Part IV: Catalogue of Cremations', *East Anglian Archaeology* (1987), p. 34.

(2) Mucking belt fitting

A copper-alloy Roman-style military belt set found in an early fifth-century grave in Mucking, Essex.

The Mucking belt buckle may have belonged to one of the German mercenaries employed by the Romans to protect the south coast from invasions and incursions. Mucking, situated close to the Thames estuary, was finally abandoned in the 700s but for millennia it had been an important coastal site.

Sue Hirst and Dido Clark, *Excavations at Mucking: The Anglo-Saxon Cemeteries* (London, 2009).

(3) The first folio of the poem *Beowulf*

The manuscript of the poem *Beowulf* dates perhaps from the late tenth century, perhaps from the early eleventh, but despite such controversies most historians and literary scholars would agree that the actual poem was composed considerably earlier, either in the late eighth or in the ninth century.

A turning point in the reception of the work followed the publication in 1936 of the lecture by J. R. R. Tolkien (of Lord of the Rings fame) in which he proposed that the monsters of the poem, and what they might mean, be taken seriously. Just recently (in 2014) Tolkien's own translation of the poem has finally been published. The edition cited in this chapter has been chosen since it includes both text and translation.

J. R. R. Tolkien, 'Beowulf, the Monsters and the Critics', *Proceedings of the British Academy* (1936), vol. 22.

J. D. Niles, *Beowulf: The Poem and its Tradition* (Cambridge, MA, 1983).

BL, Cotton Vitellius A. xv, f.13.

(4) Replica of the helmet from the Sutton Hoo burial ship, mound 1

When mound one at Sutton Hoo was first excavated in 1939, one of the most spectacular finds were the remnants of this helmet, pictured here in re-constructed form; the helmet, wrapped and placed to the left of the body, had rusted so that when the chamber roof collapsed it had broken into hundreds of fragments.

At the time of its discovery the helmet was remarkable for its rarity; the evidence for helmets from the Staffordshire hoard now provides a different perspective, but the Sutton Hoo helmet is unlikely to ever lose its interest, not least because it was one of the first archaeological finds that could corroborate the splendour of the weapon-loving world depicted in the poem *Beowulf*.

But, of course, it was not simply its iron construction which gave the Sutton Hoo helmet its protective powers. Consider also its iconography: the menacing dragon and the sharp-teethed bird, both with eyes of garnet; the eyebrows of silver wire; the scenes of triumphant warriors. This was indeed a helmet fit for both life and beyond.

British Museum, M&LA 1939, 10-10, I.

(5) Belt buckle from the Sutton Hoo burial ship

The great gold belt buckle from the Sutton Hoo ship burial (mound 1) is remarkable not only for the elaborate beauty of its decorative motifs with its intricately woven pattern of writhing snakes but also for the skilfully hidden catches that fasten it. The belt looks solid but it is in fact hollow, though no evidence has survived of what, if anything, was kept inside.

British Museum

Martin Carver, *Sutton Hoo: A Seventh-Century Princely Burial Ground and its Context* (London, 2005).

(6) Detail from the south face of the Ruthwell Cross, Dumfries and Galloway

Ruthwell lies in the north west corner of Northumbria close to Hadrian's wall. Its cross is particularly famous not simply because of its size (5 metres of red sandstone) but because carved on it, as well as Gospel scenes, are also lines, in runes, from the Anglo-Saxon poem *The Dream of the Rood*. The speaker in the poem is the tree cut down to make the cross on which Christ must hang.

Manchester's Art Museum contains a painted replica of the Ruthwell Cross which gives a startling sense of how the cross would originally have looked.

The cross (cf. the Sandbach crosses) suffered at the hands of iconoclasts in the seventeenth century.

Eamonn O. Carragain, *Ritual and the Rood: Liturgical Images and the Old English Poems of the Dream of the Rood Tradition* (Toronto, 1995).

CHAPTER 2

(7) St Martin's Church, Canterbury

When King Aethelbert of Kent took as his wife the Frankish princess, Bertha, it was understood that provision would need to be made for her to attend Christian services. She had arrived in England accompanied by her own priest, Liudhard; what was needed now was a church. The solution seems to have been to give to Liudhard the old Roman church, dedicated to St Martin of Tours, that stood outside the city walls. Traces at St Martin's of seventh-century work are still visible today.

Nicholas Brooks, *The Early History of the Church at Canterbury* (Leicester, 1984).

(8) St Luke from St Augustine's Gospels

The portrait of St Luke comes from a sixth-century Italian Gospel book. It is thought to have been one of the books supplied by Pope Gregory the Great to the missionaries he sent to England, under the leadership of St Augustine, in 597. The manuscript would once have had pictures of all four evangelists, together with a large number of narrative scenes – possibly 72 in all – taken from the Gospels. Such a number is surprising given the size of the book's pages (250 × 195 mm). A number of captions to the illustrations were added later by an English hand, evidence that the book was in use throughout the Anglo-Saxon period.

Richard Marsden, *The Gospels of St Augustine*, in ed. R.Gameson, *St Augustine and the Conversion of England* (Stroud, 1999).

(9, 10 and 11) Staffordshire Hoard

In 2009, what is known now as the Staffordshire Hoard was unearthed.

No other hoard of such as size has been found before, either in England or abroad, and there is still much work to be done on the thousands of artefacts discovered. What is however immediately striking is that the hoard is made up almost entirely of war gear: countless pommel caps; at least 92 swords and seaxes; a thousand and more fragments of what was clearly a magnificent helmet; and numerous garnet-inlaid gold mounts thought to have come from saddles. Why, as well, the hoard should contain a mangled gold processional cross remains a matter of some controversy, but it is very clear that in some way or other God had his place in the scenario which led to the burying of all this treasure. A strip of gold bears a biblical inscription in Latin which, in translation, reads 'Rise up, O Lord, and may thy enemies be dispersed and those who hate thee be driven from thy face.' (This may come either from Numbers 10.35 or from Psalm 68:1.) Illustrated here are a gold and garnet seax fitting; a gold helmet cheek-piece, decorated with writhing animals; and a gold object (of unknown use) in which two eagles hold a fish in their talons.

Kevin Leahy and Roger Bland, *The Staffordshire Hoard* (London, 2009).

(12) Pictish stone from Aberlemno, possibly commemorating the Battle of Nechtansmere, 685

Five standing stones are to be found in the village of Aberlemno, in Angus, Scotland. On the rear of stone 2, located in the churchyard, a battle scene is in full swing. But is it a particular battle? If so, could it be the Battle of Nechtansmere, that fatal battle, for the Northumbrians, in which King Ecgfrith was killed in 685. Some figures have helmets (are these Northumbrians?) while some do not (are these Picts?) The jury is still out.

James E. Fraser, *From Caledonia to Pictland: Scotland to 795* (Edinburgh, 2009).

CHAPTER 3

(13) Jarrow Church Dedication

The dedication stone of St Paul's Church, Jarrow, is now set in the chancel arch of the present church. Translated it reads: 'The dedication of the basilica of St Paul on the ninth day before the Kalends of May in the fifteenth year of King Ecgfrith, and in the fourth of Abbot Ceolfrid, founder, by the guidance of God, of the same church.' Seemingly the occasion had been planned to take place before the king set off on that major expedition to Scotland in which he was killed; the hope must have been that Ecgfrith would sail back in glory to his newly founded minster, strategically placed as it was by the harbour at Jarrow.

Ian Wood, *The Origins of Jarrow: The Monastery, the Slake and Ecgfrith's Minster* (Jarrow, 2008).

(14) Ezra the scribe from the *Codex Amiatinus*

The Codex Amiatinus, a weighty one-volume copy of the Bible, was one of three such copies commissioned by Ceolfrith, abbot of Wearmouth-Jarrow.

Ceolfrith intended to present this particular copy to the Pope when he set out for Rome in 715. His death at Langres in 716 put an end to that plan but the Bible nonetheless reached Italy where for centuries it was housed in the monastery of San Salvatore at Monte Amiata. So sumptuous is it as a volume, and so Italianate in style, that no one recognised it for what it was: a proud sign of Northumbrian achievement and its emulation of Italian manuscripts.

Translated, the caption above the illustration reads: 'The sacred books having been destroyed by the enemies' flames, Ezra on fire with the Lord, repaired this need.' The volumes in the book cupboard, of a kind likely to have been found at Wearmouth-Jarrow, will have represented the nine volumes into which the Italian scholar Cassiodorus (d. *c.*580) divided up the Bible, but there is no reason to think, as has sometimes been suggested, that the figure is Cassiodorus himself rather than Ezra. The tale of destruction of books referred to in the caption relates to chapters of the Bible that were not included in the version generally in use in the Middle Ages (and beyond).

(15) St Wilfrid's crypt, Ripon Cathedral

The minster at Ripon, early on in his career, was given to Wilfrid in the years before he became a bishop.

The church at Ripon (together with Hexham) became Wilfrid's great showcases: here he built churches of greater magnificence than had been seen before in England. Both had crypts of a kind designed to dazzle any pilgrim. Each crypt was situated in the east end below the main altar. Their purpose was to house relics and to provide the pilgrim with an extraordinarily theatrical experience as he made his journey into a dark ante-chamber before coming upon spectacular reliquaries. Stephen (Wilfrid's biographer) does not give details of the Ripon crypt but a sense of the pilgrim's experience there can be gained from his description of Hexham which likewise had 'various winding passages with spiral stairs leading up and down.'

N. J. Higham (ed.), *Wilfrid, Abbot, Bishop, Saint* (Donington, 2013).

(16) Offa's gold coin

The grandeur of Offa's self-perception and ambitions is well caught by this gold coin, struck *c.*773/4 in imitation of a gold dinar of the Abbasid caliph, al-Mansur. Offa's moneyer has got the inscription upside down, though in other respects has made a faithful enough copy. It is of course possible that the coin was made for trading purposes rather than simply as an object of prestige.

Anna Gannon, *The Iconography of Early Anglo-Saxon Coinage, Sixth to Eighth Centuries* (Oxford, 2003).

(17) Sandbach Crosses

In the seventeenth century (if not before) the Sandbach crosses were considered an idolatrous eyesore. Divided up into pieces they ended up as part of a grotto, as part of the town well and more generally as handy stones for various building projects. But in 1816 the decision was taken to re-assemble the crosses and to restore them to the place of honour in the market place where they had certainly once stood, though where they had been positioned in pre-conquest England is less certain. The crosses depict complex narratives. The North Cross includes traditional scenes from the life of Christ (his birth; the adoration of the Magi) and, more unusually, the handing of the keys of heaven to St Peter, of the new law to St Paul and of Christ on the Road to calvary. The South Cross is enigmatic: do the figures depicted on the east face have a story to tell or are they simply part of the design? The west face also presents a puzzle: a crowd of figures appear to be awaiting the Day of Judgment – or are they? Might this not be (as Jane Hawkes suggests) a transfiguration scene?

Jane Hawkes, *The Sandbach Crosses: Sign and Significance in Anglo-Saxon Sculpture* (Dublin, 2002).

CHAPTER 4

(18) Map of territories mentioned in the Tribal Hidage

The Tribal Hidage lists the hides of 34 territories south of the river Humber, a hide being the amount of land thought necessary to support a peasant family in early Anglo-Saxon England. The text survives only in an eleventh-century manuscript and there is still much controversy as to the purpose of the list and its original date. Nonetheless, it remains a crucial document for any understanding of kingdom formation in early Anglo-Saxon England, providing as it does a sense of just how many tiny blocks of land there once were before being swallowed up by the bigger kingdoms as described by Bede.

BL, Harley MS 3271.

Stephen Bassett, *The Origins of Anglo-Saxon Kingdoms* (Lecister, 1989).

(19) All Saints' Church, Brixworth

Brixworth when it was first built, in the late eighth or ninth century, was something of a novelty. Churches of quite this size had hitherto been unusual. But Brixworth qualifies as a 'basilica' not on size alone but since, among other architectural features, it had aisles alongside and of equal length to the main body of the building. It had to the east an apse beneath which was a ring-crypt where, it is thought, were kept relics. Such relics included a throat-bone, discovered during restoration work in the nineteenth century. It is not out of the question that this was a relic of St Boniface; nor is it impossible that Brixworth was *Clofesho*, site of many a church council.

Helen Gittos, *Liturgy, Architecture, and Sacred Places in Anglo-Saxon England* (Oxford, 2013).

(20) The Priory Church of St Mary's, Deerhurst

Recent work at the church of St Mary's Deerhurst, enlarged in the early ninth century by Ealdorman Aethelric, has shown quite what an innovative building it was. Long famous for its polychrome beasts that act as label-stops, Deerhurst has too a number of other features unusual for an Anglo-Saxon church: the Virgin above the arch in the central wall of the tower stands behind Christ who is himself standing on a shield; on the second floor of the tower an external wooden balcony surrounds its three faces (presumably for use in various liturgical ceremonies); and finally a font, rescued from various locations in the nineteenth century, suggests that the survival of so few fonts is not proof that they were such a rarity at the time, as has long been supposed.

Richard N. Bailey, 'Anglo-Saxon Sculptures at Deerhurst', Deerhurst Lecture 2002.

CHAPTER 5

(21) Silver ring, *c.*775–850.

'Rings' to the Anglo-Saxons could mean finger rings, arm rings, or neck rings. 'A ring-giver' (as found for example in *Beowulf*) denoted a lord who knew how to reward, and thus how to keep, his followers. Rings however might be worn not only as a marks of favour and prestige but also for their amuletic qualities. It is striking that in the laws of King Alfred the compensation value of the ring finger is much higher than that due in the case of a lost index, middle or little finger (though worst of all was to lose a thumb since it rendered the hand especially useless). The ring here is silver-gilt, decorated with animal interlace.

Jay Gates and Nicola Marafioti, *Capital and Corporal Punishment in Anglo-Saxon England* (Woodbridge, 2014).

(22) The Fuller Brooch, British Museum

The Fuller brooch, made of silver with engravings marked with niello, would originally have been used as a cloak fastener, and worn therefore on the shoulder.

The sixteen roundels that make up the outer circle of the brooch depicts, four times over, man, beast, bird and plant. In the inner circle are four lenticular panels. The figures here represent Taste (top left), Smell (top right), Touch (bottom right), Hearing (bottom left). In the centre, is Sight. The pre-eminent value given to Sight has led to the brooch being associated with King Alfred for whom sight meant the ability to see, 'with the eyes of the mind', truths beyond the purely physical.

British Museum, MLA 1952, 4-4, I.

Leslie Webster, *Anglo-Saxon Art* (London, 2012).

(23) The Alfred Jewel

The Alfred Jewel, as it has long been called, was discovered in the seventeenth century not far from Athelney where, during his wars against the Vikings, King Alfred was known to have encamped. Around the crystal setting is an inscription in Old English which reads 'Alfred ordered me to be made.'

It is generally thought that the snout of the animal provided a socket which would have held the kind of pointer known to have been used for the reading of manuscripts. King Alfred in the preface to his translation of Pope Gregory's *Pastoral Care* specifically mentions that he is sending along with this text *aestels* of some considerable value, which the 'jewel' most certainly is. Framed in gold the central plaque is enamelled and covered in polished rock-crystal. But who is the figure? Given his large eyes, does he represent Sight? (cf the Fuller brooch for the importance of 'sight' to Alfred.)

Leslie Webster, *Anglo-Saxon Art* (London, 2012).

CHAPTER 6

(24) St Aethelthryth of Ely from the Benedictional of St Aethelwold

St Aethelthryth of Ely was a saint from the age of the conversion chosen for inclusion – twice – in the tenth century Benedictional of St Aethelwold, that sumptuously illustrated book commissioned by Aethelwold when he was bishop of Winchester (963–84).

A benedictional was a book of blessings which only a bishop had the authority to give before communion. In the first depiction of Aethelthryth in the Benedictional, at the beginning of the manuscript, is of him among a choir of virgins. The second is the full page portrait. Aethelthryth's virginity, kept throughout two marriages, deserved particular veneration as the benediction for her feast, perhaps written by Aethelwold himself, makes clear:

> May the one omnipotent and eternal God, the Father, the Son and the Holy Spirit, who made the will of blessed Aethelthryth steadfast and ablaze with the bounty of seven-fold grace, that summoned to the marriage beds of two husbands, she avoided them, remaining intact, and was taken as a chaste bride in perpetuity by the most just one, remove from you the burning desire of lust by protecting you, and kindle the fire of his own love. Amen.

Robert Deshman, *The Benedictional of St Æthelwold* (Princeton, 1995).

(25) King Edgar seated between St Aethelwold and St Dunstan, from the *Regularis Concordia*

The *Concordia* manifestly proclaims the role of the king in the monastic reform movement of the tenth century. The king is both patron and beneficiary of the reform; the prologue to the *Regularis Concordia* proclaims it was his royal duty 'even as the Good Shepherd' to give help and protection to the monks of his kingdom. Abbots and abbesses are to be elected 'with the consent and advice of the King.' Each day the monks will pray for the King (and other benefactors) 'distinctly' and not at 'excessive spend.'

Regularis Concordia Anglicae nationis monachorum sanctimonialiumque, ed. and trans. Thomas Symons (London, 1953).

(26) St Swithun of Winchester from the Benedictional of St Aethelwold

St Swithun was bishop of Winchester between 852 and 863.

Very little is known of Swithun's life but in 971 (on 15 July) Bishop Aethelwold had his relics translated from a tomb outside the west door of the minster at Winchester into a sumptuous new shrine within the minster itself. It was a grand occasion, of a kind (probably) never before witnessed in England, though not uncommon on the continent. A very full account was kept by Wulfstan, later precentor of the Minster but at the time still an oblate. According to this account, it was St Swithun himself who set in motion the translation, appearing in 968, to demand that it be done. On 9 July 971 bishop Aethelwold duly announced to his congregation his plans for the imminent translation. From the following Wednesday all were to fast for the next three days. Thereafter, on the evening of 14 July, a tent was erected around the old tomb. There throughout the night, the faithful kept vigil. On 15 July Bishop Aethelwold together with the abbots of the Old and New Minster communities processed to the tent so as to open the lid of the tomb; outside the faithful continued their chanting. In due course the relics, washed and newly wrapped were carried into the choir of the Old Minster where Aethelwold then said Mass. Further elaborate ceremonies would follow once the suitably grand new reliquary (it was made of silver and gold and rubies) commissioned by King Edgar was ready.

Robert Deshman, *The Benedictional of St Æthelwold* (Princeton, 1995).

(27) Preface to the blessing for Palm Sunday, from the Benedictional of St Aethelwold

Traditionally, those accompanying Christ as he made his way to Jerusalem the week before the crucifixion were the apostles. However, in Aethelwold's Benedictional it seems to be 'the faithful' who are represented: they do not wear 'apostle-style' clothing, nor do they have haloes. This group carry palms but others in the scene hold flowers. From the writings of Abbot Aelfric of Eynsham it is very clear that processions with palms or branches (and almost certainly flowers) formed an important part of the Palm Sunday devotions of the laity.

CHAPTER 7

(28) Nineteenth-century representation of the treacherous moment before the murder of Edward the Martyr

On the death of King Edgar in 975, the succession was disputed between two of his sons: Edward and his younger half-brother Aethelred. Who Edward's mother was is unknown but Aethelred was the son of a woman of determination: Aelfthryth. Nonetheless in 975 Edward, backed by Dunstan archbishop of Canterbury, was crowned king. Three years later, as he was making his way to visit his step-mother at Corfe Castle, he was murdered, allegedly at the hands of a number of his step-mother's retainers who had ridden out to meet him. His burial, at Wareham, was unceremonious but the following year Edward was re-buried with due solemnity in Shaftesbury and in 1001 he was canonised. No one was ever held responsible for the murder and the suspicion that it was Aelfthryth herself who had planned it never entirely lifted, however in the illustration here blame is squarely laid at the hands of the retainers who have poisoned the welcoming drink which the guiltless Aelfthryth is offering to her king.

Christine Fell, *Edward King and Martyr* (Leeds, 1971).

(29) Lenborough Hoard

Late in 2014 a metal detectorist found over 5000 coins wrapped in a lead sheet in the village of Lenborough in Buckinghamshire. The coins date from the reigns of Kings Aethelred and Cnut but it is not yet clear (if it ever will be) who hid them and why. But the discovery of the hoard is yet one more reminder of how archaeology has transformed our knowledge of the wealth and splendour of Anglo-Saxon England, from the discovery of the ship at Sutton Hoo, to the battle hoard of Staffordshire, and now to a massive coin hoard in a Buckinghamshire village.

(30) The Gokstad Ship, Vikingskipmuseet, Oslo

For the Anglo-Saxons, the speed at which Viking ships could travel was unnerving. The geography of Scandinavia had necessarily fostered ship-building techniques and by the seventh century the Vikings had rediscovered the use of sail. The Gokstad ship pictured here was built around 900. It was exceptionally sturdy, well able to cross the Atlantic (as replicas have shown) and grand enough also for use as a burial chamber – placed in a mound sealed with clay it was rediscovered only in 1880. The keel (*c.*58 foot long) was constructed of a single piece of oak. It would have been manned by 32 rowers (16 on each side) and decorated on each side with shields.

In the *Life of King Edward* (p. 14) Earl Godwine (himself of Anglo-Danish ancestry) gives King Edward as a present on his accession a ship of enormous splendour:

A golden lion crowns the stern. A winged
And golden dragon at the prow affrights
The sea, and belches fire with triple tongue.
Patrician purple pranks the hanging sail
On which are shown th'instructive lineage
And the sea battles of our noble kings.

Sea-power belongs now, too, to the Anglo-Saxons.

Peter Sawyer (ed.), *The Oxford Illustrated History of the Vikings* (Oxford, 2001).

The Life of King Edward who Rests at Westminster, ed. and trans. Frank Barlow (London, 1962).

(31) Encomium of Queen Emma

The purpose of this book, entitled *In Praise of Queen Emma*, has long intrigued both historians and literary critics. Queen Emma may well have had a guilty conscience (she had after all abandoned the children she had had by King Aethelred in favour of her sons by Cnut) and the book indeed does its best to exculpate Emma from having paid any part in the capture and blinding of her son Alfred on his visit to England in 1036. The book was written by a Flemish monk (Emma had spent a short time in exile in Flanders after Cnut's death) seemingly to reconcile the queen with her two sons, and possibly with each other. The frontispiece here depicts Emma as the central figure, with both Harthacnut and Cnut somewhat deferential and marginalised.

Pauline Stafford, *Queen Emma and Queen Edith: Queenship and Women's Power in Eleventh-Century England* (Aldershot, 2006.)

CHAPTER 8

(32) Eadwine Psalter

The Eadwine Psalter was made at Canterbury sometime in the mid-twelfth-century. It is a triple psalter, that is to say, it gives three different versions of the Psalms, adding interlinear glosses to the Latin in both English and Anglo-Norman French.

The Eadwine Psalter is a huge book, weighing about two stone. It must have been the work of at least ten scribes. It is also magnificent, with lavish illustrations in gold leaf and lapis lazuli. Eadwine, the designer of the book, is given a portrait at the back of the Psalter, followed by two drawings of the precinct at Canterbury where a new water system had just been installed. Tempting though it might be to think that Psalm 136/7 as illustrated here ('By the Waters of Babylon there we sat down, yea we wept') might have special meaning for a conquered people, it has recently been suggested that these drawings should in fact be understood in relation to Psalm I: 'he shall be like a tree planted by the rivers of the water, that bringeth forth fruit in his season.' The Psalter, in other words, is a work of collaboration and celebration and not of lament.

Elaine Treharne, *Living Through Conquest: The Politics of Early English, 1020–1220* (Oxford, 2012).

Martin Brett and David A. Woodman (eds), *The Long Twelfth-Century View of the Anglo-Saxon Past* (Abingdon, 2015).

(33) Bayeux Tapestry: coronation of Harold

The Bayeux Tapestry provides an embroidered account of the fall (and death) of Harold Godwineson and the successful bid for the throne of England made by William Duke of Normandy.

Precisely when the Tapestry was made, by whom and for whom remain uncertain but its partisan character is clear from the start: the villain of the piece is Harold. Thus although this scene depicts Harold being crowned as King after the death of Edward the Confessor, it manages to suggest that this was a ceremony conducted with inappropriate haste (Edward's burial is depicted before his death scene) and with a measure of illegality since the archbishop who performs the consecration is named as Stigand, a prelate who had been deprived of his office for simony. It is possible that in fact it was the archbishop of York, Eadred, who officiated, but as with many of the details of the rival claims of Harold and William to the English throne, much is likely to remain forever murky.

David M. Wilson, *The Bayeux Tapestry* (London, 2004).

(34) Bayeux Tapestry: Harold's death

That Harold met his death at the Battle of Hastings is certain (notwithstanding legends that he in fact escaped and lived as a hermit, dying eventually in Chester). Whether he was or was not killed by an arrow in his eye is a more controversial problem. Next to the 'arrow in the eye' picture is a man lying on the ground hacked in the thigh by a Norman soldier with the inscription above that reads 'the king is killed'. It is of course possible that both pictures represent Harold and that there were all kinds of reasons (not least the alleged role of his family in the blinding of Edward's brother Alfred when he came to England in 1036) for depicting a scene in which Harold's eye suffers. Most striking of all, however, is the inscription: Harold the king is killed because it recognises his kingship whereas a number of Norman sources attempt to deny that this had any legality (because the coronation service had been conducted by Stigand).

(35) The initial page of the *Peterborough Chronicle*

In the early twelfth century the monks of Peterborough acquired a text of the Anglo-Saxon Chronicle, most probably from Canterbury. This text, known both as 'E' and as the Peterborough Chronicle, after 1121 focuses strongly on Peterborough itself where it was then kept up until the death of King Stephen in 1154 (but composed probably in retrospect rather than from year to year).

The continued use of Anglo-Saxon at a time when so much monastic and 'national' history was being written in Latin should not mislead the reader into assuming that the chronicler harboured particular nostalgia for a lost age. Some of the most stirring passages recount the rebellion against the Normans led by Hereward the Wake, but there is no suggestion that Hereward deserved support. What the monastery wants above all is peace; thus the final hero of the work is Abbot Martin 'a good monk and a good man' who 'planted a vineyard, and did much building and made the village better than it had ever been before.'

English Historical Documents, vol. 2: 1042–1189, ed. and trans. David Douglas and George Greenaway (London, 1981).

Malasree Home, *The Peterborough Version of the Anglo-Saxon Chronicle* (Woodbridge, 2015).

Select Bibliography

ABBREVIATIONS

ASE   *Anglo-Saxon England*
ASSAH   *Anglo-Saxon Studies in Archaeology and History*
EHR   *English Historical Review*
EME   *Early Medieval Europe*
TRHS   *Transactions of the Royal Historical Society*
ODNB   *Oxford Dictionary of National Biography*
EHD   *English Historical Documents* (vols i and ii)

PRIMARY SOURCES

Abbots of Wearmouth and Jarrow, ed. and trans. C. W. Grocock and Ian Wood (Oxford, 2013).

Aethelwulf, *De abbatibus*, ed. and trans. Alistair Campbell (Oxford, 1967).

Aldhelm, *Aldhelm: The Prose Works*, ed. and trans. Michael Lapidge and Michael W. Herren (Cambridge, 1979).

—*Aldhelm: The Poetic Works*, ed. Michael Lapidge and James L. Rosier (Cambridge and Dover, NH, 1985).

Alfred the Great: Asser's Life of King Alfred and Other Contemporary Sources, trans. Simon Keynes and Michael Lapidge (Harmondsworth, 1983).

The Anglo-Saxon Missionaries in Germany: Being the Lives of SS. Willibrord, Boniface, Sturm, Leoba, and Lebuin, Together with the Hodoeporicon of St. Willibald and a Selection from the Correspondence of St. Boniface, trans. C. H. Talbot (London, 1954).

The Annals of St-Bertin, trans. Janet L. Nelson (Manchester, 1991).

Bede, *Bede's Ecclesiastical History of the English People*, ed. and trans. Bertram Colgrave and R. A. B. Mynors (Oxford, 1969).

—*The Ecclesiastical History of the English People*, trans. Judith McClure and Roger Collins (Oxford, 1999).

Select Bibliography

Beowulf: Edited with an Introduction, Notes and New Prose Translation, ed. and trans. Michael Swanton (Manchester and New York, 1978).

The Chronicle of Æthelweard, ed. and trans. A. Campbell (London, 1962).

Councils and Synods, with Other Documents Relating to the English Church, vol. 1: A.D. 871–1204, ed. and trans. Dorothy Whitelock et al. (Oxford, 1981).

Eddius Stephanus, *The Life of Bishop Wilfrid*, ed. and trans. Bertram Colgrave (Cambridge, 1927).

English Historical Documents, vol. 1: c. 500–1042, ed. and trans. Dorothy Whitelock (London, 1979).

English Historical Documents, vol. 2: 1042–1189, ed. and trans. David Douglas and George Greenaway (London, 1981).

Eynsham Cartulary, ed. H. E. Salter (2 vols, Oxford, 1907).

Felix, *Felix's Life of Saint Guthlac*, ed. and trans. Bertram Colgrave (Cambridge, 1956).

Gildas, *The Ruin of Britain, and Other Works*, ed. and trans. Michael Winterbottom (London, 1978).

The Gododdin: The Oldest Scottish Poem, ed. and trans. Kenneth H. Jackson (Edinburgh, 1969).

Henry of Huntingdon, *Historia Anglorum: The History of the English People*, ed. and trans. Diana E. Greenway (Oxford, 1996).

Historia ecclesie Abbendonensis: The History of the Church of Abingdon, ed. and trans. John Hudson (2 vols, Oxford, 2002).

The Life of Christina of Markyate, trans. Samuel Fanous and Henrietta Leyser (Oxford, 2008).

The Life of King Edward who Rests at Westminster, ed. and trans. Frank Barlow (London, 1962).

Old English Liturgical Verse: A Student Edition, ed. Sarah Larratt Keefer (Peterborough, ON, 2010).

Old English Poems of Christ and His Saints, ed. and trans. Mary Clayton (Cambridge, MA, 2013).

Old English Shorter Poems, ed. and trans. Christopher A. Jones and Robert E. Bjork (2 vols, Cambridge, MA, and London, 2012).

Ordericus Vitalis, *The Ecclesiastical History of Orderic Vitalis*, ed. and trans. Marjorie Chibnall (6 vols, Oxford, 1969–80).

Regularis concordia Anglicae nationis monachorum sanctimonialiumque, ed. and trans. Thomas Symons (London, 1953).

William of Malmesbury, *The History of the English Bishops*, ed. and trans. M. Winterbottom (Oxford, 2007).

William of Poitiers, *The Deeds of William*, ed. and trans. R. H. C. Davis and Marjorie Chibnall (Oxford, 1998).

Wulfstan, *The Life of St. Æthelwold*, ed. and trans. Michael Lapidge and Michael Winterbottom (Oxford, 1991).

SECONDARY SOURCES

Abels, R., *Lordship and Military Obligations in Anglo-Saxon England* (Berkeley, 1988).

Atherton, Mark, *The Making of England* (forthcoming I.B.Tauris, 2017).

Bailey, Maggie, 'Aelfwynn, second Lady of the Mercians', in N. J. Higham and David Hill (eds), *Edward the Elder, 899–924* (London, 2001).

Bailey, Richard N., *Anglo-Saxon Sculptures at Deerhurst* (Deerhurst, 2005).

Banham, Debby, '"In the Sweat of thy Brow Shalt Thou Eat Bread": Cereals and cereal production in the Anglo-Saxon landscape', in N. J. Higham and Martin J. Ryan (eds), *The Landscape Archaeology of Anglo-Saxon England* (Woodbridge, 2010).

Barlow, Frank, *The Godwins: The Rise and Fall of a Noble Dynasty* (Harlow, 2001).

Barrow, Julia, 'Chester's earliest regatta? Edgar's Dee-rowing revisited', *EME*, x (2011), pp. 81–93.

Bassett, Steven (ed.), *The Origins of Anglo-Saxon Kingdoms* (London, 1989).

Baxter, Stephen, *The Earls of Mercia: Lordship and Power in Late Anglo-Saxon England* (Oxford, 2007).

—'Edward the Confessor and the succession question', in Richard Mortimer (ed.), *Edward the Confessor: The Man and the Legend* (Woodbridge, 2009).

—'Lordship and labour', in Julia C. Crick and Elisabeth M. C. Van Houts (eds), *A Social History of England, 900–1200* (Cambridge, 2011).

Bedingfield, M. Bradford, *The Dramatic Liturgy of Anglo-Saxon England* (Woodbridge, 2002).

Blair, John, 'Anglo-Saxon pagan shrines and their prototypes', *ASSAH*, viii (1995), pp. 1–28.

—'The minsters of the Thames', in John Blair, Brian Golding and Barbara F. Harvey (eds), *The Cloister and the World: Essays in Medieval History in Honour of Barbara Harvey* (Oxford, 1996).

—'The Tribal Hidage', in Michael Lapidge (ed.), *The Blackwell Encyclopaedia of Anglo-Saxon England* (Oxford, 1999).

—*The Church in Anglo-Saxon Society* (Oxford and New York, 2005).

—'Flixborough re-visisted', *ASSAH*, xvii (2011), pp. 101–07.

—'Overview: The archaeology of religion', in H. Hamerow, D. A. Hinton and S. Crawford (eds), *The Oxford Handbook of Anglo-Saxon Archaeology* (Oxford, 2011).

Brett, M. and Woodman, D. A., *The Long Twelfth-Century View of the Anglo-Saxon Past* (Farnham and Burlington, VT, 2015).

Brooks, Nicholas, *The Early History of the Church of Canterbury: Christ Church from 597 to 1066* (Leicester, 1984).

Brown, Michelle, *The Book of Cerne: Prayer, Patronage and Power in Ninth-Century England* (London and Toronto, 1996).

Brown, Michelle and Carol Ann Farr (eds), *Mercia: An Anglo-Saxon Kingdom in Europe* (London, 2001).

Campbell, James, *The Anglo-Saxon State* (London, 2000).

—'What is not known about the reign of Edward the Elder', in N. J. Higham and David Hill (eds), *Edward the Elder, 899–924* (London, 2001).

Campbell, James, John, Eric and Wormald, Patrick, *The Anglo-Saxons* (London, 1982).

Carver, Martin O. H., *The Age of Sutton Hoo* (Woodbridge, 1992).

—*Portmahomack: Monastery of the Picts* (Edinburgh, 2008).

—'Intellectual territories in Anglo-Saxon England', in H. Hamerow, D. A. Hinton and S. Crawford (eds), *The Oxford Handbook of Anglo-Saxon Archaeology* (Oxford, 2011).

Charles-Edwards, Thomas M., *Early Christian Ireland* (Cambridge, 2000).

—*Wales and the Britons, 350–1064* (Oxford, 2013).

Clarke, Peter A., *The English Nobility under Edward the Confessor* (Oxford, 1994).

Coates, Richard, 'Invisible Britons: The view from linguistics'. Available online: http://www.sussex.ac.uk/gateway/file.php?name=rc-britons.pdf (accessed May 2016).

Crawford, Barbara E., *The Churches Dedicated to St. Clement in Medieval England: A Hagio-Geography of the Seafarer's Saint in 11th Century North Europe* (St. Petersburg, 2008).

Cubitt, Catherine, 'Pastoral care and conciliar canons: The provisions of the 747 council of Clofesho', in John Blair and Richard Sharpe (eds), *Pastoral Care before the Parish* (Leicester, 1992).

—*Anglo-Saxon Church Councils c. 650–c. 850* (London, 1995).

—'Review: *The Tenth-Century Benedictine Reform in England*', *EME*, vi (1997), pp. 77–94.

—'The politics of remorse: Penance and royal piety in the reign of Æthelred the Unready', *Historical Research*, lxxxv (2012), pp. 179–92.

Davidson, Michael R., 'The (non) submission of the northern kings in 920', in N. J. Higham and David Hill (eds), *Edward the Elder, 899–924* (London, 2001).

Dendle, Peter, *Satan Unbound: The Devil in Old English Narrative Literature* (Toronto, 2001).

Deshman, Robert, *The Benedictional of Æthelwold* (Princeton, 1995).

Dickinson, Tania M., 'Overview: Mortuary ritual', in H. Hamerow, D. A. Hinton and S. Crawford (eds), *The Oxford Handbook of Anglo-Saxon Archaeology* (Oxford, 2011).

Dodwell, C. R., *Anglo-Saxon Art: A New Perspective* (Manchester, 1982).

Dornier, Ann (ed.), *Mercian Studies* (Leicester, 1977).

Dumville, David N., 'Gildas and Maelgwn: Problems of dating', in M. Lapidge and D. N. Dumville (eds), *Gildas: New Approaches* (Woodbridge and Dover, NH, 1984).

—*Wessex and England from Alfred to Edgar: Six Essays on Political, Cultural, and Ecclesiastical Revival* (Woodbridge, 1992).

Fell, Christine E., *Edward, King and Martyr* (Leeds, 1971).

Fernie, Eric, 'Edward the Confessor's Westminster Abbey', in Richard Mortimer (ed.), *Edward the Confessor: The Man and the Legend* (Woodbridge, 2009).

Fleming, Robin, 'Rural elites and urban communities in late-Saxon England', *Past & Present*, cxli (1993), pp. 3–37.

—*Britain after Rome: The Fall and Rise, 400–1070* (London, 2010).

Foot, Sarah, *Æthelstan: The First King of England* (New Haven, 2011).

Foxhall Forbes, Helen, *Heaven and Earth in Anglo-Saxon England: Theology and Society in an Age of Faith* (Farnham, 2013).

Frank, Roberta, 'King Cnut in the verse of his skalds', in Alexander R. Rumble (ed.), *The Reign of Cnut: King of England, Denmark and Norway* (London and Rutherford, NJ, 1994).

Gannon, Anna, *The Iconography of Early Anglo-Saxon Coinage: Sixth to Eighth Centuries* (Oxford, 2003).

Gelling, Margaret, *The West Midlands in the Early Middle Ages* (Leicester, 1992).

Gem, Richard, *Deerhurst and Rome: Æthelric's Pilgrimage c. 804 and the Oratory of St Mary Mediana* (Deerhurst, 2008).

Gerchow, Jan, in Carola Hicks (ed.), *England in the Eleventh Century: Proceedings of the 1990 Harlaxton Symposium* (Stamford, 1992).

Gilchrist, Roberta and Green, Cheryl, *Glastonbury Abbey: Archaeological Investigations 1904–79* (London, 2015).

Gillingham, John, '"The most precious jewel in the English Crown": Levels of Danegeld and heregeld in the early eleventh century', *EHR*, civ (1989), pp. 385–406.

—'Thegns and knights in eleventh-century England: Who was then the gentleman?', *TRHS*, v (1995), pp. 129–53.

Gittos, Helen, *Liturgy, Architecture, and Sacred Places in Anglo-Saxon England* (Oxford, 2013).

Godden, Malcolm R., 'Money, power and morality in late Anglo-Saxon England', *ASE*, xix (1990), pp. 41–65.

—'Did King Alfred write anything?', *Medium Aevum*, lxxvi (2007), pp. 1–23.

Goffart, Walter A., *The Narrators of Barbarian History (A.D. 550–800): Jordanes, Gregory of Tours, Bede, and Paul the Deacon* (Princeton and Guildford, 1988).

Gretsch, Mechthild, *Aelfric and the Cult of Saints in Late Anglo-Saxon England* (Cambridge, 2005).

Hall, Alaric, *Elves in Anglo-Saxon England: Matters of Belief, Health, Gender and Identity* (Woodbridge, 2007).

Halsall, Guy, *Worlds of Arthur: Facts and Fictions of the Dark Ages* (Oxford, 2013).

Hamerow, Helena, 'The Anglo-Saxon Settlement', in A. Clark (ed.), *Excavations at Mucking* (3 vols, London, 1993), vol. 2.

—'Anglo-Saxon timber buildings and their social context', in H. Hamerow, D. A. Hinton and S. Crawford (eds), *The Oxford Handbook of Anglo-Saxon Archaeology* (Oxford, 2011).

Hamerow, Helena, Hinton, David A. and Crawford, Sally (eds), *The Oxford Handbook of Anglo-Saxon Archaeology* (Oxford, 2011).

Harvey, Sally, *Domesday: Book of Judgement* (Oxford, 2014).

Hawkes, Jane, *The Sandbach Crosses: Sign and Significance in Anglo-Saxon Sculpture* (Dublin and Portland, OR, 2002).

Henderson, George, *Vision and Image in Early Christian England* (Cambridge, 1999).

Henig, M. and Ramsay, N. (eds), *Intersections: The Archaeology and History of Christianity in England, 400–1200: Papers in Honour of Martin Biddle and Birthe Kjølbye-Biddle* (Oxford, 2010).

Higham, N. J. (ed.), *Wilfrid: Abbot, Bishop, Saint: Papers from the 1300th Anniversary Conferences* (Donnington, 2013).

Higham, N. J. and Ryan, Martin, *The Anglo-Saxon World* (Yale, 2013).

Hill, David, *'Ethelred the Unready': Papers from the Millenary Conference* (Oxford, 1978).

Hill, David and Worthington, Margaret (eds), *Æthelbald and Offa: Two Eighth-Century Kings of Mercia* (Oxford, 2005).

Hills, C. M. and O'Connell, T. C., 'New light on the Anglo-Saxon succession: Two cemeteries and their dates', *Antiquity*, lxxxiii (2009), pp. 1096–108.

Hobley, Brian, 'Saxon London: Ludenwic and Ludenburh: Two cities rediscovered', in B. Hobley and R. Hodges (eds), *The Rebirth of Towns in the West AD 700–1050* (London, 1988).

Howe, Nicholas, *Writing the Map of Anglo-Saxon England: Essays in Cultural Geography* (New Haven and London, 2008).

John, Eric, *Reassessing Anglo-Saxon England* (Manchester, 1996).

Kabir, Ananya Jahanara, *Paradise, Death and Doomsday in Anglo-Saxon Literature* (Cambridge, 2001).

Keynes, Simon, *The Diplomas of King Æthelred 'The Unready' (978–1016): A Study in their Use as Historical Evidence* (Cambridge, 1980).

—'A tale of two kings: Alfred the Great and Æthelred the Unready', *TRHS*, xxxvi (1986), pp. 195–217.

—'Cnut's earls', in Alexander R. Rumble (ed.), *The Reign of Cnut: King of England, Denmark and Norway* (London and Rutherford, 1994).

—'An abbot, an archbishop, and the Viking raids of 1006–7 and 1009–12', *ASE*, xxxvi (2007), pp. 151–220.

Keynes, Simon and Naismith, Rory, 'The *Agnus Dei* pennies of King Æthelred the Unready', *ASE*, xl (2011), pp. 175–223.

Knowles, David, *The Monastic Order in England: A History of its Development from the Times of St. Dunstan to the Fourth Lateran Council, 943–1216* (Cambridge, 1949).

Lapidge, Michael (ed.), *The Cult of St Swithun* (Oxford, 2003).

Lapidge, Michael, *The Anglo-Saxon Library* (Oxford, 2006).

Lapidge, Michael and Dunmville, David (eds), *Gildas: New Approaches* (Woodbridge and Dover, NH, 1984).

Lapidge, M., Blair, J., Keynes, S. and Scragg, D. (eds), *The Blackwell Encyclopaedia of Anglo-Saxon England* (Oxford, 1999).

Lavelle, Ryan, *Alfred's Wars: Sources and Interpretations of Anglo-Saxon Warfare in the Viking Age* (Woodbridge, 2010).

—'Geographies of power in the *Anglo-Saxon Chronicle*: The Royal Estate of

Wessex', in Alice Jorgensen (ed.), *Reading the Anglo-Saxon Chronicle: Language, Literature, History* (Turnhout, 2010).

Lawson, M. K., 'The collection of Danegeld and heregeld in the reigns of Aethelred II and Cnut', *EHR*, xcix (1984), pp. 721–38.

—*Cnut: England's Viking King* (Stroud, 2004).

Leahy, Kevin and Bland, Roger, *The Staffordshire Hoard* (London, 2009).

Levison, Wilhelm, *England and the Continent in the Eighth Century: The Ford Lectures Delivered in the University of Oxford in the Hilary Term, 1943* (Oxford, 1946).

Lionarons, Joyce Tally, *The Homiletic Writings of Archbishop Wulfstan: A Critical Study* (Cambridge, 2010).

Loveluck, Christopher, *Rural Settlement, Lifestyles and Social Change in the Later First Millennium AD: Anglo-Saxon Flixborough in its Wider Context* (Oxford, 2007).

Maddicott, John R., 'Prosperity and Power in the Age of Bede and Beowulf', *Proceedings of the British Academy* (2002), vol. 117, pp. 49–71.

—'Edward the Confessor's return to England in 1041', *EHR*, cxix (2004), pp. 650–66.

—*The Origins of the English Parliament, 924–1327* (Oxford, 2010).

Magennis, Hugh and Swan, Mary (eds), *A Companion to Ælfric* (Boston, 2009).

Marafioti, Nicole, *The King's Body: Burial and Succession in Late Anglo-Saxon England* (Toronto, Buffalo and London, 2014).

Mayr-Harting, Henry, *Saint Wilfrid* (London, 1986).

Mitchell, Bruce, *An Invitation to Old English and Anglo-Saxon England* (Oxford, 1995).

Moffett, L., 'Food plants on archeological sites', in H. Hamerow, D. A. Hinton and S. Crawford (eds), *The Oxford Handbook of Anglo-Saxon Archaeology* (Oxford, 2011).

Molyneaux, George, 'The Old English Bede: English ideology or Christian instruction?', *EHR*, cxxiv (2009), pp. 1289–323.

—*The Formation of the English Kingdom in the Tenth Century* (Oxford, 2015).

Mortimer, Richard (ed.), *Edward the Confessor: The Man and the Legend* (Woodbridge, 2009).

Naismith, Rory, *Money and Power in Anglo-Saxon England: The Southern English Kingdoms 757–865* (Cambridge, 2012).

—'Prelude to reform: Tenth-century English coinage in perspective', in Rory Naismith, Martin Allen and Elina Screen (eds), *Early Medieval Monetary History: Studies in Memory of Mark Blackburn* (Farnham, 2014).

Newman, J., 'Exceptional finds, exceptional sites? Barham and Coddenham, Suffolk', in Tim Pestell and Katharina Ulmschneider (eds), *Markets in Early Medieval Europe: Trading and Productive Sites, 650–850* (Macclesfield, 2003).

Niblett, Rosalind, *Verulamium: The Roman City of St Albans* (Stroud, 2001).

Nightingale, Pamela, 'The origin of the court of husting and Danish influence on London's development into a capital city', *EHR*, cii (1987), pp. 559–78.

North, Richard, *Heathen Gods in Old English Literature* (Cambridge, 1997).

O'Brien O'Keeffe, Katherine, *Stealing Obedience: Narratives of Agency and Identity in Later Anglo-Saxon England* (Toronto and Buffalo, 2012).

Page, Christopher, *The Christian West and its Singers: The First Thousand Years* (New Haven and London, 2010).

Palmer, James T., *Anglo-Saxons in a Frankish World, 690–900* (Turnhout, 2009).

Pestell, T. and Ulmschneider, K. (eds), *Markets in Early Medieval Europe: Trading and Productive Sites, 650–850* (Macclesfield, 2003).

Petts, David, 'Coastal landscapes and early Christianity in Anglo-Saxon Northumbria', *Estonian Journal of Archaeology*, xiii (2009), pp. 79–95.

Reuter, Timothy (ed.), *Alfred the Great* (Aldershot, 2003).

Roach, Levi, *Kingship and Consent in Anglo-Saxon England, 871–978: Assemblies and the State in the Early Middle Ages* (Cambridge, 2013).

Rodwell, W., Hawkes, J., Howe, E. and Cramp, R., 'The Lichfield angel: A spectacular Anglo-Saxon sainted sculpture', *The Antiquaries Journal*, lxxxviii (2008), pp. 48–108.

Rollason, D., Leyser, C. and Williams, H., *England and the Continent in the Tenth Century: Studies in Honour of Wilhelm Levison (1876–1947)* (Turnhout, 2010).

Sawyer, P. H., *Anglo-Saxon Charters: An Annotated List and Bibliography* (London, 1968).

Scragg, D. G. (ed.), *The Battle of Maldon, AD 991* (Oxford, 1991).

Sherlock, S. J. and Allen, S., *A Royal Anglo-Saxon Cemetery at Street House, Loftus, North-East Yorkshire* (Hartlepool, 2012).

Simpson, Luisella, 'The King Alfred/St Cuthbert episode in the *Historia de sancto Cuthberto*', in G. Bonner, D. W. Rollason and C. Stancliffe (eds), *St. Cuthbert, his Cult and his Community to AD 1200* (Woodbridge, 1989).

Sims-Williams, Patrick, *Religion and Literature in Western England, 600–800* (Cambridge, 1990).

Spiegel, Flora, 'The tabernacula of Gregory the Great and the conversion of Anglo-Saxon England', *ASE*, xxxvi (2007), pp. 1–13.

Stafford, Pauline, *Queen Emma and Queen Edith: Queenship and Women's Power in Eleventh-Century England* (Oxford, 1997).

Stenton, F. M., 'The supremacy of Mercian kings', *EHR*, xxxiii (1918), pp. 433–52.

Story, Joanna, *Carolingian Connections: Anglo-Saxon England and Carolingian Francia, c. 750–870* (Aldershot, 2003).

Tinti, Francesca (ed.), *Pastoral Care in Late Anglo-Saxon England* (Woodbridge, 2005).

Tipper, Jess, *The Grubenhaus in Anglo-Saxon England: An Analysis and Interpretation of the Evidence from a Most Distinctive Building Type* (Yedingham, 2004).

Townend, M. (ed.), *Wulfstan: Archbishop of York* (Turnhout, 2004).

Treharne, Elaine M., *Living through Conquest: The Politics of Early English, 1020–1220* (Oxford, 2012).

Tyler, Elizabeth M., *Treasure in the Medieval West* (York, 2000).

Walton Rogers, Penelope, *Cloth and Clothing in Early Anglo-Saxon England, AD 450–700* (York, 2007).

Ward-Perkins, Bryan, *The Fall of Rome and the End of Civilisation* (Oxford, 2005).

Webster, L., *Anglo-Saxon Art* (London, 2012).

White, Roger H. and Barker, Philip, *Wroxeter: The Life and Death of a Roman City* (Stroud, 1998).

White, Stephen D., 'Kinship and lordship in Early Medieval England: The story of Sigeberht, Cynewulf, and Cyneheard', in R. M. Liuzza (ed.), *Old English Literature: Critical Essays* (New Haven and London, 2002).

Wilcox, Jonathan, 'The dissemination of Wulfstan's homilies: The Wulfstan tradition in eleventh-century vernacular preaching', in Carola Hicks (ed.), *England in the Eleventh Century: Proceedings of the 1990 Harlaxton Symposium* (Stamford, 1992).

Williams, Ann, '"Cockles amongst the wheat": Danes and English in the Western Midlands in the first half of the eleventh century', *Midland History*, xi (1986), pp. 1–22.

Williams, Howard, 'Material culture as memory: Combs and cremation in early medieval Britain', *EME*, xii (2003), pp. 89–128.

Williamson, Tom, *Shaping Medieval Landscapes: Settlement, Society, Environment* (Macclesfield, 2003).

Wilson, David, *The Bayeux Tapestry* (London, 2004).

Wilson, Richard M., *The Lost Literature of Medieval England* (London, 1952).

Wood, Ian, 'The end of Roman Britain: Continental evidence and parallels', in Michael Lapidge and D. N. Dumville (eds), *Gildas: New Approaches* (Woodbridge and Dover, NH, 1984).

Woods, David, 'The *Agnus Dei* pennies of King Aethelred II: A call to hope in the Lord (Isaiah XL)?', *ASE*, xlii (2013), pp. 209–309.

Woolf, Alex, 'Onuist son of Uuguist: Tyrannus Carnifex or a David for the Picts?', in David Hill and Margaret Worthington (eds), *Æthelbald and Offa: Two Eighth-Century Kings of Mercia: Papers from a Conference Held in Manchester in 2000, Manchester Centre for Anglo-Saxon Studies* (Oxford, 2005).

—*From Pictland to Alba: 789–1070* (Edinburgh, 2007).

Wormald, Patrick, 'Aethelwold and his continental counterparts', in Barbara Yorke (ed.), *Bishop Æthelwold: His Career and Influence* (Woodbridge, 1988).

—*The Making of English Law: King Alfred to the Twelfth Century, vol. 1: Legislation and its Limits* (Oxford, 1999).

—'Archbishop Wuflstan and the holiness of society', in D. A. E. Pelteret (ed.), *Anglo-Saxon History: Basic Readings* (New York and London, 2000).

—'Archbishop Wulfstan: Eleventh-century state builder', in Matthew Townend (ed.), *Wulfstan, Archbishop of York: The Proceedings of the Second Alcuin Conference* (Turnhout, 2004).

Worthington, Margaret (ed.), *Æthelbald and Offa: Two Eighth-Century Kings of Mercia: Papers from a Conference Held in Manchester in 2000, Manchester Centre for Anglo-Saxon Studies* (Oxford, 2005).

Yorke, Barbara, *Wessex in the Early Middle Ages* (London, 1995).

Notes

Introduction

1   Michael Wood, *In Search of England* (Harmondsworth, 1999), p. 8.
2   James Campbell et al., *The Anglo-Saxons* (London: Phaidon, 1982). p. 20.

Chapter 1: After the Romans

1   Gildas, *The Ruin of Britain, and Other Works*, ed. and trans. Michael Winterbottom (London, 1978), pp. 23, 26.
2   *Anglo-Saxon Chronicle*, in *English Historical Documents* vol. i. ed. and trans. Dorothy Whitelock (2nd edn, London, 1979), p. 152 (for both 410 and 418). For ease of reference the editions of the *Chronicle* as found in Whitelock (vol. i) and Douglas and Greenaway (eds) (vol. ii) of *English Historical Documents* (henceforth *EHD*) have been used throughout. For vol. i only years (but not recensions) have been given; for vol. ii it becomes more important to differentiate between versions C, D and E, so these will be cited. For an introduction to the complexity of the *Chronicle* see Whitelock's introduction to vol. i. pp. 109–29; also the entry by Simon Keynes in Michael Lapidge et al. (eds), *The Blackwell Encyclopaedia of Anglo-Saxon England* (Oxford, 1999), pp. 35–6.
3   Gildas, *The Ruin of Britain*, p. 27.
4   Ibid., pp. 26–7.
5   Michael Lapidge, 'Gildas's education and the Latin culture of sub-Roman Britain', in Michael Lapidge and David Dumville (eds), *Gildas: New Approaches* (Woodbridge and Dover, NH, 1984), pp. 27–50.
6   See David Dumville, 'Gildas and Maelgwn: Problems of dating', in ibid., pp. 51–84.
7   South Cadbury, excavated by Leslie Alcock in the late 1960s, was long imagined as an Arthurian site; for long-held scepticism about any such claims see Guy Halsall, *Worlds of Arthur: Facts and Fictions of the Dark Ages* (Oxford, 2013).

8 *The Gododdin: The Oldest Scottish Poem*, ed. and trans. Kenneth H. Jackson (Edinburgh, 1969).

9 Ibid., p. 125.

10 Ibid., p. 112.

11 *English Historical Documents (EHD)*, i, p. 157.

12 James Campbell et al., *The Anglo-Saxons* (Oxford, 1982), p. 19.

13 J. N. L. Myres, British Academy Lecture 1970, pp. 9–10.

14 Bede, *Bede's Ecclesiastical History of the English People*, ed. Bertram Colgrave and R. A. B. Mynors (Oxford, 1969), i, 14.

15 Ibid., i, 15.

16 For an excellent introduction to current debates see Robin Fleming, *Britain after Rome: The Fall and Rise, 400–1070* (London, 2010), Ch. 3, pp. 61–88.

17 Martin O. H. Carver, 'Intellectual territories in Anglo-Saxon England', in H. Hamerow, D. A. Hinton and S. Crawford (eds), *The Oxford Handbook of Anglo-Saxon Archaeology* (Oxford, 2011), p. 917.

18 Tom Williamson, *Shaping Medieval Landscapes: Settlement, Society, Environment* (Macclesfield, 2003), p. 29.

19 For the complexity of these issues see Howard Williams, 'Material culture as memory: Combs and cremation in early medieval Britain', *EME*, xii (2003).

20 For the excavations at Mucking see Helena Hamerow, 'The Anglo-Saxon settlement', in A. Clark (ed.), *Excavations at Mucking* (3 vols, London, 1993), vol. 2.

21 For a comprehensive study see Jess Tipper, *The Grubenhaus in Anglo-Saxon England: An Analysis and Interpretation of the Evidence from a Most Distinctive Building Type* (Yedingham, 2004). Helena Hamerow, 'Anglo-Saxon timber buildings and their social context', in H. Hamerow, D. A. Hinton and S. Crawford (eds), *The Oxford Handbook of Anglo-Saxon Archaeology* (Oxford, 2011), Ch. 9, pp. 146–55.

22 See Bryan Ward-Perkins, *The Fall of Rome and the End of Civilisation* (Oxford, 2005).

23 For London, see Brian Hobley, 'Saxon London: Ludenwic and Ludenburh: Two cities rediscovered', in B. Hobley and R. Hodges (eds), *The Rebirth of Towns in the West AD 700–1050* (London, 1988), p. 69: 'notwithstanding an unprecedented programme of excavations over the last 12 years little or no evidence of permanent occupation in the sub-Roman period has been found'. But see Alison Telfer, 'New evidence for the transition from the Late Roman to the Saxon Period at St Martin-in-the-Fields', in M. Henig et al. (eds), *Intersections: The Archaeology and History of Christianity in England, 400–1200: Papers in Honour of Martin Biddle and Birthe Kjølbye-Biddle* (Oxford, 2010), pp. 49–58, which suggests sixth-century occupation near Trafalgar Square. For Canterbury, see Nicholas Brooks, *The Early History of the Church of Canterbury: Christ Church from 597 to 1066* (Leicester, 1984), p. 21.

24 For Wroxeter see Roger H. White and Philip Barker, *Wroxeter: The Life and Death of a Roman City* (Stroud, 1998).

25 For Queensford see Tania M. Dickinson, 'Overview: Mortuary ritual', in Hamerow, Hinton and Crawford (eds), *The Oxford Handbook of Anglo-Saxon Archaeology*, p. 230, but note also, as cited by Dickinson, C. M. Hills and T. C. O'Connell, 'New light on the Anglo-Saxon succession: Two cemeteries and their dates', *Antiquity*, lxxxiii (2009), pp. 1096–108.

26 For spelt see L. Moffett, 'Food plants on archeological sites', in Hamerow, Hinton and Crawford, *The Oxford Handbook of Anglo-Saxon Archaeology*, pp. 348–9; for breeds of sheep, see Penelope Walton Rogers, *Cloth and Clothing in Early Anglo-Saxon England, AD 450–700* (York, 2007), pp. 13–14.

27 Ian Wood, 'The end of Roman Britain: Continental evidence and parallels', in Michael Lapidge and D. N. Dumville (eds), *Gildas: New Approaches* (Woodbridge and Dover, NH, 1984), pp. 1–25; for Verulamium, see Rosalind Niblett, *Verulamium: The Roman City of St Albans* (Stroud, 2001).

28 For the virtual disappearance of Brittonic, see Richard Coates, 'Invisible Britons: The view from linguistics'. Available online at: http://www.sussex.ac.uk/gateway/file.php?name=rc-britons.pdf (accessed May 2016).

29 For Sutton Hoo see Martin Carver (ed.), *The Age of Sutton Hoo* (Woodbridge, 1992).

30 For Prittlewell, see Sue Hirst, *The Prittlewell Prince: The Discovery of a Rich Anglo-Saxon Burial in Essex* (Museum of London Archaeology, 2004).

31 For Coddenham, see J. Newman, 'Exceptional finds, exceptional sites? Barham and Coddenham, Suffolk', in Tim Pestell and Katharina Ulmschneider (eds), *Markets in Early Medieval Europe: Trading and Productive Sites, 650–850* (Macclesfield, 2003), pp. 97–109.

32 S. J. Sherlock and Steve Allen, *A Royal Anglo-Saxon Cemetery at Street House, Loftus, North-East Yorkshire* (Hartlepool, 2012).

33 Cambridge Archaeological Unit website: 16 March 2012.

34 *Beowulf*, ed. and trans. Michael Swanton (Manchester and New York, 1978), p. 185. Numerous translations of *Beowulf* exist; Swanton's is preferred here since it includes both the Anglo-Saxon text as well as a translation.

35 For a preliminary account of the Staffordshire Hoard see Kevin Leahy and Roger Bland, *The Staffordshire Hoard* (London, 2009).

36 See Steven Bassett (ed.), *The Origins of Anglo-Saxon Kingdoms* (London, 1989), in particular Bassett's chapter 1, 'In search of the origins of Anglo-Saxon Kingdoms', pp. 3–27.

37 Bede, *Ecclesiastical History*, i, 15.

Chapter 2: The Arrival of Christianity

1 Bede, *Ecclesiastical History*, ii, 1.
2 Ibid., i, 23.

3   For such silver see Kenneth Painter, 'A Roman silver jug with Biblical scenes from the treasure found at Traprain Law', in M. Henig et al. (eds), *Intersections: The Archaeology and History of Christianity in England, 400–1200: Papers in Honour of Martin Biddle and Birthe Kjølbye-Biddle* (Oxford, 2010), pp. 1–2.

4   In recent years the argument as to what in any case should be classified as 'pagan' and what 'Christian' has become considerably more sophisticated. For an excellent analysis, see John Blair, 'Overview: The archaeology of religion', in H. Hamerow, D. A. Hinton and S. Crawford (eds), *The Oxford Handbook of Anglo-Saxon Archaeology* (Oxford, 2011), pp. 727–41.

5   See Leo the Great's sermon preached in 441and the analysis – to which this paragraph is much indebted – by Thomas M. Charles-Edwards, *Early Christian Ireland* (Cambridge, 2000), pp. 202–14.

6   See John Blair, 'Anglo-Saxon pagan shrines and their prototypes', *ASSAH*, viii (1995), pp. 1–28; for Goodmanham, see in particular pp. 22–3.

7   Bede, *Ecclesiastical History*, i, 30. For the suggestion that Gregory is here following an Old Testament custom, see Flora Spiegel, 'The tabernacula of Gregory the Great and the conversion of Anglo-Saxon England', *ASE*, xxxvi (2007), pp. 1–14. Thus the huts, which may indeed have been built, are comparable to those constructed for the Jewish festival of Sukkot as described in Deuteronomy 16.13–16 and 31.10.

8   See J. Blair, 'Anglo-Saxon pagan shrines and their prototypes', *ASSAH*, viii (1995), pp. 1–28.

9   Bede, *Ecclesiastical History*, ii, 13.

10   Ibid.

11   Ibid.

12   Ibid.

13   Richard North, *Heathen Gods in Old English Literature* (Cambridge, 1997), pp. 330–40.

14   Bede, *Ecclesiastical History*, ii, 14.

15   Ibid., ii, 16.

16   Ibid., ii, 17.

17   See Thomas M. Charles-Edwards, *Wales and the Britons, 350–1064* (Oxford, 2014), pp. 354–55.

18   Bede, *Ecclesiastical History*, ii, 14.

19   Bede, Preface to the *Ecclesiastical History*.

20   Bede, *Ecclesiastical History*, iv, 26.

21   Ibid., iv, 26.

22   The text and translation of Bede's letter to Ecgbert can be found now in *Abbots of Wearmouth and Jarrow*, ed. and trans. C. W. Grocock and Ian Wood (Oxford, 2013), pp. 124–61.

23   Bede, *Ecclesiastical History*, iii, 14.

24   Ibid., iii, 14. Richard M. Wilson, *The Lost Literature of Medieval England* (London, 1952), pp. 105–06 suggests that, as well as the story of Oswine's death, so too the death of Oswald was most probably recounted in vernacular verse.

25 *Beowulf*, ed. and trans. Michael Swanton (Manchester and New York, 1978), p. 155.

26 Bede, *Ecclesiastical History*, iii, 22.

27 Ibid., iii, 24.

28 Ibid.

29 Kevin Leahy, Portable Antiquities scheme: www.finds.org.uk.

30 Bede, *Ecclesiastical History*, iii, 21.

31 Ibid., ii, 4. For the problematic nature of the term 'bretwalda' see Simon Keynes, 'Bretwalda of *Brytenwalda*', in Michael Lapidge et al. (eds), *The Blackwell Encyclopaedia of Anglo-Saxon England* (Oxford, 1999).

32 *The Life of Bishop Wilfrid by Eddius Stephanus*, ed. and trans. Bertram Colgrave (Cambridge, 1927), c.xiii, pp. 27–9 for the first encounter; c.xli, pp. 81–3 for the second.

33 Bede, *Ecclesiastical History*, iv, 13.

34 Ibid., iv, 16.

35 Ibid., v, 7.

36 See Catherine Cubitt, *Anglo-Saxon Church Councils c. 650–c. 850* (London, 1995), pp. 8–14.

37 Bede, *Ecclesiastical History*, iii, 18.

38 For Aldhelm's letter to Aldfrith see Aldhelm, *Aldhelm: The Prose Works*, ed. and trans. Michael Lapidge and Michael W. Herren (Cambridge, 1979), pp. 34–47, in particular pp. 45–6.

39 William of Malmesbury, *The History of the English Bishops*, ed. and trans. Michael Winterbottom (Oxford, 2007), vol. 1, bk. 5, p. 507.

40 Bede, *Ecclesiastical History*, iv, 22.

41 *Letter to Bishop Egbert*, in Bede, *The Ecclesiastical History of the English People*, trans. Judith McClure and Roger Collins (Oxford, 1999), p. 345.

42 Cuthbert's letter is appended to Colgrave and Mynor's edition; see Bede, *Ecclesiastical History*, pp. 581–87.

43 Ibid., ii, 20.

44 Ibid., iv, 2.

45 Aethelwulf, *De abbatibus*, ed. Alistair Campbell (Oxford, 1967), pp. 20–2.

46 For graphic descriptions of the wiles of the devil and of his minions, see Peter Dendle, *Satan Unbound: The Devil in Old English Narrative Literature* (Toronto, 2001). But note also the presence of those more ambiguous 'elves' who robustly survived the conversion to Christianity, continuing to add complexity to any concept of the supernatural in Anglo-Saxon England. For a wide-ranging study see Alaric Hall, *Elves in Anglo-Saxon England: Matters of Belief, Health, Gender and Identity* (Woodbridge, 2007).

Chapter 3: Monks and Mission

1 Bede, *Ecclesiastical History*, i, 27.

2 *Beowulf*, ed. and trans. Michael Swanton, p. 85.

3   For what follows see Henrietta Leyser, *Medieval Women: A Social History of Women in England, 450–1500* (London, 1995), Ch. 2, pp. 19–39.
4   Bede, *Ecclesiastical History*, iii, 24.
5   Ibid., iv, 8. It is indeed very possible that Bede himself, oblated at the age of 7 to the newly founded monastery of Wearmouth, may have been an orphan, a possibility to be considered by Sarah Foot in her forthcoming biography of Bede.
6   A suggestion I owe to Conor O'Brien, in a paper given to the Oxford Medieval Church and Culture seminar.
7   Bede, *Ecclesiastical History*, iii, 25.
8   *The Life of Ceolfrith*, ed. and trans. C. W. Grocock and I. N. Wood (Oxford, 2013), xxvi–xxvii, pp. 105–07.
9   *Beowulf*, ed. and trans. Michael Swanton, p. 37.
10   *Life of Ceolfrith*, xxxviii, p. 119.
11   Nicholas Howe, *Writing the Map of Anglo-Saxon England: Essays in Cultural Geography* (New Haven and London, 2008), pp. 101–02.
12   See also, for a more wide-ranging analysis of the journeys than is offered here, I. N. Wood, 'The continental journeys of Wilfrid and Biscop', in N. J. Higham (ed.), *Wilfrid: Abbot, Bishop, Saint: Papers from the 1300 Anniversary Conferences* (Donnington, 2013), pp. 200–11.
13   See Christopher Page, *The Christian West and its Singers: The First Thousand Years* (New Haven and London, 2010), pp. 269–74.
14   For Jarrow and Wearmouth and their separate identities see the introduction to *Abbots of Wearmouth and Jarrow*, ed. and trans. C. W. Grocock and I. N. Wood (Oxford, 2013), pp. xxix–xxxii.
15   For an authoritative dating by Catherine Cubitt of Wilfrid's career, see her revised chronology in *Wilfrid: Abbot, Bishop, Saint*, ed. N. J. Higham (Donnington, 2013), pp. 342–47.
16   For Wilfrid's buildings, see Chapters 9–12 in ibid.
17   Eddius Stephanus, *The Life of Bishop Wilfrid*, ed. and trans. Bertram Colgrave (Cambridge, 1927), xvi, p. 35.
18   Ibid., xvii, p. 37; for Hexham, ibid., xxii, p. 47.
19   Ibid., xvii, p. 35.
20   Ibid., xxi, p. 43.
21   Ibid., xxiv, p. 49.
22   *Abbots of Wearmouth and Jarrow*, p. 49.
23   Stephanus, *The Life of Bishop Wilfrid*, lxiii, p. 137.
24   Ibid., lxv, p. 141.
25   Ibid.
26   One of the most apologetics for Wilfrid's career remains Henry Mayr-Harting, *Saint Wilfrid* (London, 1986).
27   Walter A. Goffart, *The Narrators of Barbarian history (A.D. 550–800): Jordanes, Gregory of Tours, Bede, and Paul the Deacon* (Princeton and Guildford, 1988), can be said to have started the debate. See his 'Bede and the Ghost of Bishop Wilfrid', ibid., pp. 235–325.
28   Bede, *Ecclesiastical History*, v, 19.
29   Ibid., iii, 27.

30   James Campbell, in James Campbell et al., *The Anglo-Saxons* (London, 1982), p. 78.

31   Bede, *Ecclesiastical History*, iii, 28.

32   Ibid., iv, 26.

33   Stephanus, *The Life of Bishop Wilfrid*, cxi, p. 115.

34   Bede, *Ecclesiastical History*, v, 9.

35   Ibid.

36   For Boniface and his circle, see Wilhelm Levison, *England and the Continent in the Eighth Century: The Ford Lectures Delivered in the University of Oxford in the Hilary Term, 1943* (Oxford, 1946), remains fundamental, but see also James T. Palmer, *Anglo-Saxons in a Frankish World, 690–900* (Turnhout, 2009).

37   *The Anglo-Saxon Missionaries in Germany: Being the Lives of SS. Willibrord, Boniface, Sturm, Leoba, and Lebuin, together with the Hodoeporicon of St. Willibald and a Selection from the Correspondence of St. Boniface*, ed. C. H. Talbot (London, 1954).

38   Ep. 21 in ibid.

39   For this importance of letter-writing at this juncture, see Patrick Sims-Williams, *Religion and Literature in Western England, 600–800* (Cambridge, 1990), Ch. 8, 'Letter-writing'.

40   Bede, *Ecclesiastical History*, v, 24.

41   For the holdings of these libraries, see Michael Lapidge, *The Anglo-Saxon Library* (Oxford, 2006).

42   See Roberta Gilchrist and Cheryl Green, *Glastonbury Abbey: Archaeological Investigations 1904–79* (London, 2015), pp. 234–37.

43   Eric John, *Reassessing Anglo-Saxon England* (Manchester, 1996), notes at p. 6 how Ine was the first Wessex king whose name did not begin with a C suggesting that thereafter Wessex ceased to have rulers with Celtic names and became 'Englished'. John nonetheless never discusses Ine's reign itself. But cf. Barbara Yorke, *Wessex in the Early Middle Ages* (London, 1995), 'The creation of Wessex, *c.* 600–802', pp. 52–93.

44   For his riddles see *Aldhelm: The Poetic Works*, ed. and trans. Michael Lapidge and James L. Rosier (Cambridge and Dover, NH, 1985), pp. 70–93.

45   *Aldhelm: The Prose Works*, ed. and trans. Michael Lapidge and Michael W. Herren (Cambridge, 1979), pp. 45–6.

46   For Ine's lawcode see *EHD*, i, pp. 398–407.

Chapter 4: A Mercian Century

1   *EHD*, i, p. 848.

2   For an overview of this developing commercial world see John Robert Maddicott, 'Prosperity and Power in the Age of Bede and Beowulf', *Proceedings of the British Academy* (2002), vol. 117, pp. 49–71. Essential also is Ch. 7, 'The rebirth of trading communities: The seventh to the mid-ninth century' in Robin Fleming, *Britain after Rome: The Fall*

    and Rise, 400–1070 (London, 2010), pp. 183–212, together with the recommended bibliography, ibid., pp. 293–401.

3   Bishop Daniel, *EHD*, i, p. 795.

4   John Blair, 'The minsters of the Thames', in John Blair, Brian Golding and Barbara F. Harvey (eds), *The Cloister and the World: Essays in Medieval History in Honour of Barbara Harvey* (Oxford, 1996), pp. 5–28; David Petts, 'Coastal landscapes and early Christianity in Anglo-Saxon Northumbria', *Estonian Journal of Archaeology*, xiii (2009), pp. 79–95.

5   For Flixborough see Christopher Loveluck et al., 2007–09, in particular vol. 4, Christopher Loveluck, *Rural Settlement, Lifestyles and Social Change in the Later First Millennium AD: Anglo-Saxon Flixborough in its Wider Context* (Oxford, 2007). For a vigorous defence of its likely monastic status, see John Blair, 'Flixborough re-visisted', *Anglo-Saxon Studies in Archaeology and History*, xvii (2011), pp. 101–06.

6   *The Life of Ceolfrith*, ed. and trans. C. W. Grocock and I. N. Wood (Oxford, 2013), xxviii, p. 107.

7   Ibid., xxxiv, p. 115.

8   Anna Gannon, *The Iconography of Early Anglo-Saxon Coinage: Sixth to Eighth Centuries* (Oxford, 2003), p. 132. See also ibid., pp. 186–93 for the rich iconography of coins found from minster sites. Note in particular p. 190: 'The use of religious iconography may also have been a way of justifying the possession of wealth that was becoming embarrassing.'

9   The notion of the 'supremacy' of Mercia was imprinted long ago by F. M. Stenton, 'The supremacy of Mercian kings', *EHR*, xxxiii (1918), pp. 433–39. Since Stenton's article huge advances in our understanding of Mercian power have been made, in particular through the contributions of archaeologists. The use of their work by John Blair in his recent Ford Lectures (publication forthcoming) is of paramount importance; only rather inadequate lecture notes inform what follows. Fundamental also is the need to see Mercia in its continental context; see Joanna Story, *Carolingian Connections: Anglo-Saxon England and Carolingian Francia, c. 750–870* (Aldershot, 2003). See also David Hill and Margaret Worthington (eds), Æthelbald and Offa: Two Eighth-Century Kings of Mercia: *Papers from a Conference Held in Manchester in 2000, Manchester Centre for Anglo-Saxon Studies* (Oxford, 2005).

10   For a succinct summary, see John Blair, 'The Tribal Hidage', in Michael Lapidge et al. (eds), *Blackwell Encyclopaedia of Anglo-Saxon England* (Oxford, 1999), pp. 455–56.

11   Felix, *Felix's Life of Saint Guthlac*, ed. Bertram Colgrave (Cambridge, 1956), pp. 149–51.

12   See George Henderson, *Vision and Image in Early Christian England* (Cambridge, 1999), p. 216 for the possibility of a 'dark political undertow' to Guthlac's life.

13   For Theodore's role in the settlement see Bede, iv, 21.

14   Ibid., iii, 11.

15   Ibid., v, 24.

16   Ibid., iv, 21.

17 Ibid., v, 23.
18 Boniface's letter is no. 32, in *The Anglo-Saxon Missionaries in Germany: Being the Lives of SS. Willibrord, Boniface, Sturm, Leoba, and Lebuin, together with the Hodoeporicon of St. Willibald and a Selection from the Correspondence of St. Boniface*, ed. and trans. C. H. Talbot (London, 1954), pp. 120–26.
19 For *Clovesho*, see Catherine Cubitt, 'Pastoral care and conciliar canons: The provisions of the 747 Council of Clofesho', in John Blair and Richard Sharpe (eds), *Pastoral Care before the Parish* (Leicester, 1992), pp. 193–211.
20 *EHD*, i, p. 502.
21 *EHD*, i, p. 515.
22 For a judicious analysis of the tale see Stephen D. White, 'Kinship and Lordship in Early Medieval England: The story of Sigeberht, Cynewulf, and Cyneheard', in R. M. Liuzza (ed.), *Old English Literature: Critical Essays* (New Haven and London, 2002), pp. 157–81.
23 *EHD*, i, p. 176.
24 For this suggestion see Alex Woolf, 'Onuist Son of Uuguist: Tyrannus Carnifex or a David for the Picts', in Hill, David and Worthington, Margaret (eds), *Aethelbald and Offa: Two Eighth-Century Kings of Mercia: Papers from a Conference Held in Manchester in 2000, Manchester Centre for Anglo-Saxon Studies* (Oxford, 2005), pp. 35–42.
25 See Alcuin's letter of 797 to the Mercian Ealdorman Osbert: 'you know very well how much blood his father shed in order to secure the kingdom for his *son*'. *EHD*, i, p. 855.
26 For Offa's coinage, see in particular Rory Naismith, *Money and Power in Anglo-Saxon England: The Southern English Kingdoms 757–865* (Cambridge, 2012); Gannon, *Iconography of Early Anglo-Saxon Coinage*.
27 For 'black stones', see Story, *Carolingian Connections*, Ch. 4, pp. 106–09.
28 For what follows, see ibid., Ch. 3, pp. 55–92.
29 *EHD*, i, p. 862.
30 Ibid., p. 849.
31 Ibid., p. 855.
32 For Offa's Dyke, see Hill, David and Worthington, Margaret (eds), pp. 91–5.
33 John Blair, Ford Lectures (forthcoming).
34 For charters issued from Tamworth at Christmas see Cyril Hart, in Ann Dornier (ed.), *Mercian Studies* (Leicester, 1977), p. 60, n.2; for a reconstruction of the water mill see Helena Hamerow, David Alban Hinton and Sally Crawford (eds), *The Oxford Handbook of Anglo-Saxon Archaeology* (Oxford, 2011), p. 442. See also Margaret Gelling, *The West Midlands in the Early Middle Ages* (Leicester, 1992), pp. 146–53, both for the water mill and more generally for the importance of Tamworth.
35 See David Hill, 'The eighth-century urban landscape', in Hill, David and Worthington, Margaret (eds), Æthelbald and Offa: Two Eighth-Century Kings of Mercia: Papers from a Conference Held in Manchester

in 2000, Manchester Centre for Anglo-Saxon Studies (Oxford, 2005), pp. 97–101.

36 Cf. also Gelling, *The West Midlands*, pp. 122–24 and for the particular significance of Burton and associated names, ibid., pp. 119–22.

37 See Alan Hardy, Bethan Mair Charles and Robert J. Williams (eds), *Death and Taxes: The Archaeology of a Middle Saxon Estate Centre at Higham Ferrers, Northamptonshire* (Oxford, 2007).

38 For the Lichfield angel see Warwick Rodwell et al., 'The Lichfield angel: A spectacular Anglo-Saxon painted sculpture', *The Antiquaries Journal*, lxxxviii (2008).

39 Bede, *Ecclesiastical History*, iv, 3.

40 For Alcuin's letter, see *EHD*, i, p. 846.

41 See Michelle Brown, *The Book of Cerne: Prayer, Patronage and Power in Ninth-Century England* (London and Toronto, 1996).

42 For Breedon, see Rosemary Cramp, 'Schools of Mercian sculpture', in Ann Dornier (ed.), *Mercian Studies* (Leicester, 1977), Ch.11, pp. 191–233.

43 Richard Jewell, 'Classicism of Southumbrian sculpture', in Michelle Brown and Carol Ann Farr (eds), *Mercia: An Anglo-Saxon Kingdom in Europe* (London, 2001), pp. 256–57.

44 Jane Hawkes, *The Sandbach Crosses: Sign and Significance in Anglo-Saxon Sculpture* (Dublin and Portland, OR, 2002), pp. 146–47.

45 For what follows, see Richard Gem, *Deerhurst and Rome: Æthelric's pilgrimage c. 804 and the Oratory of St Mary Mediana* (Deerhurst, 2008). See also Richard N. Bailey, *Anglo-Saxon Sculptures at Deerhurst* (Deerhurst, 2005).

Chapter 5: King Alfred, the Vikings and the Rise of Wessex

1 *The Annals of St-Bertin*, ed. and trans. Janet L. Nelson (Manchester, 1991), p. 43.

2 *EHD*, i, p. 845.

3 P. H. Sawyer, *Anglo-Saxon Charters: An Annotated List and Bibliography* (London, 1968), no.133, p. 105. *EHD*, i, p. 845.

4 Martin O. H. Carver, *Portmahomack: Monastery of the Picts* (Edinburgh, 2008).

5 *EHD*, i, p. 186.

6 See Joanna Story, *Carolingian Connections: Anglo-Saxon England and Carolingian Francia, c. 750–870* (Aldershot, 2003), pp. 144–45.

7 Nicholas Brooks, *The Early History of the Church of Canterbury: Christ Church from 597 to 1066* (Leicester, 1984), p. 146.

8 For what follows, see Story, *Carolingian Connections*, pp. 232–43.

9 See notably Malcolm Godden, 'Did King Alfred write anything?', *Medium Aevum*, lxxvi (2007), pp. 1–23.

10 See James Campbell, 'Asser's *Life of King Alfred*', reprinted in James Campbell, *The Anglo-Saxon State* (London, 2000), pp. 129–55.

11 For what follows see *EHD*, i, pp. 191–5.

12 See Ryan Lavelle, 'Geographies of power in the *Anglo-Saxon Chronicle*: The royal estate of Wessex', in Alice Jorgensen (ed.), *Reading the Anglo-Saxon Chronicle: Language, Literature, History* (Turnhout, 2010), pp. 204–10.

13 *EHD*, i, p. 195.

14 Asser, *Life of King Alfred*, Ch. 55, p. 84. See also the *Chronicle* for 876, *EHD*, i, pp. 194–95.

15 Asser, *Life of King Alfred*, Ch. 49, pp. 82–3.

16 *EHD*, i, p. 196.

17 Cf. Story, *Carolingian Connections*, pp. 237–38, who argues that Alfred was chosen 'not because of some foreordained destiny' but simply because at the time he was 'the most expendable member of the family'.

18 Asser, *Life of Alfred*, Ch. 23, p. 75.

19 From the translation of Gregory's *Pastoral Care*, in ibid., p. 125.

20 Ibid., p. 126.

21 The bibliography here is immense, concerned as it is both with estimating Alfred's personal role as a translator and the extent to which the king had a sense of 'England' or of 'Englishness'. See Malcolm Godden (above) and George Molyneaux, 'The Old English Bede: English ideology or Christian instruction?', *EHR*, cxxiv (2009), pp. 1289–323. See also Mark Atherton, *The Making of England* (forthcoming).

22 From the translation of Gregory's *Pastoral Care*, in Asser, *Life of Alfred*, p. 125.

23 Ibid., p. 126.

24 Ibid., p. 110.

25 Ibid., p. 133.

26 For the importance of the Battle of Conwy, see Thomas M. Charles-Edwards, *Wales and the Britons, 350–1064* (Oxford, 2013), pp. 490–96.

27 Asser, *Life of Alfred*, p. 98. Cf. also Derek Keene, 'Alfred and London', in Timothy Reuter (ed.), *Alfred the Great: Papers from the Eleventh-Centenary Conferences* (Aldershot, 2003), pp. 235–50.

28 Alfred's organization of his army, both in the field and on garrison duty, has caused considerable controversy. For a careful calculation of how the 27,000 may have been deployed see Ryan Lavelle, *Alfred's Wars: Sources and Interpretations of Anglo-Saxon Warfare in the Viking Age* (Woodbridge, 2010), Ch. 3, pp. 47–140. For Asser on Alfred's system for organizing his 'fighting men' see Asser, *Life of Alfred*, Ch. 100, p. 106.

29 *EHD*, i, p. 205.

30 Asser, *Life of Alfred*, p. 102.

31 Ibid., xci, pp. 101–02.

32 For an introduction to the *Chronicle*, see ibid., pp. 275–81.

33 For Fulco's letter, see ibid., pp. 182–6; for the 'visible wolves', p. 184.

34 For the sword hilt and its significance, see James Campbell et al., *The Anglo-Saxons* (London, 1982), p. 156, n.144.

35 *EHD*, i, p. 184.

36 Ibid., p. 205: 'in the summer of this year the Danish army divided, one force going into East Anglia and one into Northumbria; and those that

were moneyless got themselves ships and went south across the sea to the Seine'.

37   Ibid.
38   See James Campbell, 'What is not known about the reign of Edward the Elder', in N. J. Higham and David Hill (eds), *Edward the Elder, 899–924* (London, 2001), p. 21: 'Had it not been for the chances of battle and of war, Aethelwold might very well have been regarded as one of the greatest figures in our island's story.'
39   *EHD*, i, p. 208.
40   Ibid., p. 208.
41   This account of the battle is taken from *The Chronicle of Æthelweard*, ed. A. Campbell (London, 1962), p. 53. For the suggestion that it was the booty which proved fatal to the Vikings see Lavelle, *Alfred's Wars*, p. 198.
42   *EHD*, i, p. 197.
43   For the disappearance from the scene of Aelfwynn, Aethelflaed's daughter, see Maggie Bailey, 'Aelfwynn, second Lady of the Mercians', in N. J. Higham and David Hill (eds), *Edward the Elder, 899–924* (London, 2001), pp. 112–27.
44   *EHD*, i, p. 217.
45   See Michael R. Davidson, 'The (non) submission of the northern kings in 920', in N. J. Higham and David Hill (eds), *Edward the Elder, 899–924* (London, 2001), pp. 200–11.
46   But cf. the caution of David N. Dumville, *Wessex and England from Alfred to Edgar: Six Essays on Political, Cultural, and Ecclesiastical Revival* (Woodbridge, 1992), in his chapter 'Aethelstan, first king of England', p. 146.
47   *EHD*, i, p. 217.
48   For the reign of Athelstan see now Sarah Foot, *Æthelstan: The First King of England* (New Haven, 2011).
49   *EHD*, i, p. 218.
50   For the Eamont meeting as the opening scene of 'a contest in seven rounds' see Thomas Charles-Edwards, *Wales and the Britons, 350–1064*, pp. 521–23.
51   Levi Roach, *Kingship and Consent in Anglo-Saxon England, 871–978: Assemblies and the State in the Early Middle Ages* (Cambridge, 2013), pp. 8–9.
52   See Alex Woolf, *From Pictland to Alba: 789–1070* (Edinburgh, 2007), p. 161.
53   *EHD*, i, p. 201. For a study of the poem, see the essays in *The Battle of Brunanburh: A Casebook*, ed. Michael Livingston (Exeter, 2011).

Chapter 6: *Godes Rice*: God's Kingdom

1   Michael Lapidge (ed.), *The Cult of St Swithun* (Oxford, 2003), p. 607.
2   F. M. Stenton, *Anglo-Saxon England* (3rd edn, Oxford, 1989), p. 368.
3   *EHD*, i, p. 225.

4   For what follows see in particular Levi Roach, *Kingship and Consent in Anglo-Saxon England, 871–978: Assemblies and the State in the Early Middle Ages* (Cambridge, 2013).

5   For the revival of the word, see the introduction to ibid., pp. 3–6.

6   For the scribe see ibid., pp. 32–43.

7   John Maddicott, *The Origins of the English Parliament, 924–1327* (Oxford, 2010), pp. 20–1.

8   Patrick Wormald, *The Making of English Law: King Alfred to the Twelfth Century, vol. 1: Legislation and its Limits* (Oxford, 1999), pp. 290–308.

9   Ibid., p. 298.

10 George Molyneaux, *The Formation of the English Kingdom in the Tenth Century* (Oxford, 2015), pp. 114–15.

11 Quoted Wormald, *The Making of English Law*, pp. 302–03.

12 King Athelstan's laws used at Grately, *EHD*, i, p. 422. See also the striking observation in John Blair, *The Church in Anglo-Saxon Society* (Oxford and New York, 2005), p. 464, that this is 'the first European reference to consecrated ground for burial'.

13 *EHD*, i, p. 225, n.3.

14 Fundamental here is the work of James Campbell. See his collected essays, James Campbell, *The Anglo-Saxon State* (London, 2000).

15 Key here is Molyneaux, *The Formation of the English Kingdom, passim*.

16 Wormald, *The Making of English Law*, p. 319.

17 For such connections see in particular D. Rollason et al., *England and the Continent in the Tenth Century: Studies in Honour of Wilhelm Levison (1876–1947)* (Turnhout, 2010).

18 For an illuminating review of biographies of 'the Reform's trio of leaders', see Catherine Cubitt, 'Review: *The Tenth-Century Benedictine Reform in England*', *Early Medieval Europe*, vi (1997), pp. 77–94.

19 See Edgar's privilege for the New Minster at Winchester in *Councils and Synods, with Other Documents Relating to the English Church, vol. 1: A.D. 871–1204*, ed. and trans. Dorothy Whitelock et al. (Oxford, 1981), p. 125.

20 See Wulfstan, *The Life of St. Æthelwold*, ed. and trans. Michael Lapidge and Michael Winterbottom (Oxford, 1991), p. 31.

21 See David Knowles, *The Monastic Order in England: A History of its Development from the Times of St. Dunstan to the Fourth Lateran Council, 943–1216* (Cambridge, 1949), pp. 697–701.

22 *Regularis concordia Anglicae nationis monachorum sanctimonialiumque*, ed. Thomas Symons (London, 1953), p. 3.

23 See Patrick Wormald, 'Aethelwold and his continental counterparts', in Barbara Yorke (ed.), *Bishop Æthelwold: His Career and Influence* (Woodbridge, 1988), pp. 30–2.

24 But cf. the discussion in Katherine O'Brien O'Keeffe, *Stealing Obedience: Narratives of Agency and Identity in Later Anglo-Saxon England* (Toronto and Buffalo, 2012), pp. 3–54.

25 For what follows, see Lapidge, *The Cult of St Swithun*.

26 Wulfstan, *The Metrical Life of St Swithun*, in ibid., pp. 494–5. Cited by

Helen Gittos, *Liturgy, Architecture, and Sacred Places in Anglo-Saxon England* (Oxford, 2013), p. 103 in her chapter 'Going between God's houses: Open-air processions in Anglo-Saxon England', pp. 103–45.

27   Lantfred, *Translatio et Miracula S. Swithuni*, in Lapidge, *The Cult of St Swithun*, p. 297.

28   The major study of the iconography of the *Benedictional* remains Robert Deshman, *The Benedictional of Æthelwold* (Princeton, 1995).

29   For Edgar's coinage reform see Rory Naismith, 'Prelude to reform: Tenth-century English coinage in perspective', in Rory Naismith et al. (eds), *Early Medieval Monetary History: Studies in Memory of Mark Blackburn* (Farnham, 2014), Ch. 3, pp. 39–83.

30   Julia Barrow, 'Chester's earliest regatta? Edgar's Dee-rowing revisited', *EME*, x (2011), pp. 81–93.

31   See Lantfred, *Translatio et Miracula S. Swithuni*, in Lapidge, *The Cult of St Swithun*, p. 277.

32   For Aelfric, see in particular Hugh Magennis and Mary Swan (eds), *A Companion to Ælfric* (Boston, 2009).

33   See Jonathan Wilcox, 'The use of Aelfric's homilies: MSS Oxford, Bodleian Library, Junius 85 and 86 in the field', in Magennis and Swan, *A Companion to Ælfric*, pp. 345–68.

34   See Mechthild Gretsch, *Aelfric and the Cult of Saints in Late Anglo-Saxon England* (Cambridge, 2005).

35   See Luisella Simpson, 'The King Alfred/St Cuthbert episode in the *Historia de sancto Cuthberto*: Its significance for mid-tenth-century English history', in Gerald Bonner, D. W. Rollason and Clare Stancliffe (eds), *St. Cuthbert, his Cult and his Community to AD 1200* (Woodbridge, 1989), pp. 397–411.

36   Quoted in Francesca Tinti, 'The "costs" of pastoral care', in Francesca Tinti (ed.), *Pastoral Care in Late Anglo-Saxon England* (Woodbridge, 2005), p. 34. See also Helen Foxhall Forbes, *Heaven and Earth in Anglo-Saxon England: Theology and Society in an Age of Faith* (Farnham, 2013), p. 286.

37   For the complexity and paradoxes of Aelfric's ideas on the fate of the soul after death see Ananya Jahanara Kabir, *Paradise, Death and Doomsday in Anglo-Saxon Literature* (Cambridge, 2001), Ch. 2, pp. 14–48.

38   See M. Bradford Bedingfield, *The Dramatic Liturgy of Anglo-Saxon England* (Woodbridge, 2002), p. 57.

39   Sarah Larratt Keefer, *Old English Liturgical Verse: A Student Edition* (Peterborough, ON, 2010), p. 27.

40   *Old English Shorter Poems*, ed. and trans. Christopher A. Jones and Robert E. Bjork (2 vols, Cambridge, MA and London, 2012), pp. 231, 199.

41   Ibid., p. 249.

42   *Old English Poems of Christ and His Saints*, ed. and trans. Mary Clayton (Cambridge, MA, 2013), p. 63. See also Clayton's note to this passage, p. 370: 'The Latin sources on which this poem draws make no reference

to confession, and it would appear the poet took this motif from vernacular homilies.'

43 These extracts from Edgar's law code are taken from Blair, *The Church in Anglo-Saxon Society*, p. 442.

44 See in particular Gittos, *Liturgy*, Ch. 4, pp. 103–45.

45 Text and translation in Bedingfield, *The Dramatic Liturgy*, p. 55.

46 Ibid., p. 60.

47 Ibid., p. 81.

48 Deshman, *The Benedictional of Æthelwold*, p. 83.

49 *Regularis concordia*, pp. 44–5; 49–50.

50 Bedingfield, *The Dramatic Liturgy*, p. 313.

Chapter 7: The Viking Return

1 *EHD*, i, p. 932.

2 For the speed with which the cult developed see Christine E. Fell, *Edward, King and Martyr* (Leeds, 1971), pp. xx–xxv.

3 Wulfstan, *The Life of* St *Æthelwold*, ed. and trans. Michael Lapidge and Michael Winterbottom (Oxford, 1991), xl, p. 61.

4 *EHD*, i, p. 235.

5 *Historia ecclesie Abbendonensis: The History of the Church of Abingdon*, ed. and trans. John Hudson (2 vols, Oxford, 2002), i, p. 143.

6 See the collection of essays in D. G. Scragg (ed.), *The Battle of Maldon, AD 991* (Oxford, 1991).

7 *EHD*, i, p. 235.

8 See the classic article on the sources for the reign, in comparison with those available for the reign of Alfred: Simon Keynes, 'A tale of two kings: Alfred the Great and Æthelred the Unready', *TRHS*, xxxvi (1986), pp. 195–217; see also Simon Keynes, *The Diplomas of King Æthelred 'The Unready' (978–1016): A Study in their Use as Historical Evidence* (Cambridge, 1980).

9 Note: There has been a fierce debate about the actual figures paid: see on the one hand M. K. Lawson, 'The collection of Danegeld and heregeld in the reigns of Aethelred II and Cnut', *TEHR*, xcix (1984), pp. 721–38 and on the other, John Gillingham, '"The most precious jewel in the English crown": Levels of Danegeld and heregeld in the early eleventh century', *EHR*, civ (1989), pp. 385–406.

10 See Malcolm R. Godden, 'Money, power and morality in late Anglo-Saxon England', *ASE*, xix (1990), pp. 41–66.

11 *History of the Church of Abingdon*, p. 145.

12 But cf. now Catherine Cubitt, 'The politics of remorse: Penance and royal piety in the reign of Æthelred the Unready', *Historical Research*, lxxxv (2012), pp. 179–92.

13 For the next stage of this reign, see in the first instance Keynes, *The Diplomas*, 'The years of maturity, c. 993–1006', pp. 186–208.

14 Aethelwold was not the only saint to be translated in these years: Edith

of Wilton (daughter of King Edgar) was followed by a number of others, including Edward (Aethelred's murdered half-brother). Keynes (*OBNB* sub Aethelred) discusses alongside these translations the 'intense productivity' of the last decade of the eleventh century, both in the fine arts and in writings both in Latin and the vernacular, and observes: 'Perhaps it is paradoxical that so much activity could take place when the country was under Viking attack, or perhaps the reign of Alfred shows that this is precisely what should be expected' (p. 415).

15 *EHD*, i, p. 236.

16 Ibid., i, pp. 238–39.

17 Aethelred's justification for his order, as given in his charter to St Frideswide, was that he, together with 'his leading men and magnates', had determined upon extermination of 'all the Danes who had sprung up in this island, sprouting like cockle amongst the wheat'. *EHD* no. 127, pp. 590–93.

18 For what follows see Ann Williams, '"Cockles amongst the Wheat": Danes and English in the Western Midlands in the first half of the eleventh century', *Midland History*, xi (1986), pp. 1–22.

19 *EHD*, i, p. 238.

20 Ibid., p. 239.

21 Ibid., p. 239.

22 For what follows see Simon Keynes, 'An abbot, an archbishop, and the Viking raids of 1006–07 and 1009–12', *ASE*, xxxvi (2007), pp. 151–220.

23 Simon Keynes' term: see also his entry in *ODNB* sub Eadric Streona.

24 *Eynsham Cartulary*, ed. and trans. H. E. Salter (2 vols, Oxford, 1907), i, 19.

25 See Jonathan Wilcox, 'The dissemination of Wulfstan's homilies: The Wulfstan tradition in eleventh-century vernacular preaching', in Carola Hicks (ed.), *England in the Eleventh Century: Proceedings of the 1990 Harlaxton Symposium* (Stamford, 1992), p. 202, n.21.

26 Joyce Tally Lionarons, *The Homiletic Writings of Archbishop Wulfstan: A Critical Study* (Cambridge, 2010), p. 52.

27 *EHD*, i, p. 241.

28 Ibid., p. 445.

29 Ibid., p. 241.

30 Ibid., p. 241.

31 Ibid., p. 442.

32 Ibid., p. 242.

33 Ibid., pp. 447–48.

34 See Simon Keynes and Rory Naismith, 'The *Agnus Dei* pennies of King Æthelred the Unready', *ASE*, xl (2011), pp. 175–223. Cf. David Woods, 'The *Agnus Dei* pennies of King Aethelred II: A call to hope in the Lord (Isaiah XL)? ', ibid., xlii (2013), pp. 299–309, for his suggestion that the reverse of such coins portrays an eagle, not a dove.

35 *EHD*, i, p. 243.

36 Ibid., p. 244.

37 Ibid., p. 245.

38 For this sum – 'heregeld' – and the distinction that should be made

between this tax and the arbitrary amounts paid out as Danegeld, see
Simon Keynes' entry under *Heregeld* in Lapidge et al., *The Blackwell
Encyclopaedia of Anglo-Saxon England*, p. 235.

39   *EHD*, i, p. 246.
40   Ibid., i, p. 931.
41   Ibid., p. 934.
42   Ibid., p. 247.
43   Ibid., p. 449.
44   Henry of Huntingdon, *Historia Anglorum: The History of the English
       People*, ed. and trans. Diana E. Greenway (Oxford, 1996), ii, 17,
       pp. 17–18.
45   For what follows, see M. K. Lawson, *Cnut: England's Viking King*
       (Stroud, 2004), in particular, pp. 124–28, for Cnut and crowns.
46   *EHD*, i, p. 476.
47   Ibid., p. 250.
48   See Lawson, *Cnut*, p. 84, n.6.
49   See Jan Gerchow, in *England in the Eleventh Century: Proceedings of the
       1990 Harlaxton Symposium* (Stamford, 1992), pp. 226 and 232.
50   *EHD*, i, p. 452.
51   See in particular Patrick Wormald, 'Archbishop Wuflstan and the holiness
       of society', in David Pelteret (ed.), *Anglo-Saxon History: Basic Readings*
       (New York and London, 2000), pp. 191–244, and further Patrick
       Wormald, 'Archbishop Wulfstan: Eleventh-century state builder', in
       Matthew Townend (ed.), *Wulfstan, Archbishop of York: The Proceedings
       of the Second Alcuin Conference* (Turnhout, 2004), pp. 9–27.
52   Quoted in Roberta Frank, 'King Cnut in the verse of his skalds', in
       Alexander R. Rumble (ed.), *The Reign of Cnut: King of England,
       Denmark and Norway* (London and Rutherford, NJ, 1994), p. 119.
53   See Barbara Yorke, *Wessex in the Early Middle Ages* (London, 1995),
       pp. 143–44.
54   Elaine M. Treharne, *Living through Conquest: The Politics of Early
       English, 1020–1220* (Oxford, 2012), p. 45.
55   See Treharne, op. cit., p. 44, n.45.
56   See Pamela Nightingale, 'The origin of the court of husting and Danish
       influence on London's development into a capital city', *EHR*, cii (1987),
       pp. 559–78.
57   Barbara. E. Crawford, *The Churches Dedicated to St. Clement in
       Medieval England: A Hagio-Geography of the Seafarer's Saint in 11th
       Century North Europe* (St. Petersburg, 2008).
58   Debby Banham, in N. J. Higham and Martin J. Ryan (eds), *The
       Landscape Archaeology of Anglo-Saxon England* (Woodbridge, 2010),
       p. 188.
59   Robin Fleming, 'Rural elites and urban communities in late-Saxon
       England', *Past & Present*, cxli (1993), pp. 3–37.
60   For Emma and for what follows see Pauline Stafford, *Queen Emma
       and Queen Edith: Queenship and Women's Power in Eleventh-Century
       England* (Oxford, 1997).

61 *EHD*, i, p. 258.
62 Ibid., p. 259.
63 Ibid.
64 Ibid., p. 260.

Chapter 8: England *Tempore Regis Edwardi*

1 *EHD*, i, p. 260.
2 See Richard Sharpe's translation of 'Argumentum' to *Quadripartitus*, Ch. 9, cited by John Maddicott, 'Edward the Confessor's return to England in 1041', *HER*, cxix (2004), p. 650.
3 Ibid., pp. 650–66.
4 For Edward's earls see Peter A. Clarke, *The English Nobility under Edward the Confessor* (Oxford, 1994).
5 For the question of who was and who was not a thegn see John Gillingham, 'Thegns and knights in eleventh-century England: Who was then the gentleman?', *TRHS*, v (1995), pp. 129–53.
6 *EHD*, i, p. 247.
7 *EHD*, ii, p. 105. Variations between versions of the *Chronicle* become more and more marked after its first compilation in the 890s. It thus becomes increasingly necessary to distinguish one version from another. For an introduction to the complexity of the recensions see Dorothy Whitelock's introduction to *EHD*, i, pp. 109–25.
8 For what follows, see the respective entries in the *ODNB*; see also Simon Keynes, 'Cnut's earls', in Alexander R. Rumble (ed.), *The Reign of Cnut: King of England, Denmark and Norway* (London and Rutherford, 1994), pp. 43–88.
9 *The Life of King Edward who Rests at Westminster*, ed. Frank Barlow (London, 1962) pp. 21, 52.
10 Henry of Huntingdon, *Historia Anglorum: The History of the English People*, ed. and trans. Diana E. Greenway (Oxford, 1996), p. 381.
11 For his family and for every turn of Morcar's career, Stephen Baxter, *The Earls of Mercia: Lordship and Power in Late Anglo-Saxon England* (Oxford, 2007), is fundamental.
12 See Frank Barlow, *The Godwins: The Rise and Fall of a Noble Dynasty* (Harlow, 2001), Ch. 1.
13 See Stephen David Baxter, 'Edward the Confessor and the succession question', in Richard Mortimer (ed.), *Edward the Confessor: The Man and the Legend* (Woodbridge, 2009), p. 85, n.36.
14 *EHD*, ii [D], p. 119.
15 *The Life of King Edward*, p. 24.
16 *EHD*, ii [D], p. 121.
17 Ibid. [C; D], p. 125.
18 Ibid. [C; D], p. 126.
19 *The Life of King Edward*, p. 28.

20 For the landholding of the nobility see Clarke, *The English Nobility under Edward the Confessor* (Oxford, 1994).
21 *EHD*, ii [D], p. 137.
22 *The Life of King Edward*, p. 30.
23 Ibid.
24 Ibid., pp. 32–3.
25 Ibid., p. 40.
26 See Robin Fleming, *Britain after Rome: The Fall and Rise, 400–1070* (London, 2010), pp. 295–307.
27 For Aelfgar, see Baxter, *The Earls of Mercia*, pp. 42, 45–7.
28 According to Thomas M. Charles-Edwards, *Wales and the Britons, 350–1064* (Oxford, 2013), p. 567, the murderer was almost certainly Cynan ab Iago.
29 *EHD*, ii [D], p. 141.
30 *EHD*, ii [D and E], pp. 143–44.
31 For the architectural novelty of the abbey, see Eric Fernie, 'Edward the Confessor's Westminster Abbey', in Richard Mortimer (ed.), *Edward the Confessor: The Man and the Legend* (Woodbridge, 2009), pp. 139–50.
32 For Edward and Westminster, see Nicole Marafioti, *The King's Body: Burial and Succession in Late Anglo-Saxon England* (Toronto, Buffalo and London, 2014), pp. 40–52.
33 John Maddicott, *The Origins of the English Parliament, 924–1327* (Oxford, 2010), pp. 18–19. It is notable that one of the earliest depictions of the three wise men who came to Bethlehem as crowned kings appears in the *Benedictional* of Aethelwold. See Robert Deshman, *The Benedictional of Æthelwold* (Princeton, 1995), p. 194.
34 *The Life of King Edward*, p. 41; see also Pauline Stafford, 'Edith, Edward's wife and queen', in Richard Mortimer (ed.), *Edward the Confessor*, p. 127.
35 See Elizabeth M. Tyler, 'When wings incarnadine with gold are spread: The *Vita Aedwardi regis* and display of treasure at the court of Edward the Confessor', in Elizabeth M. Tyler (ed.), *Treasure in the Medieval West* (York, 2000), pp. 99–107.
36 *The Life of King Edward*, p. 36.
37 C. R. Dodwell, *Anglo-Saxon Art: A New Perspective* (Manchester, 1982), p. 75.
38 See Tyler, 'When wings incarnadine', pp. 90–1.
39 For such plunder see Dodwell, *Anglo-Saxon Art*, Ch. 8, 'Anglo-Saxon art and the Norman Conquest'; for the quotation by William of Poitiers, ibid., p. 217.
40 See Robin Fleming, 'Rural elites and urban communities in late-Saxon England', *Past & Present*, cxli (1993), pp. 3–37.
41 Harold's body was later claimed by Waltham Abbey but for doubts about this location see Marafioti, *The King's Body*, pp. 230–39.
42 William of Poitiers, *The Deeds of William*, ed. and trans. R. H. C. Davis and Marjorie Chibnall (Oxford, 1998), pp. 139–41.
43 Edward Creasy, in his *Fifteen Decisive Battles*, published in 1909, lists

it fifth, after Charles Martel's victory at the Battle of Tours in 732 and before Joan of Arc's victory at Orleans in 1429.

44 See Sally Harvey, *Domesday: Book of Judgement* (Oxford, 2014), for the compelling argument that the making of the Domesday Book was William's response to the threat of invasion from Swein of Denmark.

45 *EHD*, ii [E], p. 164. The figures quoted by Stephen Baxter, 'Lordship and labour', in Julia C. Crick and Elisabeth M. C. Van Houts (eds), *A Social History of England, 900–1200* (Cambridge, 2011), p. 104, give substance to this verdict.

46 *The Ecclesiastical History of Orderic Vitalis*, ed. and trans. Marjorie Chibnall (Oxford, 1969), iv, p. 269.

47 See the collection of essays M. Brett and D. A. Woodman, *The Long Twelfth-Century View of the Anglo-Saxon Past* (Farnham and Burlington, VT, 2015).

48 See Tony Hunt, 'The Life of St Alexis', in Samuel Fanous and Henrietta Leyser (eds), *Christina of Markyate: A Twelfth-Century Holy Woman* (London, 2005), pp. 217–38.

49 *The Life of Christina of Markyate*, trans. Samuel Fanous and Henrietta Leyser (Oxford, 2008), p. 42.

Epilogue

1 Marjorie Chibnall (ed), *The Ecclesiastical History of Orderic Vitalis*, vol. II, Bk IV (Oxford, 1969), p. 273.

2 David Carpenter, *The Struggle for Mastery: Britain 1066–1284* (London, 2003), p. 8.

Index